SCAPEGOAT JUSTICE

LLOYD MILLER
AND THE FAILURE OF THE
AMERICAN LEGAL SYSTEM

SCAPEGOAT JUSTICE

LLOYD MILLER
AND THE FAILURE OF THE
AMERICAN LEGAL SYSTEM

Willard J. Lassers

INDIANA UNIVERSITY PRESS
Bloomington and London

PUBLISHED IN CANADA BY FITZHENRY & WHITESIDE LIMITED,
DON MILLS, ONTARIO
LIBRARY OF CONGRESS CATALOG CARD NUMBER: 73-80378
ISBN: 0-253-17820-7
MANUFACTURED IN THE UNITED STATES OF AMERICA

to ELISABETH  KIPPI

wife daughter

CONTENTS

PRINCIPAL PERSONS MENTIONED

The Victim and her Family

Janice Elizabeth May   *The Victim, 8*
Mrs. Jeane May   *Her Mother*
Dean Eugene May   *Her Father*
Willard Dean May   *Her Brother, 14*
James Allen May   *Her Brother, 12*

The Accused and his Family

Lloyd Eldon Miller, Jr.   *The Accused*
Mrs. Jewel Miller   *His Mother*
Lloyd Eldon Miller, Sr.   *His Father*
Mrs. Margaret Isaak   *His Sister*

The People of Canton, Illinois

Mrs. Alice Baxter   *Miller's Landlady*
Robert Baxter   *Husband of Mrs. Baxter*
David A. Bennett, M.D.   *Canton Surgeon*
Mrs. Joyce Hardy   *Clerk at Carver & Denny Cleaners*
Ira Johns   *Son of Teke*
Lawrence ("Teke") Johns   *Proprietor of Yellow Cab Co.,*
Miller's Employer
June Lang (Later June Gross)   *Canton Waitress*
Harold Largent   *Gas Station Proprietor*
Edward R. Lewis, Jr.   *Proprietor of Lewis Pharmacy*
Hugh Max   *Testified regarding waving incident at Kellogg School*
Adrian Watters
Rebecca Watters   *Grandchildren of Mrs. Baxter*

Others

Sally Abbott   *Miller's first wife*
Richard Applegate   *WAIT Reporter*

Brahm Baittle, M.D. *Psychiatrist*
Alexander I. Dunsay *Men's clothing salesman*
Mrs. Jean Erkes *Administrative Assistant, Illinois Division, American Civil Liberties Union, Chicago*
Bernadine Martin *Reporter for Peoria Journal-Star*
James S. Martin *Chemist at Walter C. McCrone and Associates, Chicago*
Leon N. Sussman, M.D. *Hematologist, New York*
Donald Sweezey, M.D. *Psychiatrist*
Sue Ann Williams *Miller's second wife*

The Judges

William M. Bardens *1956 Trial Court Judge*
Keith F. Scott *1963 Sanity Hearing Judge*
Bernard M. Decker *Federal Court Judge who granted 1963 stay 7½ hours before execution*
J. Sam Perry *Federal Trial Court Judge at 1963 hearing*

Other Public Officials

John ("Jocko") Anderson *Treasurer of Fulton County*
Raymond G. Ball *Canton Police Officer*
Virgil ("Buck") Ball *Sheriff of Fulton County*
Neil Baxter *Canton Police Officer*
William G. Clark *Attorney General of Illinois*
Sergeant Robert Hardy *Canton Police Officer*
Roger W. Hayes *State's Attorney of McDonough County; assisted Ramsey*
Oral Kost *1963 State's Attorney of Fulton County*
Kenneth Lindzey *Canton Police Chief*
Forrest R. ("Jess") Litterley *Chemist at Illinois Bureau of Criminal Identification and Investigation*
John Lynch *Polygraph Operator*
Raymond J. Mercey, M.D. *Coroner of Fulton County*
Frank J. Pate *Warden of Stateville Prison*
Blaine Ramsey *Fulton County State's Attorney*
Dwight Whitlock *Polygraph Operator*
Ronald Wilkerson *Canton Police Officer*

Miller's Attorneys; 1956 Counsel

William Howard Malmgren
George K. Meuth

*Miller's Attorneys; Counsel in First Federal Court Case
(1960–1962)*

Donald Page Moore
George K. Meuth

Counsel in Second Federal Court Case (1963–1971)

George M. Leighton
Willard J. Lassers
Arthur G. Greenberg
Edwin C. Conger
Harry Golter
George Pontikes
Robert Grossman
Maurice Rosenfield (for amici curiae)
W. Robert Ming, Jr. (for amici curiae)

CHRONOLOGIES

General

1955
NOV. 26 Janice May murdered
NOV. 28 Miller arrested in Danville, Illinois
NOV. 30/ Miller signed confession to murder
DEC. 1

1956
JUNE 11 Trial opened in Lewiston
JUNE 20 Judge Bardens declared mistrial; case moved to Carthage
SEPT. 10 Trial opened in Carthage
SEPT. 28 Miller found guilty
NOV. 15 Miller sentenced to die

1957
JAN. 18 Death date 1 (set Nov. 15, 1956, stayed Nov. 28, 1956)

1958
JAN. 24 Illinois Supreme Court affirms conviction
APRIL 11 Death date 2 (set Jan. 24, 1958, stayed March 18, 1958)

1960
DEC. 9 First Federal Court suit filed
DEC. 16 Death date 3 (set Nov. 16, 1960, stayed Dec. 9, 1960)

1961
JUNE 7 Federal Judge Igoe ruled against Miller

1962
FEB. 15 Federal Court of Appeals affirmed Judge Igoe
NOV. 5 Supreme Court denied review

1963
MAY 17 Death date 4 (set March 26, 1963, stayed May 14, 1963)

MAY 22 Petition filed to determine Miller's sanity
JUNE 20 Miller declared sane
JUNE 21 Death date 5 (set May 14, 1963, stayed June 17, 1963)
JULY 26 Death date 6 (set June 17, 1963, Reprieve granted July 17, 1963.)
AUG. 12–14 Commutation hearing before Illinois Pardon and Parole Board
AUG. 21 Second Federal Court suit filed
AUG. 23 Death date 7 (set July 17, 1963). Execution set for 12:01 A.M. Stayed 4:30 P.M., August 22, 1963.
DEC. 4 Judge Perry opened trial of second Federal Court suit
DEC. 24 Trial concluded. Judge Perry set aside conviction.

1965
FEB. 15 Federal Court of Appeals reversed Judge Perry's decision

1966
JUNE 20 Supreme Court granted review

1967
JAN. 11–12 Case argued in Supreme Court
FEB. 13 Supreme Court upheld Judge Perry
MARCH 20 Judge Perry freed Miller and barred a retrial
APRIL 19 Hayes appealed order barring retrial

1970
JUNE 23 Federal Court of Appeals reversed bar on retrial

1971
SEPT. 15 Indictment dismissed. All proceedings ended after 15 years, 9 months and 19 days.

Chronology of November 26–27, 1955 as Reported by Witnesses

A.M. NOV. 26
9:00 Miller returned from work and went to bed
P.M.
2:30 Dean May drove Mrs. May to work at Graham Hospital, leaving children at home
2:45 Teke Johns called Miller to wake him up

3:35	J. C. Penney clerk called Miller regarding a purchase
4:00	Janice May attacked and killed at mine cars (Time as fixed by prosecution in 1963)
4:00	Miller awakened by grandchildren of landlady
4:30	Miller left landlady's residence
4:32	First call to police
5:00	Miller had supper at Maid-Rite Restaurant
5:25–5:30	Miller at Lewis Pharmacy for prescription refill Took prescription to landlady
5:45	Miller reported to cab stand
5:57	Janice died
10:45	Miller drove June Lang to St. David

A.M. NOV. 27

3:45	Miller left Canton with cab

Chronology of November 26, 1955 as set out in Confession

P.M.

2:30	Miller arose
2:30[1]	Coffee at Mac's Drive-In
4:00[2]	Rape–murder at the mine cars Ran to Van Buren Court ("The Flats") and removed jockey shorts To room, put on clean pants
5:15[3]	To Carver and Denny Cleaners. Picked up pants and shirt. Returned to room Walked back to The Flats Walked to railroad. Threw clothes in boxcar. Returned to room
5:45	Left room. Went to cab stand.
11:00	Took June Lang to St. David

1. Time set by waitress
2. Time as set by prosecution in 1963
3. Time set by Carver and Denny clerk

SCAPEGOAT JUSTICE

LLOYD MILLER
AND THE FAILURE OF THE
AMERICAN LEGAL SYSTEM

INTRODUCTION

Tragedy shook the town of Canton, Illinois, on Saturday afternoon, November 26, 1955. An eight-year-old child, Janice May, was murdered. Later, a twenty-nine-year-old cab driver, Lloyd Eldon Miller, Jr., was arrested for that crime, tried, convicted, and sentenced to death. For seven years Miller's attorneys battled in the state and federal courts to save him. Ten execution dates were set. On four occasions the Supreme Court of the United States denied review.

In Spring 1963, Miller's death date was approaching. The Illinois Division of the American Civil Liberties Union in Chicago asked for volunteer attorneys to represent Miller in a commutation plea and to take whatever other steps they could to help Miller. Several attorneys responded. In Summer 1963, by an act of providence, they uncovered evidence sufficient to convince Judge Bernard M. Decker of the Federal Court in Chicago to grant a stay only hours before the scheduled execution.

Subsequent investigation unearthed a mass of facts that undermined the conviction. Investigation revealed also that the prosecution had misrepresented the facts regarding a key portion of the evidence. Federal Judge J. Sam Perry set aside the conviction. Early in 1967 the Supreme Court upheld his ruling.

On March 20, 1967, after eleven years, three months, twenty-two days of imprisonment, Miller was ordered released by Judge Perry.

There is a dramatic intensity to Miller's story. The case against him, as presented by the prosecution, was superficially persuasive. But there were peculiar flaws of logic and strange inconsistencies. Under probing by the defense attorneys, the case disintegrated piece by piece, until it collapsed and lay in ruins.

Because of its drama, the tale is worth telling for its own sake. But this is not the primary reason for telling the story of the Miller-May case. The case illuminates with fearful clarity many of the major evils of the American system of criminal justice—its frequent ineptness, crudity, and unfairness.

These are harsh words. The constitutional guarantees afforded by the Bill of Rights to criminal defendants are the pride of American justice. All provisions of the Bill of Rights apply to federal proceedings and nearly all to state court trials. It guarantees against unreasonable searches and seizures. It requires probable cause before the issuance of a warrant. It forbids double jeopardy and self incrimination. In sweeping language it forbids deprivation of life, liberty or property without "due process of law." It guarantees to the accused a speedy and public trial by an impartial jury. It guarantees to the accused the right to be informed of the nature and the cause of the accusation. It guarantees him the right to be confronted with the witnesses against him. It guarantees the right to subpoena witnesses. It guarantees the right to the assistance of counsel. It prohibits excessive bail and excessive fines and prohibits cruel and unusual punishments.

Yet, in spite of these broad constitutional guarantees, interpreted and amplified by the Supreme Court, constitutional rights remain empty words for many an accused person. American justice is capable of extraordinary refinement and discernment but it is capable also of gross, shocking and scandalous abuses. Why is this so?

The criminal process can be understood by taking an extensive and an intensive view of the Miller-May case. An extensive view is necessary because the case must be observed in its setting—of time, of place, of the development and state of the law. If we view the Miller-May case simply as an isolated failure of the criminal process, we have missed its significance, for it is not that but rather a demonstration of the weakness of an institution.

But such a view, while important, is incomplete. It is necessary also to focus intensively on the specifics of the case in order to reveal the working of the judicial process. Laymen often think of a criminal trial as a dispassionate search for truth. It is not that. It never was that. It is more nearly a combat conducted under rather imprecise rules, an adversary system. The protagonists both fight within the rules and seek to alter them.

As a result, the outcome often is not dictated by "truth" or by "innocence" or "guilt" in the abstract. Rather the outcome frequently is controlled by the evidence available and permissible under the rules. The Miller case vividly illustrates how large a role chance often plays.

Since the system is adversary the advocate at each step is confronted with questions of strategy. We shall see what those questions were, how they were resolved, and why. Many of these tactical questions played a fundamental role in the case, drastically altering its course.

In scarcely any sense is a criminal trial what the public thinks it is. Some of its weaknesses are curable. There has been progress, indeed striking progress, in some areas of criminal procedure. In 1964, the Supreme Court in the historic *Escobedo* decision declared that upon request an accused has a right to counsel during police interrogation. In 1966, the even more historic *Miranda* decision spelled out in detail the rights of an accused person during police interrogation. Unfortunately, more recently the Supreme Court has undermined these decisions. Nonetheless, there is hope that they may make a fundamental change in American police interrogation practices. But in the Miller case, evils were not confined to the practices condemned in the *Escobedo* and *Miranda* cases. Some of the problems raised are part of the fibre of the system. Recognition of this fact should give us a deeper appreciation of the problems facing our courts. If one understands the truly subtle issues involved, then one can appreciate the limitations of the judicial process. Its judgments are made by fallible men, but they are necessary to ordered life in society.

Did the prosecution suppress facts out of malice to Miller, deliberately seeking the execution of an innocent man? This is a key question, difficult for an adversary of the prosecution to answer objectively. Let me attempt an answer: early in the case, the prosecution became convinced, genuinely convinced, of Miller's guilt. Evidence that we, as Miller's counsel, felt clearly favored him, or even exonerated him, was not seen in that light by the prosecution.

Consequently they did not feel compelled to reveal such evidence to the defense and the court. The adversary system of criminal justice has its strengths (and I do not advocate abandoning it) but a failing is that an advocate speedily finds it difficult to evaluate facts objectively. In my view, the prosecution suppression of evidence was very wrong. But the prosecution did not act maliciously. Indeed, had it done so, the Miller case, while shocking and tragic to the participants, would scarcely merit a book. A central concern of the adversary system or of any system of criminal justice should be to ensure that all the facts are fully and honestly presented. The Miller case illustrates that the failure here is not an isolated instance of wrongdoing but an inherent problem of the criminal law.

In June 1972, the Supreme Court held that capital punishment, at least within the framework of present law, is unconstitutional because it violates the Eighth Amendment bar on "cruel and unusual" punishments. We hope that this decision ends the death sentence for all time in the United States and that the present drive to restore capital punishment to the statute books and in practice will come to nothing. Since the Miller case was a capital case, its lessons present themselves with dramatic intensity, but they relate to the criminal process generally and not to the death penalty.

The Miller-May case had a profound impact on the lives of scores of persons, whose parts in the story are given in this book. In some cases, the names used are not their real ones. Many attorneys, including the author, devoted effort to it for years. We did other things, too, of course. All of the attorneys earned their livings in private practice. But there were periods when we worked on the case for days and weeks together, while writing a brief, preparing an oral argument, or preparing for trial. Long periods of inactivity would follow. Yet, even during quiet periods, the case was not far from our thoughts. For some of us it was the most exciting and rewarding professional work we undertook during this period.

An extraordinary number of people contributed to the freeing of Lloyd Miller. At least thirteen lawyers participated in one phase or another of the litigation. All of us advanced money for out-of-pocket costs, and one of the attorneys particularly spent large sums for investigation, the printing of briefs, and other expenses. Nonlawyers, too, played a vital role. Experts gave freely their time and energies to study complex matters.

Secretaries are the spear carriers of the law. They do much of the essential laborious work, but receive too little recognition. Our secretaries and even our friends volunteered to work after hours. Without their trained help, the work could not have been done.

My partners, Alex Elson and Aaron S. Wolff, willingly gave us their experienced counsel at several critical points in the case. The facilities of our office and the out-of-pocket disbursements by the firm represented a most significant contribution by them to the outcome. They were patient and understanding when the demands of the case kept me from my usual firm duties.

A massive outpouring of money, time, and volunteer human effort was necessary to achieve the final result. Much of it was devoted to uncovering and presenting to the courts facts that the prosecution had long known but suppressed. It is shocking that a man condemned to death and penniless must, in the United States, rely on volunteer help to pursue all the roads of redress open to him.

In this case, extraordinary events happened to ordinary persons. The tragedy touched deeply the lives of two families. For the Mays, a daughter was lost under frightful circumstances. Because of our role as Miller's attorneys, it was inappropriate for us to meet or interview Janice May's father, mother, or brothers. We saw her parents on one occasion only. But we did not have to know them to understand their anguish. In helping Lloyd, we did not forget Janice. For the Miller family—father, mother, brother and sister—a son stood accused and then convicted of murder. Through years of heartbreak, agony, and broken hopes, they found the courage to live and endure, to demonstrate again man's capacity to overcome adversity.

It is our duty as defense counsel, prosecutors, judges, and citizens to study a shocking crime and trial and to learn from them. If the Miller-May case helps us to improve American criminal justice, then in one special sense the death of Janice May and Miller's long ordeal will not have been for nothing.

1

MURDER

Teke Johns, owner of a cab company in Canton, Illinois, said that on Saturday, November 26, 1955, it was "misting all day long. It was cold. I can't remember any sun shining. I know the next morning there was a little sciff of snow here and there."

That morning, Janice Elizabeth May, aged 8, attended a movie for children at the Capitol theater in downtown Canton.

Her mother, Mrs. Jeane May, described her only daughter, a third-grade pupil:

> "Well, she was fifty-three and one-quarter inches tall and weighed ninety pounds, at the end of September at the school record, and she had an "A" positive blood count. She was blond-haired, blue-eyed, big deep dimples."

She and her brother, James Allen May, aged 12, were taken to the Capitol by their father, Dean Eugene May. The oldest child, Willard Dean, aged 14, did not attend.

The morning show was popular with children. Mrs. May explained, "They have a bids from kids, they call it, an auction sale where they sell toys to children for points from one of the dairies."

Canton, population 12,000, is the center of a coal mining region. Dean May worked for one of the largest employers, the International Harvester Company. He had been employed there as an assembler since 1936. He, his wife, and three children lived in a modern ranch home at 743 South Sixth Avenue.

Dean did not work on Saturdays. The family arose late that morning and watched television until Dean took Janice and Jim to the movies. About 1:50 P.M., Janice called home and asked her daddy to pick her up. Jeane and Bill held off lunch until everyone was home, and then together they had "the children's favorite Saturday lunch," according to Mrs. May—hamburgers, potato salad, baked beans and fruit. After Jeane, a registered nurse, had changed into her uniform, Dean drove her to Graham Hospital where she was to go on duty at 2:50 P.M.

The children did the dishes and watched television again after lunch. Sometime later (the exact time was never established), Bill and Jimmy left the house with a basketball intending to play at the Kellogg School, a few blocks away at Third and Hickory Street. They told Janice to stay home until they returned.

But after going a short distance toward Kellogg School, Jimmy said, they circled back to the house "to see if Janice did her work right." She was gone. The boys had a third television session and then Jimmy went to look for her. "I went to Aunt Clara's but I didn't knock on the door because I didn't know whether she was home or not. I then went to my grandmother's who lives across the street from Kellogg School. Then I went out the back gate and cut over to the cars. . . . My dog Cuddles went with me. My brother was not with me. I got to the cars and heard a noise. I looked under one car and I thought it was a dog hit that went under there to die. I ran home to tell my brother."

The cars mentioned by Jimmy were a group of abandoned mine cars stacked on end along the right of way of the Chicago Burlington and Quincy Railroad, which runs through Canton from north to south. The cars were just east of the railroad tracks at Fourth and Hickory Streets.

Jimmy told Bill that he thought he heard a noise among the cars near the tracks. Jimmy and Bill ran over there, and then Bill said, they "followed Cuddles between the pretty good sized hole between the separated cars. I saw it was Janice. I told [Jimmy] to call Dad. . . ."

The scene under the mine cars was dreadful. Bill continued:

> Janice was on her knees, knees under her and her face was down in the dirt, and her arm was lying out with a piece of cement on it. I pulled that off. The only thing I saw that she had on was just a shirt and shoes.

> I can't remember the color of the shirt. It was on her shoulders, but it was sort of bloody. I saw no clothing from her shirt to the shoes. That area of her body was nude. I spoke to Janice but all she did was moan.

Jimmy ran a block east to the filling station and adjoining residence of Harold Largent. He asked to use the phone and added:

"Oh, please, Mr. Largent, my sister is hurt." Largent directed Jimmy to a phone and looked in the direction from which he had come. There he saw Bill "waving and excited." Largent went over at once. When he saw Janice, he rushed back to tell Jimmy to call the police and ask for an ambulance.

At 4:32, a call was relayed to Sergeant Robert Hardy and Officer Neil Baxter on routine police car patrol. They went to the mine cars, and with the help of two other officers, Raymond G. Ball and Ronald Wilkinson, who arrived moments later, moved the mine cars so that Janice could be lifted out.

Within a few minutes, an ambulance arrived from the Murphy Memorial Home, driven by Thomas J. Simon and his partner, Ralph McFall. Simon remembered:

> She was very bloody. A great amount of blood there. I picked her up in my arms and moved her out to where my partner could help me get her on the ambulance cot. There was a little passageway into these cars and the ambulance cot had been placed just outside of that. We then put the little girl in the ambulance and took her immediately to the hospital. There we took her to surgery and called Dr. Bennett. I don't know the approximate time of our arrival in the surgery room. She was alive when I arrived at the scene. There were audible sounds from her, but she was not able to talk.

After the ambulance left Officer Ball remained and took charge of the scene. He roped off the area, kept everybody away, and assembled all objects he thought important, including the block of concrete, wet with blood, that Bill had removed from his sister's arm.

The ambulance brought Janice to Graham Hospital at approximately 4:45. Mrs. May, who had had supper at 4:30, was told that she was wanted in surgery. Later, Mrs. May said:

> I went to surgery and saw Janice lying on the cart. Her breathing was labored and I knew she was hurt very badly. She had a large cut over her head and around the side of her face. The cuts were very deep and I could see her brains.

Dr. David A. Bennett, the surgeon, said that when he arrived "Janice was alive and in a terminal condition." He added that she had a crushing injury to the right side of her face, multiple skull fractures, and laceration of the vagina. The rectum was bulging into the vaginal vault.

> By terminal condition, I mean the girl was in a complete coma, breathing very slowly and shallow, and pulseless, and it was obvious she was going to die, and she did soon afterwards at 5:47 P.M.

Immediately after the death of Janice, Dr. Raymond J. Mercey, a physician and the coroner of Fulton County, was called to Graham Hospital. He made a preliminary examination of the body and then was present at the autopsy performed by Dr. Bennett Sunday afternoon in the Murphy Memorial Home.

The funeral for Janice was conducted Tuesday afternoon, November 29, at the Murphy Memorial Home by the Rev. Willis Reed, pastor of the First Baptist Church where Janice had attended Sunday school. The casket was closed and there was no music. Included among the flowers was a wreath from the Anderson School pupils. "Though our eyes may be blinded with tears," Dr. Reed said, "we must pray for courage."

Most of the mourners attended brief gravesite rites at White Chapel Memory Gardens, in bitter wind and subfreezing cold.

The children in Janice's Sunday School class had been studying Psalm 100. Dr. Reed included it in the service:

> Make a joyful noise unto the Lord, all ye lands.
> Serve the Lord with gladness:

Come before his presence with singing.
Know ye that the Lord he is God:
it is he that hath made us,
and not we ourselves; we are his people,
and the sheep of his pasture.

Enter unto his gates with thanksgiving,
and into his courts with praise:
be thankful unto him, and bless his name.

For the Lord is good; his mercy is everlasting;
and his truth endureth to all generations.

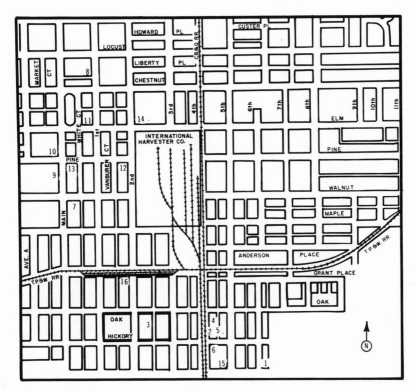

1. May home.
2. The old mine cars—scene of the crime.
3. Kellogg School.
4. Largent gas station.
5. Largent home.
6. Canton Transfer Company.
7. Baxter residence.
8. Yellow Cab Stand.
9. Maid-Rite Cafe.
10. Lewis Pharmacy.
11. Carver and Denny Cleaners.
12. Van Buren Flats.
13. Mac's Coffee Shop.
14. Harriet's Lunch.
15. Miller Auto Body.
16. TP&W Railroad Station.

The Walnut Creek Bridge is about four blocks west of the area covered by the map.

2

SATURDAY, NOVEMBER 26, 1955—
MONDAY, NOVEMBER 28, 1955

THE JOURNEY

When cab driver Lloyd Eldon Miller, Jr., soon to face trial for Janice's murder, began work on Saturday evening, November 26, 1955, he had left fifty hours of freedom. He went to his room, which he rented from Mrs. Alice Baxter at 28 East Walnut Street, packed his suitcase and called the dispatcher at "21 Yellow Cab," asking to be picked up. The dispatcher at the taxi company was Ira Johns, son of Lawrence "Teke" Johns, the proprietor. The cab didn't come and so Lloyd walked to the cab stand at First Avenue and East Chestnut. There he picked up his cab, No. 1, a 1953 Plymouth. The cabs were equipped with two-way radio.

Part of the dispatcher's job was to maintain a daily log for each driver showing the time and place of origin of each call, the destination, and the fare. Miller's log for November 26 shows that his first call was at 5:45 P.M., and the fare, fifty cents. Between then and 2:30 on Sunday morning, he made seventeen runs in all, taking in a total of $13.00. At 10:45 P.M. he had a two dollar fare from the cabstand to St. David, a small community south of Canton. The passenger and the trip were destined to have a momentous impact upon Lloyd.

When I studied the log to write about this Saturday evening, I noticed a strange notation: After the last call shown on the log (a $2.00 fare), at the bottom of the column, someone printed in block letters, a single word. The word was "DEAD."[1]

Patrolman Raymond Ball, who had assumed command of the

---

1. The word "DEAD" appears also at 7:05 P.M. Numerous pages of this log relating to several drivers were introduced into evidence. The "DEAD" notation appears only twice, each time with reference to Miller.

scene of the crime, testified at Lloyd's trial in 1956 that about eight o'clock and several times thereafter, he saw Miller near the scene driving his cab. Later that evening, or early Sunday morning, Ball added, he saw Miller in front of police headquarters and Lloyd asked whether the police were going to check the 3:00 A.M. bus from Canton to Peoria. Ball told Miller that he didn't know whether such a search would be made. Lloyd's testimony was that he did go by the scene at Fourth Avenue and Hickory Street three times, and during the evening he did stop by the police station. There he met Virgil Ball, Sheriff of Fulton County, whom he knew only by his nickname, "Buck" Ball. Lloyd asked whether he had any additional news. "I mean by that, there was a policeman down there at the cab-stand and told us about it. We had strict orders to be on the lookout for any suspicious persons." Buck Ball did not answer and Lloyd continued with his calls.

Lloyd continued with his calls until 3:45 A.M., then went to Mrs. Baxter's residence, picked up his suitcase and put it in the back seat of his cab. Since he had missed the three o'clock bus, he headed north in the cab. He drove to Farmington and then east to Peoria. He stopped at a Hopkins Service Station to call the bus station about a bus for Detroit. He was told that he could catch an Illini-Swallow bus at Pekin on the east side of the Illinois River, south of Peoria. As he crossed the bridge over the Illinois River into Pekin, he turned left a block and a half, turned left again, and left the cab down a cinder road. It was chilly. Lloyd removed his rayon gabardine uniform jacket and put on a heavy blue jacket from his suit-case. Then he walked to a drugstore a short distance from the bus stop.

At 5:55 Sunday morning, Lloyd boarded the bus and paid the fare from Pekin to Champaign. According to the bus driver, Joseph McGraw, Miller was the only passenger and took a seat directly behind the driver. McGraw did not recall any of the conversation between him and Lloyd, but did remember that he was bareheaded, wearing a jacket, and carrying a black suitcase. The bus arrived at Champaign at 7:50.

In Champaign, Lloyd bought a ticket to Danville. Upon arriving there about eleven o'clock he registered at the Grier-Lincoln Hotel under his own name. He went to bed and slept until about 10:30 or

11:00 the next morning, Monday, November 28. There were ten hours of freedom left.

After breakfast, Lloyd went back to his hotel, picked up his suitcase and checked it in a lock box at the bus depot. From there he went to a movie and then to a restaurant. While drinking a cup of coffee, Lloyd testified, "I heard the radio news that I heard my name said, that I was under suspicion for murder. Then I didn't know what to think. I mean, I thought it was all in a dream—and I looked at a newspaper, and it said, 'Miller wanted for suspicion of murder.' I got scared—I didn't know what to do. Then I stayed there in the restaurant and I decided I would go on to Detroit." He went back to the bus station. It was about 8:30 Monday evening.

When Lloyd asked the ticket agent for the next bus to Detroit, the agent, Earl Sutton, said, "Just a second. I will look it up." Lloyd sat down on a bench. He did observe that it seemed to take the agent quite a bit of time to obtain the information.

Sutton's version of the incident was substantially the same as Lloyd's. Only Miller and he were in the station. Lloyd first asked for a bus to Detroit, and was told there was one leaving via Indianapolis at 9:10 P.M. He next inquired for a bus to Evansville, Indiana. There was none until the following morning. While Lloyd was in the restroom, Sutton called the city police to tell them that there was a man at the station who resembled the one they were looking for. After calling the police, Sutton returned to the ticket window and gave Lloyd the schedule to Indianapolis. As Sutton put it, "It seemed just a few seconds then until Glen and Jocko Anderson walked in. There was just the four of us present at that time. The defendant, John Anderson, myself and Glen Miller." John Anderson said, "Do you know me, boy?" The reply was, "Yes, I know you." Then he said, "But if it's about the little girl over at Canton, you are wrong. I didn't do it."

Jocko Anderson was John B. Anderson, County Treasurer of Fulton County and former Sheriff of Fulton County. On November 28 he was acting as special deputy sheriff for Virgil Ball. He had known Lloyd for about four years.

According to Lloyd, when Anderson and Glen Miller stepped up to him, Lloyd said to them, "I admit taking off in a cab, but you are all wrong. I didn't do anything like that over there. Then Jocko said, 'Let me put the cuffs on you.' " Anderson snapped on a pair of thumb cuffs.

For Lloyd, then a few months past his twenty-ninth birthday, freedom had ended. He was not to know liberty again for over eleven years, until some months past his fortieth birthday.

Who was Lloyd Eldon Miller, and what had brought him to the moment when Jocko Anderson snapped on the thumb cuffs? Lloyd told his story at his trial in Carthage, Illinois, in 1956. He was born September 8, 1926, in Chicago. His father, Lloyd Eldon Miller, Sr., was born in Kansas in 1906 and his mother, Jewel, also a Kansas native, was born in 1907. Lloyd was the oldest of three children. After him came a daughter, Esther Margaret, called Margaret, now Mrs. Margaret Isaak, and after her, another son, Carl Leonard. Between 1929 and 1932, the depression forced the Millers to work in California as migrant laborers in the orchards. Margaret was born during that time in 1929 and Carl in 1931. About 1932, the family settled in the Canton area, and in 1937 Miller Sr. obtained a position as a plumber with International Harvester Company in Canton where he remained until compelled to an early retirement about 1964.

In 1945, after completing two years in high school, nineteen-year-old Lloyd was drafted, served time in Italy, and was honorably discharged in 1947. From then until his arrest in 1955, he was a wanderer. At his trial in 1956, Miller described his life:

> After my discharge I lived with my parents in Canton, Illinois. After my discharge, I sent money home to my mother while I was overseas—about $1,200—and she saved it for me—and I went to work at the Caterpillar Tractor Company in East Peoria. I worked there about one week and my dad got me a job at International Harvester Company around the first of March, 1947. I worked there until almost June of the same year. My father and I got into it about spending my money and I just took off and got out to Denver, Colorado, and enlisted in the U.S. Coast Guard. I don't know exactly when this was, but it was in about June, 1947.
>
> After I was sworn in in the Coast Guard, I was shipped

to Government Island, Alameda, California. I was there
about three months and I got homesick and went AWOL
and came back to my folks. Then I lived with my parents.
I worked at A.B.C. over at East Peoria. I was then living
at home, Route 2, Canton, Illinois, and riding back and
forth to work with other riders. I worked at A.B.C. about
two months, then I got scared that they would pick me up
on being AWOL so I left home and went up to Chicago. I
got a bus boy job in a Thompson Restaurant there in Chicago. I was staying with my grandpa up there. I worked
there about one month. Then I got acquainted with a
waitress there [Sally Abbott] and a few days later we
agreed to get married and we did marry [on May 25, 1948].
I had known her just a few days before we were married. I
told her before we got married that I was AWOL from the
Coast Guard, and then in about one week we talked it
over and we both decided it would be better for me to give
myself up.

Lloyd gave himself up; he and Sally separated, and, with money
from her allotments, Lloyd divorced her in Peoria on December 23,
1948. Lloyd's pattern of living for the next several years was like
that of 1942–1948—enlistment in the military, difficulties in the
service, hasty marriages with the girls he had known a few days
followed by a speedy separation. For the Coast Guard AWOL he
served thirty days in the brig. Again he went AWOL, again did thirty
days and received a bad conduct discharge. Nonetheless, in 1949, he
enlisted in the Army. After a few months, he and a friend, Tom
Nelson, went AWOL in a rented car. On September 19, 1949, in Dalton, Georgia, under the name of Jack Franklin Warner he met Sue
Ann Williams. Lloyd added,

About one week later after we was married I told her
that the car was—"you might as well say it was rented—but
you might as well say it was stolen—and I was AWOL from
the army—my own name was Lloyd Eldon Miller, Jr." We
decided it would be best to give myself up. She agreed with
me and I told her after this was all cleared up we would
come back and get married under my real name. Then
Tom Nelson and me went to Chattanooga, Tennessee,

and gave ourselves up.[1] We went from Chattanooga with the M.P. from a camp down at Atlanta. We was there a few days and then the M.P.'s from California came and got us. Then our company commander gave us each thirty days in the stockade. Then, Tom was shipped overseas and I was held there and turned over to the civilian authorities for the automobile. I guess I was held for the civilian authorities because it was my driver's license it was on. I was taken by the civilian authorities to the county jail and about December of 1949[2] I plead guilty, that I was in the wrong, and I was sentenced to seven months[3] in the Alameda Prison Farm; it was about July 10, 1950, that I was released to civilian grounds.

Upon my release from the Alameda Prison Farm I learned, for the first time I was discharged from the Army—dishonorable discharge.

Lloyd rejoined his wife in Dalton. They lived briefly in Canton, but Sue insisted on returning to Dalton. A son, Steven Eldon Miller, was born on May 5, 1951. Lloyd had the usual succession of jobs and finally enrolled in school under the G.I. Bill of Rights. A few months later, Lloyd and Sue separated. In April 1952, he enlisted in the Air Force, but was separated when his record came to light. Lloyd returned to Sue and lived with her off and on until October 1953, sometimes in Dalton, sometimes in Canton. Next came a hitchhiking spree. On December 4, 1953, he married Nan James in Bedford, Pennsylvania. Lloyd divorced Sue on June 21, 1954, but soon sought a reconciliation with her. The reconciliation was brief and Lloyd left. On February 9, 1955, in Rock Island, Illinois, he married Lynn Marin, a divorcee with a four-year-old son. Lloyd and Lynn roamed about the country. They split up, reunited, and split up again. In August, Lynn told Lloyd that he was "not too good a husband." Lloyd left and headed for Canton. On the way, he heard that Sue Ann had a warrant out for his arrest for delinquent child support. On September 16, he was back in Canton where he was hired by Teke as a cab driver.

1. On September 30, 1949 according to Army records.
2. The date was December 21, 1949.
3. Actually eight months. Lloyd may have served only seven months because of good conduct.

And that same week, the sixteenth of September, Teke says I could go to work for him if I could get my driver's license renewed. I got it renewed that same day and started work that night. Then I continued working for Teke: I worked odd hours on Friday, Saturday and Sunday, and then went on regular on Monday, working days, driving the cab up until the last of October, which I went on nights regularly.

I worked for the Yellow Cab but it was known at that time as Reliable Cab. But when I went to work nights we had got a franchise to be called '21 Yellow Cab.' I was living with my parents on Rural Route 2, Canton, Illinois, when I first started working for the Reliable Cab Company. I lived there until the first of October. Then I lived at 28 East Walnut Street in Canton up until 3:45 A.M. November 27, 1955.

From the latter part of September until November 26, 1955, I was continuously employed as a taxicab driver. My duty hours, when I first worked days was from 6:00 A.M. to 6:00 P.M. and when I was working nights it was from 6:00 P.M. to 6:00 A.M.

What was Miller's marital status? So far as we know, the marriage to Sally Abbott on May 25, 1948, was valid. Lloyd divorced her on December 23, 1948. Hence the marriage to Sue Ann Williams on September 19, 1949, was valid. But his marriage to Nan James on December 4, 1953, was void because of the prior marriage to Sue Ann Williams. Hence when Lloyd divorced Sue Ann on June 21, 1954, he was presumably a single man, even though Nan did not obtain a divorce decree until June 11, 1956. It follows that the marriage to Lynn on March 9, 1956, was valid. Lynn divorced Lloyd in the Circuit Court of Rock Island County on September 20, 1962. The ground: conviction of a felony.

Thus Lloyd married four girls in seven years. Two he divorced; two divorced him. Even-steven.

3

CONFESSION

After Anderson put thumb cuffs on Lloyd, they and Glen Miller went to the office of the Sheriff of Vermilion County in Danville, taking Lloyd's suitcase with them. According to Anderson the following conversation took place while Lloyd and he were alone: "Miller said, 'I sure hope that they catch that fellow.' I said, 'Who?' He said, 'The fellow that killed that little girl.' I said, 'We have caught him.' He said, 'Who is it?' I said, 'It is you.' He just kind of buried his head in his hands—he didn't say anything at that time. He did not deny the accusation at that time."

Lloyd's version of the conversation was this: " 'Jocko,' I says, 'You got the wrong man.' He says, 'No, I think we have the right man.' I says, 'You are wrong,' I says, 'You are crazy.' Jocko didn't say anything else."

Eight years later, Blaine Ramsey, State's Attorney of Fulton County, explained how Jocko Anderson and Glen Miller happened to be at the bus depot in Danville to arrest Miller Monday evening. Ramsey was informed of the crime immediately, at 4:45 on Saturday afternoon. He went at once to the hospital and from there to the Canton Police Station, arriving between five-thirty and six o'clock. The station was crowded and it was difficult to find out what was happening. Every Canton policeman had been called in, including men off duty. State police were there, several deputy sheriffs, and also police officers from nearby Peoria, Bellevue, Pekin, Havana, and other communities. At one time the station was teeming with sixty or seventy officers. Ramsey complained, "The problem was what to do with them as much as anything, all offering to help."

About five-thirty on Sunday morning, Teke Johns reported a cab missing. "My first reaction was, 'Don't bother me over a stolen cab.'

At the time I did not know the significance." But sometime on Sunday, Ramsey decided that there was a connection between the murder, the missing cab, and the missing cab driver. Soon word came that the cab had been seen in Peoria. The bus driver, Joseph McGraw, was found at home and informed the officials that Lloyd had been a passenger on the early morning bus from Pekin to Champaign. Later that day, the cab was found near the Illinois River in Pekin. Since Miller seemed to be going east, the authorities checked the schedules of buses from Champaign to Indianapolis. Miller had not been a passenger on a bus which arrived in Indianapolis from Champaign shortly before the check was made, so, according to Ramsey, "We started backtracking. I sent out John Anderson, who is the former sheriff of Fulton County to Danville, for the reason that he would know Lloyd himself, and would know him on sight. It was Mr. Anderson who found him at the bus depot at Danville on Monday afternoon, and he was attempting to purchase a ticket to Evansville, Indiana."

At the trial, the events from arrest until 12:15 A.M. on Thursday, December 1, when Miller signed a confession, were related twice by the witnesses, once before the judge alone, and again before the judge and the jury. Under Illinois law, before a confession may be presented to a jury, the judge must determine that it was made "voluntarily." While the jury is out of the courtroom, he hears evidence regarding the circumstances under which the confession was obtained. If the judge rules the confession voluntary, then it is presented to the jury. But the jury may reject the confession if it finds that it is untrue. For the jury to make its decision, it must hear all the facts surrounding the confession. Hence, the tale, from arrest to confession, was twice told. What follows is an amalgam of the two versions.

President at the jail when Miller arrived were Virgil Ball, Sheriff of Fulton County, Edward P. Fuller, a deputy sheriff, William C. Hendrickson, Sheriff of Vermilion County and other Vermilion County officials. Miller's personal effects were taken from him and examined.

The two sheriffs took Miller to an interrogation room, off the kitchen in the basement of the jail, where everyone had coffee. After the coffee, Lloyd said, Virgil Ball asked, "Why did you take off in that cab?" Miller answered, "Well, I says, You have threatened me down there before—a warrant—about keeping up child support. I received a letter from my former wife, Sue Ann [Williams], on—November 25, 1955. I received a letter from her that she—I didn't get no money down there, she would have a warrant out for me." Miller continued, "I told Virgil I wanted a lie detector test and Virgil says, 'Well, we will think about it.' "

According to Ball, Ball asked Miller whether he would be willing to take a lie detector test in Springfield. Lloyd agreed.

About eleven o'clock that evening, a two-car convoy left Danville for Springfield. In the lead car were Miller, Sheriff Ball, and Deputy Sheriff Fuller. Anderson and another official followed.

During the trip, according to Ball, there was "general conversation more or less." Ball added that he remembered one of the stories that Lloyd told them: ". . . he had picked up a fare in Canton about 2:00 or 2:30 and this fare held a knife in his back to make him drive to Peoria."

When they arrived in Springfield about 2:00 A.M., November 29, they went directly to the Sangamon County jail where Miller was placed in a cell alone after being booked for larceny. Miller was allowed to sleep until six o'clock when he and about a half a dozen other prisoners were routed up in the bullpen. Breakfast was a cup of coffee and two donuts. The day was spent in the bullpen with the other prisoners. The only furnishing was a long bench and a steam radiator.

About five o'clock that afternoon, Sheriff Ball and Fuller returned to the Sangamon County jail to take Miller to the Illinois Bureau of Criminal Identification and Investigation in the State armory in Springfield. On the way, they stopped to buy Lloyd a package of Kool cigarettes. Upon arrival, Ball introduced Miller to John Lynch and Dwight Whitlock, both polygraph operators. After a few preliminary questions, Lynch and Ball took Lloyd to a laboratory where they drew blood from Lloyd's right index finger, took fingernail scrapings, and took his fingerprints. Also, as Lloyd put it, ". . . they took a small quantity of hair from around my privates."

A serious interrogation then began.

During the evening, the prosecution's theory of the case began to unfold. Anderson's comment to Miller, made in the Vermilion

County Jail at Danville, reflected the authorities' deep suspicion of Miller. Ramsey's statement in a federal court in 1963 put into words what the authorities had then concluded: the man who left Canton in a stolen taxicab in the early morning hours of Sunday was the man who had murdered Janice May.

There are two versions of what occurred in the offices of the State Crime Lab on Tuesday evening, November 29, the version of the authorities—principally the two polygraph operators, Lynch and Whitlock, supplemented by Sheriff Ball and Chief Lindzey—and the version of Miller himself. At the trial, in September 1956 in Carthage, the authorities told their version swiftly. The interrogation was conducted in an office about twelve feet square, furnished with a table, a desk, and several chairs. Questioning began about five-thirty or six that evening. Lynch said that he told Miller that he had been informed that he was there to take a voluntary lie detector test. "I asked him if that was true, and he said 'Yes.' I further told him that any statement that he would make could be used against him in a court proceedings at a future date. He said that he understood that." After Ramsey and Sheriff Ball left the office, Miller was seated in a chair between Lynch and Whitlock and facing them. First Whitlock obtained a brief biographical statement and then shifted inquiries to the crime itself. Questioning continued until about eight o'clock for a supper break. Next came a lie detector test and then more questioning until about 1:00 or 2:00 A.M. Lloyd was then taken back to jail.

What happened during the questioning itself? From the prosecution witnesses, we have only a sketchy version of a session that lasted, by their own account, approximately eight hours.

Lloyd's account of the session was more detailed:

> When I was taken back into this little room Mr. Lynch, Mr. Whitlock, and Virgil Ball was then present. Then Mr. Lynch he said, "Lloyd," he says, "Why did you leave Canton?" I says, "Well, I had a—been threatened by a child abandonment warrant from my first wife." He says, "Don't give me that stuff." He said, "What is the real reason why you left Canton?" I says, "I am telling the real truth." So he went out to the laboratory and he brung in—at that

time it was a gray wet jacket. He says, "Does this belong to you?" He says, "We found this at the West Walnut Creek. Does this jacket belong to you?" I said, "No, it does not." He says, "You are a liar." I says, "You are the one that is a liar."

Next Lloyd said he was shown a pair of white jockey shorts with, in his words, "dried blood on them." (The shorts had been found on Monday afternoon in an abandoned apartment building called The Flats, not far from the crime scene.) Lloyd was asked whether the shorts were his. He said they were not. He was shown the piece of concrete found near the body and asked if he recognized it. Lloyd said he did not. After that, Lloyd testified,

> So I asked Virgil Ball if I could see my parents. He says, "Your parents told us that they didn't want to have anything to do with you." I says, "Virgil," I says, "you are lying." I says, "I know my parents."[1]

Lloyd was asked if he recognized photographs of the slain child. He denied recognition. He was shown a Carver and Denny cleaning ticket and asked if he had picked up garments there in downtown Canton the preceding Saturday. He denied that he had.

Then the authorities adopted a new tack. According to Lloyd,

> Then Virgil—he went out and Mr. Whitlock, he come back in and, "Lloyd," Mr. Lynch said, "Why don't you admit this so we can get you to a mental institution for mental care?" I says, "I am not admitting to no crime that I didn't do. I am not admitting to no crime that I did not commit."

According to Lloyd, the session ended at 3:00 A.M. when Sheriff Ball and Deputy Fuller returned him to his cell.

Lloyd added other details regarding his first interrogation. He was told that his landlady, Mrs. Alice Baxter, had told the authorities that she had not seen Lloyd until 5:45 on Saturday night. In re-

---

1. At the time, Lloyd's parents were exerting every effort to see their son. They were not allowed to visit him until after he had confessed.

sponse to this statement, Lloyd gave his questioners his version of his activities between 4:00 and 5:45 P.M. on Saturday:

He got up at four o'clock, bathed, shaved, and dressed (green shirt, green pants, green jacket, cab cap). At four-thirty he came downstairs and met Mrs. Baxter. At this point Lloyd said Lynch accused him of lying. Miller said he replied, "You are wrong. I know my innocence."

There is little dispute about what happened the next day from the time Lloyd returned to the Sangamon County Jail until about 5:00 P.M. He slept until about 6:00 A.M. After breakfast (again two donuts and a cup of black coffee), he was taken upstairs for finger-printing (again) and returned to the bullpen. At 3:30 P.M. he was placed in a lineup and then returned to the jail. Supper at 4:30 P.M. was two baloney sandwiches and a cup of coffee.

The second and crucial interrogation took place Wednesday night in the same room in the Springfield armory. Miller was brought back about 5:30 P.M. but before the interrogation as such began, a confrontation occurred that would play a paramount role in his life. The participants were Lloyd and a 23-year-old waitress, June Lang. Earlier that day, Lynch had taken a statement from June. This statement, in June's presence, Lynch read to Lloyd.

The statement itself was not introduced into evidence in the 1956 trial. No copy came into the possession of Miller's attorneys until 1963 when it was produced by the prosecution pursuant to a federal court subpoena.

The statement, dated November 30, 1955, was on three legal size sheets of paper and was written entirely by June Lang herself in question and answer form in a neat precise hand and was signed by her. June stated that she had met Lloyd about five weeks before. On their third date he had proposed. She deferred her answer. That same night June rode as a passenger in Lloyd's cab to visit her brother in St. David, a small town a few miles south of Canton. On arrival, she took Lloyd to see her baby nephew.

> Before I went in the house, he laid his head on my shoul-
> der and said, "June, why do people do things they are
> ashamed of?" When I came out with the little boy, he said,
> "Get him back in the house." I took my little nephew back

in the house and came back out to the cab. I got in and sat down. He was staring straight ahead and I said, "Lloyd what is the matter with you?" and he said "You know they will blame me for it" and I said, "What are you talking about?" He turned and looked at me with a very strange look of shock on his face, and said "June, you know I done it" and he said "they won't take me in for it. I got rid of it." I didn't say anything to him for a long time, and when I went to get out of the cab he reached over and took hold of the door handle and told me to sit still. He told me "if you say anything, you will get the same thing" and he said again "they won't get me because I got rid of it." On the way to St. David he said "wasn't it a coincident that that train passed just then."

According to Lynch, at the confrontation June turned to the defendant and said, "Lloyd, you too, know that it is true." The defendant answered, "June, you will be sorry for this."

According to Miller his interrogators did not read June's statement to him but simply told him its contents:

At this time I asked June, I says, "Tell these people that I didn't say no such thing to you." I said "Do you want me to go to the chair for something I didn't do?" June just grinned and she was about to say something and Mr. Lindzey motioned for her to take her out of the room.

After June Lang left, Lynch and Whitlock resumed their interrogation, which lasted from about 5:30 to about 8:30 P.M. We don't know what happened during that time. According to Lloyd, during part of it he was given a lie detector test. Lynch and Whitlock, however, stated that the test was given late Tuesday evening. Miller insisted that it was given early Wednesday evening. According to Lloyd, about this time he was again shown the block of concrete and again he was asked, "Why don't you admit this so we can get you to a mental institution?" Again he denied his guilt.

Another of the deeply significant events of the case occurred during the first part of Wednesday evening. When the specimen of pubic hair was taken from Miller on Tuesday night, it was not a mere matter of laboratory routine. The purpose was to compare

Miller's pubic hair and a hair connected with the crime. Not until many years later, during the course of the 1963 federal court proceedings, did we learn the incredible truth.

Miller said,

> I was in this little room at all times on the evening of November thirtieth except for one time which I demanded to look through the microscope my own self because they said these hairs belonged to me. Mr. Lynch made a statement to me that certain hairs belonged to me. He showed me some hairs there. I demanded to go back there and he took me there; back in the laboratory in a small room which appeared to me to be a microscope room and I looked there and said "Them hairs don't match." I says, "Them hairs don't belong to me." And this chemist just looked at me and smiled.

"This chemist" was a man named Litterly.

Immediately afterwards, according to Lloyd, came the lie detector test. After it was over, Lloyd said,

> I was then unhooked from the machine. After I was uncoupled from the lie detector Mr. Lynch said I was lying and I started crying.[1] I said, "I know that lie detector is telling the truth. I mean it too."

At 8:35 P.M., Lynch and Whitlock left for supper. According to the prosecution testimony, Sheriff Ball went out and got Lloyd a sandwich and a piece of pie. Miller, however, said that he requested food but that food was denied him until after midnight.

When Lynch and Whitlock left, a new team of interrogators took over, James Christensen, Superintendent of the State Bureau of Criminal Identification, and the Canton Chief of Police, Kenneth Lindzey. Christensen was to accomplish what Lynch and Whitlock had failed to do. According to Christensen, about 10:30 P.M., Miller broke down:

> I said that it may have been possible that he was over emotional. He said that he was. I said possibly he might have

1. The test, according to the examiners, was "inconclusive."

needed treatment and possibly had he had treatment these
things may never have happened. That was the trend of the
conversation. He appeared to be filled up and more or less
becoming emotional. I sensed that he might be getting
tears in his eyes and I reached over and put my hand on
his knee and said, "Lloyd, why don't you get it off your
chest?" He said, "I did it." I said, "You mean you took the
life of Janice May?" He said, "Yes." I asked him to just tell
in his own words what happened on that particular day of
November 26, 1955.

There followed a recital by Christensen of the substance of the confession soon to be signed by Miller.

The confession was actually put down on paper by Christensen in
the presence of Miller, Sheriff Ball, and Chief Lindzey. But the confession was not entirely in the words of Miller. Christensen explained the difficulty:

> There are one or two paragraphs when it was difficult for
> him to phrase into words what he meant to say, and in that
> case I would assist in the phrasing of that part of the state-
> ment and then I would read it back to him and write it and
> ask him again if that is the way he wanted it.

The confession was signed at 12:15 A.M., December 1, 1955. According to Christensen, Miller then said, "Do you think I will get
the electric chair?" Christensen replied, "I do not know. That will
be entirely up to the Fulton County authorities and the courts."

Christensen said, "I believe the last thing I did before I left the
defendant, I shook hands with him and thanked him for his co-
operation."

According to Lloyd, he eventually signed a confession after Christensen told him he would be tried by a jury "picked from the people
around Canton." Lloyd said that at some point during the evening
Christensen left the room and returned with a tablet that already
had the confession written on it. Then Christensen said,

> "Lloyd," he says, "we will see, if you will admit this, we
> will see that nothing won't happen to you." I says, "I am
> not going to admit to no crime I did not commit." He

says, "You are a damned liar." And he—Mr. Christensen says, "I want you to sign this." And I says, "I am not signing nothing." He says, "If you don't sign this," he says, "we will see that you get the electric chair." And constantly they kept saying for me to admit the crime. I says, "I am not admitting no crime I did not commit." And I was so worn out and tired and I did not know what to do. Trying to pin a crime on me for something I did not do.

Miller added,

> Then, I finally signed the paper. I did not read it and it was not read to me. I signed the paper because, I tell you, I don't want to go to the electric chair for something I didn't do.

About 1:00 A.M. Sheriff Ball and John Young took Miller from Springfield to the Tazewell County jail at Pekin. During the interval before departure, Sheriff Ball said, "I recall one thing during that thirty to forty-five minutes; the defendant stood by a window and I got beside him because I was afraid he was going to jump out." When they got to the Tazewell county jail, Sheriff Ball requested Dr. Lloyd F. Teter to examine Miller: "The reason for a doctor examining the defendant at the Tazewell county jail was to determine if he was in the frame of mind where he might take his own life."

When Ray Crafton, Sheriff of Tazewell County, took him to a cell, Lloyd said later,

> I told Sheriff Crafton I was innocent, they forced me to sign the paper. Sheriff Crafton, he says, "Well," he says—he says, "If you are innocent," he says, "if they done," he says, "in your own mind, if you are innocent," he says, "you are innocent." That is just all he said. And he put me right into the cell there.

Sheriff Crafton denied this conversation.

Lloyd's confession, dated November 30, 1955, first noted that he

had been warned it could be used against him and that he had a
right to remain silent. It continued:

CHRISTENSEN: You have read the above. Are you willing to make a
statement?

ANSWER: Yes.

CHRISTENSEN: Just tell in your own words what happened last Saturday, November 26, 1955, in Canton, Illinois, in regard
to the death of Janice May.

ANSWER: I got up about 2:30 P.M. and I went to Mac's Drive Inn
and got a cup of coffee. Then I went down to Mr. Miller.
On the way I met Janice. She said, 'Hello,' and was joyful.
She walked with me to the railroad tracks and we walked
behind the cars where we could not be seen. I molested
her without force until she started screaming and crying.
She said she was going to tell her mother on me. I went
hysterical. Then I struck her with my hand. Then she fell
and hit her head on a cement block.

LINDZEY, QUESTION: Did you push the body back under a car?

ANSWER: I tried to hide her body under a car and also threw the
large rock under the car by the body.

CHRISTENSEN, QUESTION: Just what happened when you molested
her?

ANSWER: I started intercourse with her and she started to cry and
scream, then tried to get up, and that is when I struck her
and she fell against the rock. Then I moved her body and
the rock as before mentioned.

CHRISTENSEN, QUESTION: Then what did you do?

ANSWER: I ran north down the tracks to a place on Van Buren Court
called the Flats. Then I took off my jockey shorts and put
my trousers back on. Then I went back to my room and
took off my pants that were bloody, put on a clean pair,
and left on my gray jacket that had blood on it. Then I
went up town to the corner—to the Carver and Denny
Cleaners on Elm Street and got a pair of brown trousers

and a blue and green plaid shirt, then went back to my room.

CHRISTENSEN, QUESTION: Then what did you do?

ANSWER: I changed clothes. I wrapped my bloody trousers, shirt, and shoes in a newspaper.

CHRISTENSEN, QUESTION: Then what did you do?

ANSWER: I took the wrapped up, soiled clothes and went back to get the bloody shorts in the flat at Van Buren Court. When I got there a car came along, so I went on to Second Avenue, south to Maple Street, and then East to the railroad where a train was going by. Then I throwed the bundle into an empty box car and went back to my room. I think I stayed in my room until about 5:45 P.M.

CHRISTENSEN, QUESTION: Then what did you do?

ANSWER: The first chance I got after I went to work I drove by and got my gray jacket that I had left at home and drove out West Walnut Street to the creek and threw it out of the car. I continued making my regular calls until about 11:00 P.M. I was at the cab station and June Lang came there. She said she wanted me to take her to her brother's home in St. David which I did, was there a short time, and then came back to Canton. I felt that I had to talk to someone and I told June what I had done as mentioned before in this statement and that I was sorry. I told her this at St. David.

The confession concluded by describing the Sunday night departure for Danville and the arrest.

As we shall see, the prosecution formulated its theory of the crime and the identity of the criminal during the four-day period from Saturday evening to five-thirty on Wednesday evening. Shortly after, it obtained a confession consistent with that theory.

The confession appeared to be corroborated by the jacket and jockey shorts, but it was not because those garments had been found before the confession was signed. Even the statement that bloody garments had been disposed of in the box car of a passing train seemed to be an elaboration of Lloyd's remark as reported by June in her statement, "Wasn't it a coincident that a train passed just then?" From the moment of confession, the prosecution essentially stopped developing the case and concentrated almost exclusively upon supporting and refining its theory.

Such an approach was a grave and fundamental error. We shall see that the prosecution was satisfied when it should have been dissatisfied. It stopped asking questions at the very moment that the most pressing questions remained to be asked and answered.

4

DECEMBER 1, 1955—SEPTEMBER 10, 1956

PRELUDE
TO TRIAL

Fall 1955 was a troubled time for the Miller family. Lloyd's sister Margaret had married Donald Isaak in May 1953. During 1954 and 1955 Donald was in military service. In April 1955, he was sent overseas, and Margaret, then pregnant, returned home to live with her parents during her husband's absence. The baby, born at the Great Lakes Naval Hospital in September 1955, lived only a few hours. The doctors asked Margaret to remain at home for several weeks. She left on Friday, November 25, to rejoin her husband who was then stationed in Norfolk, Virginia. The senior Millers were in Chicago on the weekend of November 25–26 because the son of Mrs. Miller's sister was near death; they knew nothing of the tragic events of Saturday afternoon until they returned Sunday evening.

After Lloyd was arrested on Monday evening, November 28, his parents tried to learn where he was and to speak to him. Not until the authorities had the signed confession were the Millers permitted to see their son. Their first interview was at approximately eleven o'clock on the morning of December 1 in the Tazewell county jail in Pekin. At the September 1956 trial, Mr. Miller recalled,

> I asked him if he done this and he couldn't hardly talk. He was so hoarse he couldn't hardly talk, and he said no.
>
> Well, he was—his eyes was all swollen and he looked pretty bad to me.

While Lloyd himself was not permitted in 1956 to testify as to the conversation that took place between him and his parents, he did say: "I was taken out to my mother and mother—she—mother—she started in crying."

That afternoon, the Millers retained an attorney, William Howard Malmgren. They paid him $1,000 and later mortgaged their home to pay additional fees. It was his first criminal case.

William Malmgren became a lawyer in middle life. He had been a resident of Canton since 1935 and for seventeen years had worked for Harvester. He and Miller, Sr., belonged to the same union, the United Automobile Workers.

About 6:30 that evening, Lloyd was taken from Pekin to Lewistown, the seat of Fulton County, for a preliminary hearing before a police magistrate on a charge of murder. Malmgren first met his client in the courthouse there, in the presence of Mr. and Mrs. Miller. Before the Pardon and Parole Board in 1956, Malmgren remembered the meeting:

> At that time he was introduced and he said either "Hello. I did not do this thing" or "I did not do this thing. Hello." Those were his words, but I don't know the order which they were.

Sometime in January 1956 Malmgren asked George K. Meuth (pronounced Moit) to join him as co-counsel. Like Malmgren, Meuth was admitted to the bar in 1952 and from September 1952, until June 1953, had been a teaching associate at Northwestern Law School in Chicago. When approached by Malmgren, he was a law clerk for Walter C. Lindley, a judge of the Federal Court of Appeals in Chicago. In order for him to participate actively in the case, he had to drive almost every weekend from his home in Wheaton, a Chicago suburb, to confer with Malmgren in Canton. In addition to his weekend visits, he was in Canton and Lewistown during June 1956, when there was a abortive effort to select a jury.

In 1963, before the Illinois Parole Board, he told of his complete lack of experience and added:

> I think that lack of experience on the part of defense counsel was a substantial factor in this case. I have so publicly stated and I so publicly state now.

On January 11, 1956, the grand jury of Fulton County returned an indictment for murder. On March 6 Lloyd Miller was arraigned and filed a plea of "Not Guilty." On the same date the State's Attorney was ordered to furnish to defense counsel an "up to the present" list of witnesses and their addresses. The case was set for trial in Lewistown on June 6.

The six-month interval from December 1955 to the opening of the trial in June 1956 was crowded with important developments destined to have a vital influence upon the case.

The defense counsel received the list of witnesses by March 7. The problem was not that the list was incomplete. It was more than complete. As ultimately supplemented, the list contained ninety-three names, some of them followed by a brief description of the individuals. The role of many of the persons—members of the May family, the coroner, Dr. Mercey, and James Christensen—was perfectly apparent. But it was difficult to determine the possible role of many other individuals. For example, what might be the possible testimony of Jim Klockenkenper, identified as "special deputy sheriff"? Malmgren (and later Meuth) had to learn, if possible, the role of every person on the list and his possible testimony before the trial. By the time defense counsel would know precisely the prosecution's case, it would be too late for effective investigation. The case for the defense would immediately follow that of the prosecution.

In fact, the prosecution made no effort to keep its case secret—from the press. Because of its sensational nature, the case was given space by the column yard in central Illinois, notably in the Peoria *Journal Star* and Canton *Daily Ledger*. First press coverage was on Sunday, November 27. The Peoria *Journal Star* devoted a full column to the facts of the crime, including the discovery of Janice's body by her two brothers and her death in Graham Hospital.

By Monday, November 28, Lloyd was the prime suspect. The Canton *Daily Ledger* for that date headlined:

CAB DRIVER HUNTED IN GIRL'S SLAYING

The article told of an unsuccessful search for the killer with bloodhounds flown in from the State Penal Farm at Vandalia.

Also, on November 28, the *Journal Star* reporter, "Shivers in Wake of Canton Child Slaying":

Canton—This small city still shivers and shudders. Mixed with the fear and horror is a frustrated rage over the unsolved Saturday rape-murder of third-grader Janice May.

More parents are picking up their children after school. Puzzled children told teachers Monday that their working mothers are "getting somebody to look after us."

* * *

In Havana, 18 miles away, a woman sipping a cup of coffee in a drug store analyzed the shock of the area.

"You expect such things to happen in Chicago or New York but not around here."

The *Journal Star*, in an article appearing early Tuesday, November 29, also identified Lloyd Miller as the prime suspect. Chief Lindzey was quoted as saying on Monday night that he was "almost positive" that Miller was the man who killed Janice May. According to Lindzey, there was a "very good chain of evidence" pointing to Miller. State's Attorney Ramsey was quoted as saying, "We sat down today and went over our notes and found a few loopholes that still need checking." Lindzey added, "The public will have to have patience. We want him and we will get him."

The Fulton *Democrat*, which quoted Jackson in its masthead, "I'll take the responsibility," had little doubt as to the killer of Janice May. In its November 30 issue a headline was "Evidence Against Cabbie as Girl's Rapist-Killer Grows."

Almost immediately after the murder the press regarded Miller's guilt as an accepted truth. The view was clearly shared by the public. Consider: the Canton *Daily Ledger* for November 30 carried a simple display ad in a black border:

NOTICE

Lloyd Miller
Was Not Employed
at the

B&B TAXI

A brief story in the Peoria *Journal Star* on December 2 ran as follows:

CABBIE KILLS WORRY, TOO

Canton—A worried Canton couple hurried home from a "night out" last Saturday night after they heard of the rape-murder of little Janice May.

They were so concerned about the safety of their young baby sitter that they called a cab and sent her home in it.

Lloyd Miller drove the baby sitter home.

The press showed great interest in Lloyd's personality. Bernadine Martin, a *Journal Star* writer, wrote her first story on the case on December 1. The headline: "Friends Can't Believe Miller Murdered Girl." Bernadine wrote that the "few acquaintances of Lloyd Miller found it 'hard to believe' that he had raped and murdered eight-year-old Janice May. . . . His portrait emerged as that of a person not given to acts of violence." A fellow cab driver said that in his opinion Miller "did not have the capacity to commit murder." The article continued:

Ira Johns, brother of the cab stand owner, could not believe that Miller had confessed to the crime.

He said that Miller had driven many youngsters to school and that at no time had there been a complaint at any time from the parents of the children.

Some sympathy was shown for Lloyd's parents in an article she wrote for the *Journal Star* of December 2:

WILL SPEND LIFE SAVINGS IN HIS DEFENSE
MILLER'S PARENTS BELIEVE SON INNOCENT

For over eleven years Bernadine Martin continued reporting the case.

The press was interested in Miller's attorney. On December 2, the *Journal Star* reported:

Questioned as to why he had taken the case, Malmgren said it was a "moral obligation." He pointed out that according to the laws of our society "no man is guilty until proven so."

Malmgren evidently felt community pressure for representing Lloyd because on December 5 the *Ledger* stated that Malmgren had resigned as Chairman of the Canton Police and Fire Commission because, Malmgren said, the thought had been advanced that his position on the Board might prove incompatible with his function as an attorney in the Lloyd Miller case.

On December 2, the *Ledger* reported: "Miller Repudiates His Confession In Murder of Child. Claims He Admitted Crime Because He Tired of Questions."

The same day the *Ledger* ran an article on a subject destined to perplex and trouble the authorities, especially in light of Lloyd's prompt repudiation of the confession: "Case Not Closed, Chief Lindzey Says." Why? Because, explained Lindzey, "Some of the articles of clothing worn by Miller Saturday have not been recovered, and we are extremely anxious to find them, if possible."

By December 3, large scale efforts to find the missing garments were reported. The principal headline of the *Journal Star* was "Seek Blood Stained Bundles—Hunt Goes on for Clues in Canton Death." Illustrating the story was a picture showing Tazewell County Sheriff Ray Crafton and two other men dragging the Illinois River for the garments.

In the following days, attention centered on the search for the articles allegedly abandoned by Miller. The *Journal Star* reported on December 7, "Clothing Search Continues In Try For Confession Proof." The article stated that in the view of Chief Lindzey, even the fact that clothing had not been discovered substantiated the confession.

Despite the energetic efforts by the authorities and the mobilization of large portions of the community, the missing garments were never found. No bloody garments were ever discovered in a boxcar on the Chicago, Burlington & Quincy or on an east–west railroad, the Toledo, Peoria & Western. The dragging of the Illinois River near the place where Lloyd abandoned the taxicab was unsuccessful.

On December 6, the *Journal Star* reported that laboratory tests showed that a pair of undershorts, identified as Lloyd's in the confession, was stained with type "A" blood, the same type blood as that of Janice May, and that Miller has blood type "O."

By December 2, June Lang was the focus of attention. The *Journal Star* published a stark, unsmiling portrait of her on that date under the heading, "June Lang . . . Marriage Is Out, So Is Job." The story was captioned "Rape-Slayer Killed Wedding Plans Too."

> Waitress June Lang was to be married this Sunday to confessed rape-slayer Lloyd Miller. She helped authorities crack the brutal case and lost her fiance, her job and plans for the future.
>
> "Sunday was to be our day," Mrs. Lang said Thursday afternoon. The 23-year-old divorced mother added, "Lloyd and I were to get married in Pekin and then go to Rochelle where both of us could have worked in a factory."
>
> The heavy-set brunette said she has been fired from her restaurant job and doesn't know whether she will remain in Canton, where she has resided two months.
>
> Authorities did not win an admission from Miller until Wednesday night after he had been confronted by Mrs. Lang. Her statement about his confession to her was read and he replied, "Lord, June, do you want me to go to the chair for something I didn't do?"
>
> The waitress also said that Miller showed remorse when he broke down two hours later. He sobbed wildly, said he was sorry. . . .

Had the authorities been alert, the June Lang interview would have troubled them. June had not told the police that Sunday was an agreed-on wedding date. More serious, the wild sobbing scene was clear invention. June did not see Lloyd on Tuesday night after he had confessed. These were but the first in a lengthy series of June Lang embellishments.

The next day a *Star* headline was "Story of Suspect's Reunion with Girl Denied, Confirmed." The story contained a strange hint of mystery and love:

> William Malmgren, counsel for Lloyd Miller, Jr., accused killer, reported Friday night that no "romantic

reunion" has occurred between his client and Miller's accuser—"girl-friend"—"as far as I know."

Mrs. June Lang, however, contacted by The Journal-Star Friday evening after she had apparently returned from a visit with Miller, said she had something to say, but that she had "to talk to someone first" before saying anything.

What was this tale of "a romantic reunion" with June Lang? Before the Parole Board, years later, Mrs. Miller and Malmgren told the story of the "reunion." On Friday, December 2, June Lang appeared at the residence of Mr. and Mrs. Miller. At the Millers' request Malmgren came to the house immediately. June informed Malmgren that she had come to tell him about the case, but refused to make any statements until she had seen Lloyd. They drove to the Lewistown jail. First Malmgren saw Lloyd briefly alone, leaving June in his car. When he came back, June Lang was gone. She did not talk to Miller nor did she stay to convey her information to Malmgren.

On February 11, the Grand Jury of Fulton County returned an eight-count murder indictment and a five-count rape indictment (No action ever was taken on the latter).

The next day, February 12, was the arraignment. Miller, brought to court, entered a plea of not guilty.

Soon June Lang and William Malmgren figured in another strange episode. Commencing about ten-thirty on the evening of March 16, 1956, and concluding sometime after midnight, June Lang gave a seven-page statement to Malmgren. In June 1963, Malmgren sent us a copy of her statement and subsequently sent to us the original statement. Appended to the copy sent to us in June was a note as follows:

6/10/63:
    This is copy of statement given me by Lang on 3/17/56. The original consists of 7 legal size sheets each signed "June Ann Lang." In addition, the last sheet bears the longhand statement by Lang: "I have read this and it is true." The original contains inked changes by Lang, primarily date corrections.

The circumstances giving rise to the statement were as bizarre as the statement is puzzling and were these: Lang phoned me after a long period of what I will call inaccessibility. The phone call was of temperament en sotto voce but strained and insistent. The intimation was "they" were after Lang to prevent her from talking to me, that she wanted to but would only talk to me if I came alone and in my car. I phoned my wife, telling her of the situation and that I felt I would have to try to talk to Lang even under the "sitting duck circumstances" conditioned. I then did pick Lang up and, fearful of the circumstances, stopped for gas some miles out of Canton at a place where I was known, later managed a phone call to friends reporting the situation briefly and later took Lang to my home.

The statement is purely that of Lang excepting that language oft-times became my own insofar as continuity and facility is concerned. But the matters and things set forth are there by the *insistence* of Lang.

After this occasion Lang dropped out of sight until shortly before trial. I next heard from her by phone, apparently from Havana, Ill. Her proposition was that she had something of great importance to tell me. Thereafter, because of circumstances, Geo. K. Meuth and my wife went to Havana in an attempt to see Lang.

During the course of the drive related in Malmgren's memorandum, June Lang related the substance of what was to be embodied in the statement. After he picked her up at Fifth and Lind Streets in Canton, June told him to hurry quickly out of town because "they" were after her. By that, Malmgren said, she meant the local officialdom. After the automobile ride, Malmgren and June returned, according to the statement itself, to Malmgren's house at about nine o'clock, where they had coffee and ice cream. They went from there to Malmgren's law office, where, as Malmgren states, he himself typed the statement.

The statement began with a biographical sketch: June became pregnant when a high school sophomore. The baby was given for adoption. At eighteen, she was married and had two more children. In 1953 June's husband divorced her and was awarded child custody. Two years later she was again pregnant. June left the baby with a cousin. When she tried to reclaim him, the cousin refused to give up the child and later adopted him.

About October 1955, June came to Canton and got a job as a waitress.

The statement (somewhat condensed) continued:

> Shortly after I started to work at Harriett's I met Lloyd Miller, Jr. who was driving a cab. I met him when he would come in for coffee.
>
> I liked him and about 2 or 3 weeks before the May girl was killed I started going with him.
>
> We liked one another and he asked me to marry him one night at the [cab] office.
>
> Shortly after Lloyd and I started going together he started talking that we should go away together where we could make a new start and that he wanted to get away from Canton. Lloyd said that the people in Canton were against him and that as long as we stayed around Canton we never would get a good start.
>
> We had it planned that we would leave Canton on Sunday, December 3, 1955 and go away and that we would get married the following day.

June and Lloyd went out together just after midnight on the day of the murder. Then:

> The next time I saw Lloyd was after 10:00 P.M. on Saturday, November 26, 1955. I got off work at 10:00 P.M. at Harriett's, went over to my rooming house about two blocks away, took a shower, changed clothes and then walked up to the cab stand where Lloyd worked. Teke Johns cashed my check and I told him I wanted to go to St. David and he motioned for Lloyd to take me.
>
> Lloyd and I got in the cab and started for St. David. The two of us were alone in the cab and in the front seat.
>
> We talked about leaving on Sunday morning, November 27, 1955. We decided to go. Lloyd asked me if I had my suitcase packed and I said "Part of them." He said he had his things packed and from the way he talked I think he had packed that morning. We planned to go to Pekin and leave from there by bus to go to Rochelle and from the way Lloyd talked I knew that he planned on taking the cab

over to Pekin. We also talked about the crime that had been committed in Canton. The first thing Lloyd asked me when we got in the cab was whether I had heard about the little girl who had been killed. Lloyd said something about that it was a coincidence that that train came by and that he thought whoever did the crime got on the train and got away. Lloyd said that the way people felt about him in Canton and the way they treated him that they'd lay this on to him and that he wanted to just to go ahead and go. Lloyd never said anything about the May girl crying or screaming or anything like that. He did not indicate that he knew anything about the position of her body. He never gave any indication that he knew anything about the facts of the crime. Lloyd never said, "June, you know I done this" or anything like that. In talking about leaving from Pekin Lloyd said that people would blame this thing on to him and that he wanted to leave. When he got to St. David to my brother's house we sat in the cab and talked a few minutes. We talked about the crime.

Just before I went in to my brother's house Lloyd put his head on my shoulder and we talked. He said, "June, why do people do things they're ashamed of?"

And when he said that I said, "Oh, honey," and just patted his face because I thought he was sorry for hurting me. I went in the house and woke my brother and his wife up and their baby woke up and I took the baby out to show Lloyd. Lloyd seemed angry because I didn't have a blanket on the baby and I had the feeling that he was thinking about his own little boy about whom he talked to me frequently and acted like he thought a lot of him. I got in the cab with Lloyd and he got angry and told me to take the baby back into the house and I thought he was that way because the baby didn't have a blanket on. I took the baby back into the house and came back into the cab with Lloyd. I said, "Lloyd, what's the matter with you?" He sat with his hands on the steering wheel and then turned his head casual and said, "You know I didn't do it." I said, "What?" and we just sat there. We talked a few more minutes about the May girl and then Lloyd told me when I was ready to come back to call him. We smooched a minute and he said to be sure to call him and he left.

At no time on the way to St. David or while in St. David did I have any idea that Lloyd had done anything to the May girl and nothing he said led me to believe that he had. He didn't act as if he had a guilty conscience. He didn't act like he was scared or jumpy. In fact he acted happy and glad, like a kid who was going to leave on a vacation and I thought he was glad we were going to leave Canton and get married.

After Lloyd left I didn't see him again until about 12 midnight or perhaps a little later. I went to a tavern in St. David and I heard a man tell the bartender to call a cab and to come and get him to take him back to Canton. This man was Whitney Rogers and I decided to go back in the same cab with him. So Teke Johns came down in the cab to get him and I went back to Canton with him. He let me out at Harriett's Lunch: Whitney and I both. I started walking up the street towards town: this was up Elm Street. When I got up about to the Canton Chili stand I saw Lloyd who was in the cab.

He slowed down real slow and honked and waved. I waved back and he drove on. I walked on up to King's Drug Store and turned down to Missouri's tavern on White Court. I went in there.

I drank a gin squirt (I had had four down at St. David before I came back): From Missouri's I went down to Mac's Coffee Shop and had a cheeseburger and glass of milk. When I came out Tom Richards was driving by and he asked if he could take me home. I got in the car with him and there was just the two of us. He took me up where I was rooming and then drove on past and I said, "Where're you going?" And he said, "Oh, just for a ride." I said, "O.K." He drove on a little ways and then said, "Where do you want to go?" And I said, "To Pekin." He said, "O.K." So we went to Pekin, going through Banner. We went directly there. He is married. In Pekin we went to a restaurant in downtown Pekin and we ate: both of us a ham sandwich. Then we went out to the car and got in and then he got out of the car (before we had started) and he left to get something and he went in a store after it: it seems to me he went back in to the restaurant.

As soon as he went inside I got out of the car and left.

I ran down to the corner and hid in the doorway of a building until I thought he had left. Then went to a store (little bitty place) and called a cab and went to the Pekin bus station. I stayed there until about 5 A.M. I met a guy in the bus station: I talked to him and he didn't seem to be waiting for a bus because he had his car. I talked him into taking me home: back to Canton and he did.

I slept from about 5:30 A.M. Sunday, Nov. 27, 1955, to about 11:00 A.M. and then went to work at Harriett's.

My reason for going over to Pekin was to meet Lloyd but when he didn't show up I decided to come back. I didn't pack any clothes or take any with me over to Pekin. However, I did have my clothes partly packed in my room: I did this Saturday morning after Lloyd brought me back.

When I was working at Harriett's on Sunday, Nov. 27, 1955, I heard for the first time that Lloyd was missing with the taxicab. The minute I heard it I went to the phone and called the police station. I told them at the police station that Lloyd didn't do it and that I was supposed to go with him and they said they would send someone down to talk to me. Pretty soon Ed Fuller and (I think) John Young came down.

Naturally, the police were interested in a young lady who called to say that Miller hadn't done it. The statement described briefly June's initial interviews with the authorities and then related June's version of the events at Springfield on November 30, the day of the Miller–Lang confrontation:

I had to sit around and then I had to go in to talk to Jack Lynch. While I was sitting around they were talking about pubic hairs and the evidence they had against Lloyd. They said they had a hair which they got out of the little May girl and one of them (a young fellow I think is assistant to Jack Lynch) said that he positively knew the hair was from Lloyd. They also talked about another hair which they said they found alongside the little girl and the young fellow said positively this hair was from Lloyd also and then another man came in and proved that it was a dog hair.

They took me into Jack Lynch and got my statement. They then took me out of the room and took Lloyd in to the room. Then they brought me back in to the room and Lloyd was there. They told Lloyd I had given them a statement and that they would like to read it to him. They did read it to him. I think this was between 3 and 4 P.M. After they read my statement to him they asked him if what I said was true and he just sat there and didn't say anything to them: just looked at me. Then he said: "June, you know I didn't do this. You don't want me to go to the chair for something I didn't do." Then they sent me out of the room into the next one.

Then they took turns questioning him. First one set of twos would question him; and then another set of twos. Once in a while one of them would be in with him alone.

I heard Jim Christensen say: "If you'll just tell us the truth, you'll never regret it." And he said: "If you'll tell us the truth we'll see that nothing happens to you."

There was loud talking and when Lloyd would say he didnt do this thing they would say: "We think you're a damn liar."

They had Lloyd in there talking to him for about 9 hours and the only time he got out of the room was when they took him to another room to show him evidence. I was there until after midnight and was brought directly back to Canton by Kenny Lindzey and I arrived in Canton about 2:30 or 3:00 A.M. Thursday, December 1, 1955.

The statement concluded with June's account of the romantic interlude of December 2. Why did June disappear just when Malmgren was about to bring her in to see Lloyd at the jail? Because, she said, she was frightened.

Obtaining this statement was an incredible stroke of good fortune. Malmgren had obtained from the chief witness for the prosecution a signed statement directly contradicting the statement she had given to the police on the afternoon of November 30 immediately before Miller signed the confession. While the statement was valuable, we must state that it betrayed Malmgren's legal inexperience. It should have been sworn to before a notary so that when

June testified that Miller made damning admissions to her, Malmgren would be able to impeach her by proving that she had made a sworn statement contrary to her trial testimony.

A more serious defect was that the statement contained needless personal irrelevancies which made it difficult to use effectively. Perhaps he could have persuaded June to omit irrelevancies, or to put these facts in a separate statement. As it was, they substantially reduced the utility of the statement.

The statement itself reveals June's incomprehensible unsettled behavior beginning with the trip to St. David. First, she spent the money for a cab ride of several miles to see her brother. Apparently, the visit was very brief since she left Canton at 10:45 P.M. and by midnight was already back in Canton. Part of the time was spent at a bar in St. David, where she consumed four gin squirts.

Once back in Canton, she met an acquaintance who offered her a ride home, which she accepted. But then he suggested a longer trip; June accepted and mentioned Pekin. After a snack in Pekin, June dodged him and accepted a ride from a stranger back to Canton. The Pekin trip is presented as a completely chance event, but later, June ascribes a purpose to it: she went there to meet Lloyd. The Pekin rendezvous version seems implausible since June mentions no time or place for the meeting. Additionally, her search for Lloyd seemed to be confined to the place where her friend happened to bring her.

When June told about the events in Springfield on November 30, we come to fascinating new information. So far as we can determine, there had never been one single word published in the press about the hair found in the body of Janice May. Yet in Springfield, on November 30, according to June, there was discussion among the authorities about a pubic hair and she overheard someone whom she identified as an assistant to Jack Lynch saying that he "positively knew" that a hair found in the body was from Lloyd.

Malmgren and Meuth were keenly aware of the crucial importance of the physical evidence. Even before Malmgren's interview with June Lang just described, he had filed a motion before the trial judge, William O. Bardens, for permission to "view and examine" the physical evidence. On March 15, the day before the session with June, Judge Bardens granted his request.

Malmgren promptly "viewed and examined." Included among the items were a brick, a blue button, a bright red plastic belt, a piece of red cloth or binding similar to the trimming on Janice's blue jeans, a bright blue girl's coat, a box with cockleburrs, a jagged piece of concrete, a hair, two long reddish-blonde hairs stuck to a dead leaf, a mouse-colored jacket, girl's blue jeans, a medallion, a pair of panties, scrapings from Janice's fingernails, Janice's shoes, her socks, a heavily blood-stained T-shirt, a front tooth and a valve cap.

There were other items of unusual interest. One was a Carver and Denny Cleaners ticket and customer's receipt, No. 2616, issued to "Miller" on November 21, 1955, for a pair of "Brn. Pts." and a "Grn. & Royal blue pld. sht." There was a dark stain on the receipt.

Recall the confession: it states that after leaving his shorts in the Van Buren Flats, Miller went back to his room, took off his pants, which were bloody, put on a clean pair but left on his gray jacket that had blood on it. "Then I went uptown to the corner—to the Carver & Denny Cleaners on Elm Street and got a pair of brown trousers and a blue and green plaid shirt and then went back to my room."

The following statement was in the envelope containing the ticket and receipt:

> I, Joyce Hardy while working at the cleaners of Carver and Denny on East Elm St. a man came in about 5 PM to get his cleaning. As I put the cleaning on the counter I noticed what looked like blood on the front of his clothes. He picked up his cleaning and went out the door, as he got outside he ran east on Elm Street. When he handed me the claim ticket it was folded. As I unfolded the ticket I glanced at the ticket and saw the #16. I got in the wrong line of cleaning so I had to look farther for the cleaning. This happened on November 26, 1955.
>
> s/Joyce Hardy.
> Witness: s/Kenny M. Lindzey, s/W. Paul Woods.
> [Woods was then Mayor of Canton.]

The second item of significance was a pair of jockey shorts, with a label, "Deluxe Artifit Combed Yarn Small." The shorts were in an envelope which had the notation, "Jock shorts—Nov. 29, 1955, found in Van Buren Flats at about 11:15 AM date by Henderson & Wilkinson 17. Ed Fuller 11–30–55."

The third item of special interest was a container bearing the initials "Dr. R.J.M." (Raymond J. Mercey, the coroner). Inside the container was a piece of Kleenex tissue, rolled and folded, and stained with a fluid and apparently with blood. Also in the container was a piece of cotton, rolled, as if it had been on a swab or probe. The tip was stained in the same manner as the tissue.

Malmgren had learned from June's statement that the authorities believed that a pubic hair found in Janice's body (actually in her vagina) came from Lloyd. Moreover, Lloyd himself was to testify, as we shall see, that the authorities told him the same thing. Hence Malmgren was on the lookout for a pubic hair, whose existence was probable but not certain. Malmgren asked for an order directing the state's attorney to disclose any pubic hair or other minute article "presumptively pertinent" to the case, or to declare, in effect, that there were no such items. He also asked for an order "permitting defendant to make . . . upon such terms and conditions as to the court seems necessary to adequately insure the interests of the parties, a scientific examination of the physical evidence to be introduced by the People."

Judge Bardens turned down both requests. Counsel for the defense saw the physical exhibits on one occasion only before the trial. Permission for a scientific examination was never obtained. The judge's reason for withholding permission later became a matter of controversy.

Malmgren had a struggle to see, before trial, a copy of the confession. In March, over the objections of Ramsey, Judge Bardens ordered the prosecution to deliver a copy to the defense.

The prosecution also sought discovery of evidence in the possession of its adversary. In April the prosecution became aware that June Lang had given a statement to the defense. State's Attorney Ramsey asked to inspect the statement on the ground that it was "material to the issues in this cause." Evidently June had decided once again to cooperate with the prosecution because attached to the motion was an affidavit from her dated April 23, in which she related that on March 16 she had met with Malmgren, that he had questioned her about the case, and that she had signed a statement.

This request, too, Judge Bardens denied. The reliability of the testimony of June clearly was to be a key issue in the case. Crucial evidence as to her reliability was partly in the hands of the prosecution and partly the defense. At no time were all the facts assembled to enable court and jury to render an informed judgment on a central question in the case. In the broad sweep of the case, one must say that the rulings largely denying to each side information in the posession of the other contributed powerfully to the ultimate miscarriage of justice.

Both the prosecution and defense were required to work chiefly in the dark. Apart from the copy of the confession, the defense was forced to learn of the prosecution case by surmises from the questions put to Lloyd as reported by Lloyd to his lawyers—and from the press. The lengthy newspaper accounts, while unquestionably most prejudicial to Miller, did at least outline for Malmgren, and later Meuth, the principal elements of the prosecution's case. But generally there was no discovery in the case. A consequence was that at no time before or during the 1956 trial would the facts of the case ever be thoroughly probed by anyone—prosecution, defense, judge, or jury.

June 5 saw a flurry of activity before Judge Bardens. Ramsey obtained an order from the court authorizing Roger Hayes to serve as assistant counsel in the case. Hayes was State's Attorney of McDonough County, immediately west of Fulton County. At the request of the defense, a psychiatrist was permitted to examine Lloyd in the County jail.

The trial opened on Monday, June 11.

The Canton *Daily Ledger* sketched the scene:

> Miller was escorted into the courtroom without handcuffs, which were removed outside the courtroom door. He was brought from the county jail by Deputy Sheriff James Elam.
>
> Mrs. Lloyd Miller, Sr., the defendant's mother, entered the courtroom on the arm of a daughter, approached Miller and kissed him. The defendant smiled at her and she

burst into tears. She was escorted from the courtroom by the daughter, but returned a few minutes later.

Also among the handful of persons attending the first session were Mr. and Mrs. Dean May, parents of the murdered girl. They sat quietly through the proceedings, saying little.

Bernardine Martin wrote in the *Journal Star* of the same day:

> The accused man appeared unperturbed and displayed much interest in the proceedings.
>
> Records show that there has never been a death penalty imposed in Fulton County.
>
> The courtroom in which Miller will be tried contains only 164 seats and it was expected the small enclosure would be well filled through the duration of the trial.

Selecting a jury proved to be a lengthy process. The prosecution and defense each had twenty peremptory challenges—the right to dismiss a prospective juror without stating a reason. In addition prospective jurors could be excused for cause, for instance, for holding a "fixed opinion" as to the guilt or innocence of the defendant, or for being unable to serve without suffering substantial hardship.

Since the prosecution had decided to ask for the death penalty, it was entitled under Illinois law in 1956 to qualify the jury to impose the death penalty, that is, to ask prospective jurors whether they had conscientious scruples against imposing the death sentence. It worked like this: A group of prospective jurors was assembled, sworn to answer questions truthfully, and then was asked by the judge whether any of them had conscientious scruples against inflicting the death penalty "in a proper case." Any juror who said that he did have such conscientious scruples was excused immediately without any further inquiry. As we shall see, an extraordinarily high percentage of prospective jurors were excused on this ground.

Ten years later, there was a serious challenge made to the constitutionality of this practice. In April 1968, the Supreme Court in *Witherspoon* v. *Illinois,* by a 5–4 vote, held that it was unconstitutional automatically to remove from the jury every prospective juror who expressed scruples against the death penalty. Such a jury, declared the Court, was a "hanging jury." Prospective jurors who, despite their scruples, would nonetheless consider a death sentence, were entitled to remain on the jury. Presumably, if the prosecution wished to dismiss them, it would have to use its peremptory challenges. The exclusion of scrupled jurors, the court held, affected the outcome of the trial on the penalty question only and hence did not require a new trial on the issue of guilt. It rejected the argument, supported by some statistical evidence, that persons who favor the death penalty generally favor the prosecution more than the run of citizens. Hence, it left standing Witherspoon's conviction, but set aside the death sentence.[1] Justice Douglas believed that Witherspoon was entitled to a complete new trial. Justice Black, for the dissenters, believed that the State was entitled to reject scrupled jurors. In a footnote, the Court ruled that its decision was retroactive, that is, that it applied to everyone then on death row (about 450 persons).

Witherspoon's case illustrates an important aspect of the criminal law. When Lloyd's case was tried in 1956, the outlook for challenging the death qualification rule appeared so slim that his attorneys did not even raise the question. By 1960 Witherspoon's lawyers deemed the point to be sufficiently important to raise the issue at the very outset of the trial. The point met with short shrift in the trial court and in the numerous appellate courts which considered Witherspoon's case. Yet by 1968 the United States Supreme Court made it a constitutional principle. We must think back to the hundreds, if not the thousands, of accused men who were indicted, tried, convicted, sentenced to death, and actually executed on the basis of a rule of law now declared by the highest court in the land to be a violation of a defendant's constitutional rights.

We return to Lloyd and the jury selection in June 1956 in Lewistown. Four jurors were selected the very first day, but no more that week. One after another prospective jurors were dismissed because of scruples against the death penalty, opinions as to Lloyd's guilt or innocence, personal hardship, or physical impairment. Others were rejected on peremptory challenge. Four jurors were selected on

1. The following January, the Illinois Supreme Court resentenced Witherspoon to 50–100 years.

Monday, June 18. By then about 300 prospective jurors had been questioned. Malmgren moved to terminate the proceedings and move the trial to another county on the ground that Lloyd could not receive a fair trial in Fulton County. The motion, advanced several times, was rejected by the Judge. But Tuesday brought another problem: there were no more names on the list of persons to be summoned as prospective jurors.

Bernadine Martin reported on the remedy adopted by Judge Bardens:

> Another panel of 25 potential jurors was being gathered by a special bailiff for questioning beginning at 1:30 this [Tuesday] afternoon. Circuit Judge William M. Bardens appointed Thomas Wilson, of Smithfield, to round them up from Fulton County Streets.

On Tuesday, of the twenty-nine prospects, only twenty-five appeared. Once more, on June 20, Malmgren moved for a mistrial and change of venue. Late in the day the motion was granted. The June 21 *Ledger* reported that Judge Bardens "said he was convinced Miller would not receive a fair trial in Fulton County." Judge Bardens announced that he would continue to hear the case.

State's Attorney Ramsey was angry. The *Ledger* of June 21 reported his statement:

> From the start I have relentlessly pushed the case toward final determination. I have constantly and successfully fought the delaying tactics of the defense. However, now the court has taken it upon itself to grant a change of venue because it believed Fulton County to be prejudiced. This was a surprising and shocking turn of events, which the defense will claim the dubious "honor" of causing.

On June 22, Judge Bardens ordered that the case be transferred to the Circuit Court of Hancock County sitting in Carthage. Hancock County, two counties west of Fulton County, borders on the Mississippi River. Carthage itself had a population of about 2,500, about the same as Lewistown, but was removed from any major population center. It had no daily newspaper.

Judge Bardens set September 10 as the opening date of the trial.

There was to be one more important incident before the opening of the trial and once again June Lang was to play a key role. On July 31 she met with State's Attorney Ramsey, and on this occasion signed an affidavit. Through the measured legal tones of the affidavit are related strange events. The affidavit stated that before June 20, Malmgren "had talked to her on several occasions concerning her testimony" in the case, and that "during many of these occasions had threatened her in several ways concerning her testimony including threatening to send her to the penitentiary and threatening to disclose certain of her alleged indiscretions." Further, Malmgren was alleged to have made other "indirect and implied threats if she would not testify more favorably to the said Lloyd Eldon Miller, Junior, than her previous statements to the State's Attorney of Fulton County would indicate." Further, June swore in the affidavit, that "since 20 June 1956, on four different occasions said atty. William Malmgren has approached her in public places in the City of Havana, Illinois, [a small community near Canton] and has engaged her in conversation and has made statements which did embarrass, harass and tend to intimidate her and on one of these occasions, did say to her, 'It might be convenient for you to disappear.' "

Further, the affidavit continued, "on one of these occasions said atty. William Malmgren, insisted and persisted in talking to her in a loud voice in a public restaurant in the City of Havana, Illinois, where she was working in such a way as to embarrass her in front of her employer and other customers and since that time she has been discharged from said job, and that she is now unemployed."

The affidavit concluded that "on several of these occasions since 20 June, 1956, the said William Malmgren threatened to send her to the penitentiary for perjury, if she didn't testify at the said trial of Lloyd Eldon Miller, Junior, more favorably to him." Finally, the affidavit concluded, that "as a result of the conduct, conversations and declarations of the said William Malmgren, she is embarrassed, feels intimidated, and is in fear of bodily harm, and is distressed and very upset emotionally and mentally."

Nine days later, Ramsey was ready to take action on the strength of June Lang's affidavit. On August 9, he appeared before Judge Burton A. Roeth, one of the Fulton County judges, with a petition. According to Ramsey, the conduct of Malmgren, as shown by the affidavit of June Lang was "illegal and is *per se* contemptuous and amounts to contempt of this Court." He therefore asked that the court issue a citation against Malmgren directing him to show cause why he should not be held in contempt of court.

Several phases of this matter were unusual. First, in litigation, generally when an attorney appears before the court to request an order, he informs the opposition of the request and time of presentation. Although Ramsey and Malmgren were practicing in the same small community, knew each other well, and had offices separated by only a few blocks, and although Ramsey had the June Lang affidavit in his hands for at least nine days, he did not serve notice on Malmgren before presenting the contempt citation.

A second unusual feature: presumably, the end which Ramsey sought was a court order requiring Malmgren not to intimidate June Lang (assuming he had done so). A simple motion would have accomplished this end. But Ramsey rather sought the much harsher remedy of a contempt proceeding.

Third: when Ramsey did appear before Judge Roeth on August 9, the court set the case for hearing on September 6 in Lewistown, precisely four days before the opening of the trial in Carthage on September 10.

Fourth: it is customary, in contempt proceedings, first, to conduct, a hearing on the question whether there is sufficient basis to warrant a contempt hearing. This preliminary phase was skipped.

The citation was served on Malmgren the next day, August 10.

The filing of the petition for citation against Malmgren was regarded as a sensation by the press and the local television stations. The Peoria *Journal Star,* for Friday, August 10, carried a picture of June Lang. Underneath, the cut line ran: "June Lang . . . says she was intimidated."

The article concluded with a statement attributed to Ramsey that if the attempt to have Malmgren held in contempt were successful, Malmgren would be subject to a jail sentence, fine, or reprimand by the court.

About two weeks later, on August 28, Malmgren and Meuth filed a motion to dismiss the contempt proceedings against Malmgren, alleging that the filing of the petition for contempt had created an atmosphere of suspicion and distrust toward Miller's attorney in the conduct of the case which inevitably would be prejudicial to the defendant. Their motion, together with the petition for citation, was heard by Judge Bardens in Carthage on September 6. The motion to dismiss was denied and the petition for citation was continued. It was never pushed by the prosecution during or after the trial and, technically, remains an open matter in the Circuit Court of Fulton and Hancock Counties.

The contempt proceeding was the last of the tumults preceding the Carthage phase of the case. But even the jury selection process in Carthage was to be a time of sensation.

5

TRIAL

THE CASE FOR THE PROSECUTION

At Carthage, the county seat of Hancock County, in June 1844, Joseph Smith, founder of the Mormon Church, and his brother were murdered by a mob in the city jail. In September 1956, in the one courtroom on the third floor, the trial of Lloyd Eldon Miller was held in the old-fashioned courthouse on the public square.

The trial began on Monday, September 10. At the end of the first day, four jurors had been accepted by both sides: Robert West, an Augusta farmer; Fred White, another Augusta farmer; Arlie B. Reid, a Bowen farmer; and Mrs. Hazel Wright, a Carthage housewife.

Tuesday failed to produce a single juror, but it did produce a sensation. The Canton *Daily Ledger* for that day headlined:

RUMOR MILLER MAY ENTER GUILTY PLEA.

DEFENSE, PROSECUTION ATTORNEYS

HUDDLE IN CARTHAGE CONFERENCE.

In 1963, before the Pardon and Parole Board, each side told its version. According to Ramsey, the defense proposed a plea of guilty if the prosecution would drop its demand for the death penalty and recommend to the court a prison sentence for an agreed-upon term. How long that term would be was the subject of disagreement.

According to Ramsey, he insisted on a ninety-nine-year sentence under which Lloyd would not be eligible for parole for thirty years, that is, until age fifty-nine. Malmgren, said Ramsey, asked for a sentence of "life," which would have made Lloyd eligible for parole in eleven years, or at age forty. Lloyd, Ramsey added, was not present at these discussions.

Malmgren's version was that the prosecution approached him and that there was a conference with Judge Bardens on the subject. The Judge indicated that if the parties agreed on a reasonable recommendation he would accept it. Later, Malmgren reported the discussion to Lloyd and to his parents. Lloyd insisted on his innocence and refused to plead guilty. The matter was dropped.

Thus if Lloyd had been willing to change his plea from not guilty to guilty, he would not have faced the electric chair. For the exercise of his constitutional right to a determination of his innocence or guilt by a jury, he had to stake his life.

It seems remarkable today that no issue was ever raised at the trial or on appeal about the publicity resulting from the stories that a guilty plea was being considered. Scarcely any other event reported was more prejudicial to Miller, including the confession. Only four jurors had been selected and therefore only four had been secluded from the news media. It is scarcely possible that the eight remaining to be selected were unaware of the discussions regarding the possible change of plea. They did not know that Miller had had no part in them, had not initiated them nor authorized them. They might reasonably suppose that an innocent man would never permit such discussions.

Today the courts, the prosecution, the defense, and the public are much more conscious of the barriers to fair trial raised by the mass media. The reversal by the Supreme Court of the conviction of Sam Sheppard, if it has not substantially altered practices, at least has made us acutely aware of the evil. There should have been an outcry by the defense, but there was none.

Who reported the matter to the press? We do not know. Surely, the defense did not. If the prosecution did so, it must have realized the impact the story would have on the prospective jurors. Surely this episode did much to deprive Lloyd of his constitutional right to a fair trial.

On Wednesday four more jurors were selected. They were Mrs. Ruby White, a widow of LaHarp; Mrs. Evelyn Lovell of Rock Creek, the mother of three small children; Mrs. Emma Ferris, a

Hamilton housewife; and George H. Preyt, a railroad employee from Plymouth who was on sick leave.

On Thursday, September 13, no jurors were selected. Meuth asked the court that the case be continued generally until Lloyd could secure a fair trial. According to his count, of fifty-six jurors examined, twenty-nine had been dismissed because they had an opinion as to guilt. Judge Bardens denied the motion.

No jurors were selected on Friday or Saturday. At the end of the Saturday session, the defense renewed its motion for a continuance. The motion was denied.

On Monday, September 17, the jury was finally completed. The four jurors selected were Mrs. Emeline Hogan of Niota, mother of four children; Mrs. Ruth Diew, also of Niota, a registered nurse and mother of two children; Mr. Fay Davis, a retired mailman; and John C. Antoine of Basco, a farmer.

Altogether, 255 veniremen had been called to obtain the 12-man jury.

The actual taking of testimony began on Tuesday, September 18, 1956.

The first witnesses established that a crime had been committed. We have heard much of their testimony in chapter one of this book. Dean May, Janice's father, related the events of Saturday, November 26. He was followed by Jeane May, her mother, who was asked for a description of her daughter. After complying and stating that Janice was in third grade at school, she broke down in tears. Judge Bardens declared a ten-minute recess. Mrs. May also described the events of that Saturday afternoon: the show at the Capitol, the lunch, and her departure for the hospital.

Jimmy and Bill May, Janice's brothers, told of finding their sister.

The gas station proprietor, Harold Largent, told about Jimmy's request to use the phone and his rush to the scene at the abandoned mine car.

Then came the testimony of the police officers. The ambulance men from the Murphy Memorial Home, Thomas J. Simon and Ralph McFall, told their stories. So did the physicians, David A. Bennett and Raymond J. Mercey. Sheriff Virgil Ball described his first visit to the scene of the crime and how the rock was found, delivered to Forrest Litterly at the State Crime Laboratory, and returned.

Next Sue Ann Williams Miller, Lloyd's former wife and the mother of his son testified that Lloyd had married her under the name "Jack Franklin Warner." Why this testimony? Lloyd had been indicted under his true name but the indictment added, "also known as Jack Franklin Warner." It seems clear that adding the alias to the indictment and bringing Sue Ann to testify against Lloyd prejudiced the jury against Miller at the outset. The 1949 marriage to Sue Ann under an alias had no connection whatever with the crime.

The last witness of the day was Superintendent Christensen. He testified that it was not possible to develop fingerprints from the rock found near the body. Such "negative testimony" was important to the prosecution to explain to the jury why fingerprint evidence was not introduced.

On Wednesday, September 19, Court was in session for the full day, but the jury was present for only a few minutes. It heard Canton police officer Donald Lingenfelter, assigned to guard the area around the abandoned mine cars, testify that Lloyd drove by in his cab about 9:45 P.M. and that he returned again about fifty minutes later. Why this testimony? Evidently so that the prosecution could remind the jury in its closing argument that a murderer always returns to the scene of the crime.

Next, with the jury absent, Christensen and other officials related the prosecution version of the confession as described previously. At the end of the day, the court noted that the State had introduced sufficient evidence of voluntariness to require a rebuttal from the defense. The prosecution had won an important first round.

Customarily, evidence regarding a confession is restricted to events immediately surrounding the taking of the confession. Usually the only witness for the defense is the defendant himself. In arguments addressed to Judge Bardens Wednesday evening and renewed Thursday morning, Malmgren and Meuth tried to convince the court that the traditional scope of inquiry was inadequate, at least with respect to Lloyd. They urged that, in order for the court to make an intelligent decision as to whether the confession was voluntary, it was necessary to inquire further than merely into what happened at the time of the interrogation and the confession. It was necessary also to inquire, "What sort of person was the defendant?" During argument on Wednesday evening, it became clear that the court was going to reject the contention. Nevertheless, Meuth renewed the effort Thursday. He sought leave to present to the court a rounded picture of Lloyd's life. He sought to bring in Lloyd's father, his mother, his wife,[1] his employer, and a girlfriend to testify regarding Lloyd's erratic conduct. Further, he sought permission to bring in a psychiatrist, Dr. Donald Sweezey, who had examined Lloyd.

Judge Bardens rejected the defense view saying that Illinois procedure did not contemplate inquiry "into the background of apparently normal, mature persons in order, in the first instance, to decide the admissibility of evidence." Thus, the defense evidence as to the voluntary character of the confession had to be confined to the events from Lloyd's arrest on Monday evening, November 28, until the actual signing of the confession on December 1 shortly after midnight.

There can be little question that the defense was handicapped by Judge Bardens' refusal to permit witnesses regarding Lloyd's emotional makeup. The effect of persuasion on a man certainly depends upon the man. A chain of events that would not break one individual may be sufficient to break another. Perhaps a question of physical coercion can be answered in the abstract by a judge drawing upon his own knowledge of the likely impact of force upon a suspect. But where the claimed coercion is not physical but psychological, an abstract approach is inadequate. Each of us is shaped in a different mold. It seems unfortunate that Judge Bardens declined to listen to psychiatric testimony and to lay witnesses as to the mental makeup of the man on trial.

Thus, the defense presented only a single witness on the issue of the voluntary character of the confession, Lloyd Miller. No one other than the public authorities themselves were present during the interrogation.[1]

1. Lynn Marin Miller.
2. Lloyd had no right to the presence of another person. But in 1966 the Supreme Court, in *Miranda* v. *Arizona,* ruled that a suspect, if he wishes, is entitled to have an

Late Thursday morning Miller took the witness stand and testified for five hours. Bernadine Martin described his appearance for
her readers on Friday morning, September 21:

> He went through his story with his attorney, William
> Malmgren, without confusion.
> But when cross examination by Roger Hayes, special
> prosecutor, attempted to lead him backward from the time
> of signing Miller grew confused.

The backward questioning was hard for Miller to follow. For
example:

Q. You have testified that between 11:30 or a quarter-to-twelve until midnight that Christensen and Lindzey were in the
room with you?

A. Yes.

Q. And that they had come into the room at that time. I then asked
you when the last time before that was that you had seen
them and you said about 11:00. Now, then, thereby saying
that you didn't see them between 11:00 and 11:30. Do you
understand what I mean?

A. I still don't get you, Mr. Hayes.

A question or two later, Hayes worked forward.

Q. So, in other words, now we will go the other way. They Christensen and Lindzey came into the room at 11:00 P.M. on that
night?

A. Yes sir.

Q. Where were you just before 11:00 P.M. that night?

Regarding the confession, the defense was not effective. Martin
put her finger on the difficulty:

> Miller didn't seem able to get across clearly his conten-
> tions that he had been broken mentally before he con-

---

attorney present during questioning. Confessions obtained in violation of the *Miranda*
decision are not admissible in evidence. The confession largely responsible for Miller's conviction in 1956, by 1966 would have been inadmissible as evidence. We shall
comment further on this aspect of the case.

fessed. He admitted that he had not been physically mistreated with the exception of a blow to his left shoulder, which he said was struck by Fulton County Sheriff, Virgil Ball.

The inexperience of Malmgren and Meuth contributed to Lloyd's poor impression. He was not fully protected from improper cross-examination. An illustration: It is a general rule of evidence that a witness is supposed to be asked questions about the facts in the case. He is not supposed to be questioned about "conclusions of law." But Hayes did not hesitate to ask Miller for legal conclusions. Question after question was put in which Lloyd was asked to describe which incidents had "an undue influence" on him. After a long series of such questions, Malmgren finally objected on the ground that Hayes was asking the witness for legal conclusions. Judge Bardens asked Hayes, "Don't you agree it is a conclusion?" As Hayes struggled for a reply, the court came to his rescue:

BY THE COURT. You are using it not in the sense of conclusion, but an inquiry as to what his beliefs are about the wrong?

Hayes took the hint immediately:

Q. Yes sir. Just as a way to solicit the proper answer of what incident took place or what incidents took place.

BY THE COURT. I'll overrule the objection if you are doing it for that basis.

Thus the line of questioning was allowed to continue. As a matter of law, Lloyd's beliefs as to his rights were irrelevant. The real issue was whether Miller's constitutional rights, in fact, had been invaded.

After the testimony had been heard on the voluntary character of the confession, the judge listened to arguments of counsel, rejected a defense memorandum of law as unnecessary and stated he was ready to rule. He declared, "I have never known of a case where I felt that any officer was trying to railroad or pin something on a defendant against his will and contrary to what his conscience told him was in pursuance to a solution of crime."

What was involuntary confession to the Judge? "... interrogation that becomes so oppressive that it can be readily seen that it is against the entire will of the defendant to make it." The judge declined to review the evidence to see whether it complied with this standard. Instead (and improperly in my judgment) he turned the issue over to the jury without himself passing on the question of voluntariness.

Somewhat beside the point, he added, "My decision is that an honest, competent and reasonable investigation has been made in this case and therefore the evidence of admissions and confessions will be admitted into evidence."

A second round had been lost. The confession and testimony with respect to taking the confession would be presented to the jury.

Friday, September 21, was thus a decisive day in the trial. The jury was recalled and James Christensen, "tall and self-assured," as described by the *Ledger* on September 22, resumed the stand. He related to the jury his role in Miller's interrogation. The jacket was produced and identified as the jacket which Miller said he had thrown into the creek from the Walnut Street Bridge. The shorts were brought in and these, too, were identified by Christensen as the shorts that Miller said belonged to him and that he had removed and left in the Van Buren Flats on the evening of November 26. Finally, "People's Exhibit 4," the confession, was produced and identified by Christensen as the document signed by Miller shortly after midnight on December 1.

The final witness of the day was Kenneth Lindzey, who corroborated Christensen's testimony regarding the signing of the confession.

Just before court adjourned, Judge Bardens called counsel and the defendant to the bench outside the presence of the jury and said, according to the court record:

> The bailiff informs me that one of the jurors wants to get a hair cut. He can make arrangements with the barber and they will take him to the barbershop and stay with him after the shop is closed so that the only three people that will be there will be the barber, this juror, and the bailiff. Do you have any objection to that?

BY THE DEFENDANT: Just as long as the bailiff sees——.

BY THE COURT: That they don't talk about the case—that the barber doesn't talk about the case, you mean.

BY THE DEFENDANT: Yes.

BY THE COURT: The bailiff will be instructed in that respect because as somebody mentioned, barbers are great talkers.

Lloyd was learning about legal matters.

There was a second Saturday session on September 21. The prosecution had won the battle respecting the focal point of the case and knew it. Ramsey and Hayes moved ahead rapidly to take advantage of success. The confession was admitted into evidence as People's Exhibit No. 4 and was read to the jury.

Mrs. Betty Ellis, a waitress at Mac's Coffee House in Canton, testified that she did not know Lloyd Miller personally, but that she had known who he was for several months. According to Betty, Lloyd came in at two-thirty on the afternoon of Saturday, November 26, ate a "Mac's special," stayed just long enough to eat, and behaved "like any other customer." According to Betty, Lloyd was wearing a dark green jacket, dark green pants and had on "the cap that he drove in." The significance of the testimony of Mrs. Ellis was that it took Lloyd Miller out of Mrs. Baxter's residence by two-thirty in the afternoon, approximately an hour and a half before the crime.

The last witness of the day was Chester Phillips, the Canton police officer. He related to the jury that between five and six o'clock on Tuesday afternoon, November 29, he, together with Neil Baxter, found the jacket frozen in the ice. Baxter pulled at the jacket and tore it, until Phillips told him to stop. Finally they "picked it up, ice and all," and took it to police headquarters.

The trial was adjourned until Monday morning.

The defense had cause for weekend gloom. The prosecution had struck hard blows. Worse were to come.

When the trial resumed on Monday, September 24, the prosecution called June Lang to the stand.

June Lang, as a witness, presented a supreme challenge for the prosecution. Her testimony was invaluable since her tale of Lloyd's confession to her corroborated the signed confession. The confession, despite prosecution assertions that it was uncoerced, was secured only after lengthy interrogation. The jury might not believe it. A higher court might reject it. But Lloyd's alleged confession to June was not subject to such attack.

But calling June as a witness was hazardous. The prosecution knew her penchant for switching sides. She had first given the authorities a statement that Lloyd had confessed to her. Two days later she offered to reveal information to the senior Millers helpful to Lloyd if she were permitted to see him. On March 16, June gave Malmgren a statement repudiating her tale of Lloyd's alleged confession to her.

If June's testimony on direct examination varied significantly from the written version given to Malmgren, June would be vulnerable to impeachment on cross-examination. Or suppose that while on the witness stand as a prosecution witness, June repudiated her original statement about Lloyd's supposed confession to her. She might claim that the November 30th statement in Springfield was given under intimidation.

If she, a witness, was intimidated, what about Lloyd? The jury and judge might infer that authorities who would coerce the one would coerce the other. In such event, the case could collapse.

Suppose, in addition, that June, as a defense witness, repeated her statement to Malmgren that while in Springfield she had overheard a part of Miller's interrogation. She might testify concerning acts of coercion or intimidation. The jury might reject the confession and acquit Lloyd.

But even apart from such dramatic possibilities, there was the risk that June Lang might be destroyed on cross-examination. Her behavior immediately following the taxi ride to St. David was unusual. Moreover, the prosecution knew of other facts which cast doubt on her credibility. Were these facts known to the defense? Would they be used against June? If June's credibility were destroyed, a judge and jury might well become skeptical about the case. Even if a conviction were obtained, a seed of doubt might bar the jury from imposing a death sentence; a higher court might set aside the conviction. A fiasco with June Lang could tarnish Hayes' and Ramsey's reputations as public officials, and raise public questions about Miller's guilt.

In retrospect, it appears to us that the prosecution had a great deal to lose by calling June Lang as a witness and very little to gain. The prosecution had a signed confession. What strength did a second oral confession to a girl friend add to the case? Nevertheless, not calling June Lang might have been inexpedient. Since December 1955, Lloyd's alleged confession to her had been mentioned extensively in the newspaper. The jurors, although from the Carthage area, might well have recalled those stories. Thus a failure to call her might raise a question in the minds of the jurors and perhaps in the mind of Judge Bardens.

June was accompanied to Carthage by two women deputy sheriffs assigned to her by Sheriff Virgil Ball. In 1963, at the *habeas corpus* hearing before Judge Perry, George Leighton, then Lloyd's chief attorney, asked Sheriff Ball

> . . . why it became necessary for you, as sheriff of Fulton County, to assign two persons to be with June Lang throughout the time she was there to testify, when you did not do it with any other witness in this case?

A. We were trying to treat her with all the courtesy that was possible through our office. She seemed to be a person who did not have too many friends. . . . And we thought it was no more than right to have somebody with her during the trial.

Q. . . . they were really deputy sheriffs weren't they?

A. Yes. We had to pay them as deputy sheriffs.

Q. Before you assigned these two deputy sheriffs to her, did she ever tell you that she wanted the two deputy sheriffs to be with her because she did not have any friends?

A. No.

At 10:00 A.M. court convened. The moment had come. But the prosecution tried a gambit to minimize possible loss. Before the jury came into the courtroom, Roger Hayes asked Judge Bardens to call June as a "court's witness." When a party presents a witness in court it represents to the court by implication that the witness is worthy of belief. The party is bound by the testimony of its witness and generally is not permitted to impeach or discredit its own witness. But a court witness is not a witness for either side and either side may impeach him.

Hayes avoided stating to the court that June was not worthy of belief. Instead, he said, "I think the Court knows of the situation in regard to this witness as far as the defense counsel is concerned and we are—we believe that unless we are able to do this that a miscarriage of justice might be done."

Judge Bardens denied the request. The prosecution could call June as a prosecution witness or not call her.

Bernadine Martin described the scene in the Monday evening paper:

> Wearing a gray, button-down dress trimmed in white, Miss Lang looked only occasionally at Miller as she related events leading up to the time Miller admitted to her he had killed the May girl. . . . During the testimony Miller continually stared at Miss Lang but did not show any facial expression.

After giving her name, her address, and her occupation ("waitress"), June stated that she knew Lloyd Eldon Miller, Jr., and was asked how long she knew Lloyd. Her answer was "Approximately two years." (On cross-examination she again said that she had known Miller for two years.)

Quickly June told of the cab ride to St. David with Lloyd, of showing the new nephew and returning him to the house. Then she continued:

> I came back out and he usually opened the door for me, but he didn't that time, and I got in and sat down and he was looking straight ahead and didn't say anything for a few minutes and so I said, "Lloyd, what is the matter?" Because he had acted so funny about my nephew. So, he just sat there and looked at me and he went to sigh and he says, "June, you know I did it." I just sat there and stared at him sort of dumbfounded. He went on talking and I just sat there and listened to him. I didn't know what to say.
>
> Q. And then what was said by him at that time?

A. He says, "June, why do people do things they are ashamed of?" I said, "I don't know."

She ended her story by relating that just before she got out of the cab, Lloyd said:

> "If you say anything, the same thing will happen to you," and I didn't think anything about the rape part but I was thinking about the death of the little girl."

The prosecution had successfully mastered another crisis in the trial. June Lang had not repudiated her previous statements to the prosecution and had testified as the prosecution desired. But the question remained whether she would break down on cross-examination.

Cross-examination, which should have been penetrating, was unfortunately brief and almost superficial. Malgrem began by asking, "Miss Lang, you say you had known Mr. Miller for two years." June answered, "Yes, sir." This Malmgren knew to be a lie from the statement June had given to him the previous March 16. June had known Lloyd for only a few weeks. June should have been caught in this initial falsehood. But Malmgren did not pursue the matter. Later Malmgren asked about the events in Springfield. June admitted that Lloyd and she were in adjoining rooms, but she said she did not know whether Lloyd was being questioned.

Malmgren was now getting to pay dirt and began asking a series of questions based on June's March 16 statement. Did she hear Jim Christensen say to Mr. Miller, "If you will just tell the truth, you will never regret it." ("I don't remember hearing anybody talking to him.") Did she hear Jim Christensen say, "If you will tell the truth, we will see that nothing happens to you?" Hayes objected. Malmgren was taking the first steps on the road to impeaching June, intending to use the March 16 statement to contradict her trial testimony.

Hayes tried to halt the impeaching process. He recalled to the court that there are two horns to impeaching a witness. One horn is to ask the witness whether he made such and such statements. After the witness denies having done so, the second horn is to prove that he did in fact make the statements. An attorney is not supposed to embark on Horn 1 unless he is able to prove Horn 2. There was no problem about Horn 1, but, Hayes contended, Malmgren would not be able to prove Horn 2 because he himself would have to take the witness stand since he was the only person present when the Horn 2 statements were made. A wrangle followed, during which Malmgren requested court permission to take the stand himself. Hayes contended strongly that he should not be allowed to do so. Ultimately, after a conference with the judge, Malmgren was allowed to read to June the portions of her March 16 statement. In these selections June repudiated Lloyd's alleged taxicab confession to her and told of overhearing a part of Lloyd's interrogation in Springfield during which Lloyd was called a liar and told that if he confessed, nothing would happen to him. June denied that she had ever made such statements to Malmgren.

Malmgren's cross-examination ended at this point.

There is no doubt that the cross-examination of June Lang was a delicate challenge. Cross-examining anyone presents a challenge because of the danger that vigorous cross-examination, particularly cross-examination that necessarily impugns the veracity of a woman, may arouse sympathy for the witness in the minds of the jury. June's cross-examination presented the further difficulty that she creates a good impression. When I first met her in 1963, she was pleasant and soft-spoken. When she took the witness stand in Judge Perry's Court in that year, she gave the appearance of a young lady constantly making every effort to tell the truth. She would pause before answering a question as if to recollect her thoughts, and then would answer in careful, measured tones. No doubt these qualities were also exhibited seven years earlier in the courtroom in Carthage.

Yet, it must be said that much much more could have been done with the cross-examination of June Lang. First of all, a determined effort should have been made to obtain from the prosecution a copy of June's statement given to the authorities on November 30. At that time the law did not require such statements to be given to a defendant, but certainly a demand should have been made. The very next year, the Supreme Court of Illinois ruled that a defendant is entitled to receive a copy of such statement. Had such a statement been procured, the defense counsel would have become aware of a crucial contradiction between June's statement of November 30 and her testimony in court on September 24 following. We will discuss this matter later.

Next, there were a number of inexplicable aspects to the story that she did tell in court. When Hayes was asking the questions, June stated that after Lloyd confessed the murder to her, he asked her to leave with him that night. Her response, according to her own story, was, "I tried to explain to him that neither one of us had the money to leave at that time and he still wanted to leave." Thus, we have her own statement that only money held her back from leaving with the just-confessed murderer. Another strange fact was that one would suppose that her very first response after leaving Lloyd would be to notify the police, something she certainly did not do, for on cross-examination, she said that she saw Lloyd again after her return from St. David that same evening. Had she phoned the police while in St. David, Lloyd would have been apprehended at once and not allowed to leave Canton.

Further, on cross-examination she said that when she learned that Lloyd was missing on Sunday morning with a cab, she did phone the police; but her statement to the police was not that Lloyd confessed a murder to her but rather "I told them I was supposed to have left with Lloyd." Thus, contrary to her statement on direct examination, she did agree to go away with Lloyd.

Malmgren could have attempted to explore with June her activities on Saturday night. These he knew in detail because of the March 16 statement. Certainly, it would have been worthwhile to ask June whether it was true that she stayed in St. David a short period, that she spent part of the time in a bar where she had four gin squirts, that she immediately went back to Canton, that she spent part of the evening with one man riding with him to Pekin, that she came back with another man, etc., etc., etc.

Finally, and crucially, the defense should have offered in evidence June's March 16 statement.[1] Malmgren was allowed to take the stand to contradict June but his testimony was a poor substitute for the statement. Malmgren's testimony merely pitted his oral state-

---

1. Judge Bardens did indicate that the statement wasn't "such a document as would be permitted to go to the jury." But the defense never even offered the document in evidence. They never fought to get it in.

ment against June's oral statement. While Malmgren's reputation in the community as a professional man, no doubt, was higher than June Lang's, the fact remained that he was an attorney in the case, and his testimony for that reason did not carry the weight that it ordinarily would have. No doubt, had the full June Lang statement reached the jury, its impact would have been substantial. True, destroying the credibility of June Lang would not have destroyed Lloyd's confession to the police. Nevertheless, destroying June's credibility would have destroyed the principal corroboration for the written confession and might very well have given the jury second thoughts about the entire prosecution case.

Before noon June Lang's appearance on the witness stand was concluded. The State's most vulnerable witness had emerged virtually unscathed on the stand and her story virtually unchallenged.

The session resumed at 1:15 P.M. It was to be the last part of the last day of prosecution testimony. Some hard blows were to be struck for the prosecution in the few hours that remained.

Mrs. Joyce Hardy, a clerk at Carver and Denny Cleaners in Canton, testified that about 5:15 P.M. on November 26, while she was alone in the store, Lloyd Miller came in to pick up his cleaning. She added, "As I reached over the counter to unpin this ticket, well, I noticed a large amount of blood on the man's clothing." Malmgren immediately objected to the use of the words "a large amount of blood," and Judge Bardens ordered that it be stricken from the record. Mrs. Hardy, however, was permitted to testify that the jacket was "all streaked and spotted from the waist up. That is all I could see because the counter is about my waist height."

The color was red:

> A bright red. It looked like it might have been wiped or smeared. As I started to get the cleaning he drew his arm around it. I noticed it. When I noticed it I must have looked at it in a funny way or something. I know I started to say something and then when I noticed the smudge on him I didn't say anything and he drew his arm around it to try to hide it.
>
> He took his cleaning and went out the door in a hurry and held the cleaning up in front of him and ran east on Elm Street.

His hands just—they had the red smudges on them. His hand, as he drew it around, I noticed that it was—it just looked like it had been wiped off."

Although Mrs. Hardy stated that it was a jacket that was streaked, she was not shown or asked to identify the jacket found in Big Creek.

The testimony of Forrest R. Litterly, of the State Bureau of Criminal Identification and Investigation, was important but seemed routine. It attracted hardly any attention in the press. Litterly's testimony occupies only eight pages in the typed transcript of record.

Litterly began by giving his qualification for his work with the State Bureau: He had a bachelor of science degree and had completed three-quarters of the requirements for a master's degree in chemistry. In the five years that he had been employed at the State Bureau he had made approximately 1,000 blood analyses.

Roger Hayes, who conducted the examination, then drove to the meat of the matter. Litterly testified that on the Monday following the crime, People's Exhibit 1, the concrete block found near the body, was turned over to him by Dwight Whitlock. Litterly tested the stains on the block, found that they were of human origin and that the blood was of type A. Next, Litterly testified that People's Exhibit 2, the jacket, was turned over to him on Wednesday afternoon. According to the prosecution theory, it was the jacket Lloyd was wearing at the time of the crime and when he went to Carver and Denny's at 5:15 P.M. It was presumably the jacket Joyce Hardy identified as "streaked and spotted," as "bright red." It was the jacket found in Big Creek off the Walnut Street bridge, frozen in ice, brought to the police station and identified by Lloyd in the confession as his jacket. Litterly found two "small minute stains," "one upon the right cuff and one upon the inside of the right collar." He tested these stains, determined that they were blood, but in the process of making the test, he used up all the blood and was unable to proceed with further tests. Thus, there is no evidence that the blood was of human origin and if so, as to its type. Litterly added that cold water tends "to dissolve blood and to dilute it." This point was an essential step in the prosecution's case. Under the prosecution theory, the stains on the jacket described by Joyce

Hardy were blood stains. The prosecution had to explain their disappearance.

Finally came the crucial questions respecting People's Exhibit 3, the pair of jockey shorts identified in the confession as the shorts that Lloyd had been wearing on the Saturday afternoon of the murder and which, according to the confession, he abandoned in the Van Buren Flats. The questions and answers with respect to this exhibit occupy only twenty lines in the record:

Q. Now, Mr. Litterly, I ask you what, if anything, you did in connection with "People's Exhibit 3" so named for the purpose of identification?

A. I examined and tested that exhibit to determine the nature of the staining material which was upon it.

Q. And what was the first test that you ran?

A. The first test which I ran was to determine whether or not the material was blood.

Q. What was the result of that examination or test?

A. The result was that this material upon the shorts is blood.

Q. And then did you make any further examination or test?

A. I further examined it to determine whether or not the blood was of human origin.

Q. And what was the result of that examination and test?

A. That examination disclosed that the blood is of human origin.

Q. Now then, did you make a further test upon that?

A. I further examined it to determine the group of the blood.

Q. Now then, I ask you what the result of that examination and test was?

A. That examination disclosed that the blood is of group A.

These seven questions and seven answers established a central portion of the prosecution case. Why were the shorts abandoned in the Van Buren Flats? According to the prosecution's theory of the case, because they had been stained with blood. If the confession were true, then there should have been blood on the shorts and the blood should have been of the same type as that of Janice May.

Janice's mother testified at the very start of the trial that her daughter had type A blood. Hence, Litterly's testimony supplied a short but key link in the prosecution's case: the shorts were stained with blood, it was human blood, and it was human blood of type A.

Litterly concluded his testimony by stating that he had tested Lloyd's blood and found that he had type O blood.

The cross-examination was brief. Malmgren established that 45 percent of the people in the United States have type "O" blood, 42 percent have type "A," 10 percent have type "B," and 3 percent have type "AB." This testimony pointed up a concealed, unproved assumption in the prosecution's case. Let us assume that Janice May had type "A" blood (this assumption is open to challenge) . Assume also that there was, in fact, type A blood on the jockey shorts. It does not follow that the blood on the shorts was the blood of Janice May.

There can be no question that the defense was impressed with Litterly's honesty and professional integrity and for that reason did not indulge in vigorous cross-examination.

Had the defense been more skeptical of Litterly, they could have inquired as to the basis for his statement that cold water washes out blood.

The incident points up another problem: the defense could not know until the moment Litterly testified what his explanation would be for the disappearance of almost all the blood on the jacket. (Joyce Hardy, the clerk at the dry cleaner, had testified that Lloyd's jacket was heavily stained, presumably with blood.) The defense might have anticipated the wash-out testimony, but could not be sure of it. The defense had no right to query Litterly in advance of trial.[1] If the defense could have known beforehand of such testimony, defense counsel could have made a search of the professional literature to see what in fact is the effect of immersing a blood-stained garment in a stream, permitting it to be frozen, and then causing it to be thawed out. Is it true, as Litterly's testimony suggested, that substantially all of the blood would disappear? If there were nothing in the literature on the point, the defense might have conducted a few experiments on their own account. If blood would not disappear and dissolve the way that Litterly said, then

1. Even today its rights are limited, a fact which poses serious handicaps to the defense. See further Chapter 12.

there would have been a gaping hole in the prosecution's theory of the case, for in that event the disappearance of all of the blood from the jacket would be unexplained.

Had the defense counsel been more skeptical of Litterly, it might well have asked him a series of questions inquiring exactly what areas of the shorts were tested for blood. Counsel could have asked the precise nature of the tests used and could have asked to see Litterly's laboratory notes of his examinations.

The next witness was Hugh Max, a truck driver and tree trimmer who had known Lloyd Miller for approximately twenty years. According to Max, between 4:02½ and 4:05 P.M. on the afternoon of September 23, 1955, he was passing a school at the corner of Third Avenue and East Hickory Street (site of the Kellogg School which Janice attended) where, said Max, "I saw Lloyd here, Lloyd Miller, waving a hat and making motions to a little girl, a blond-headed girl."

Ramsey, who was conducting the examination, asked Max to describe the girl and relate what happened. Max replied that she was "blond headed, she wasn't fat—she wasn't skinny—she was just a nice plump little girl. She didn't look like she was very old, though."

As Max approached the stop sign on the corner he "looked that way. That is why I saw him. I saw him all the time I was going by before I came to the corner. And there was a man on the school ground and it was a short heavy-set fellow. He had his sleeves rolled up and he hollered at Lloyd, and he told him to move on, to leave the little girl alone."

There can be no question that this testimony was highly prejudicial. The event itself occurred approximately two months before the crime. The little child was never identified as Janice but the jury was led to infer that it was she. There was no showing or even a suggestion that Lloyd had any improper purpose in "waving a hat and making motions" to the child. There was not even the suggestion that he was trying to talk to her or encourage her to approach his taxicab. Yet, it is clear that the prosecution hoped that the jury would draw the inference that Lloyd had a propensity for making improper advances to little girls, and perhaps to Janice specifically.

6

TRIAL

DEFENSE AND VERDICT

At 9 o'clock on Tuesday morning the defense opened its case. It faced a major challenge because the prosecution case had an apparent completeness and consistency.

The first effort of the defense was to establish, in the legal sense, an alibi for Lloyd, that he was not at the scene of the crime at the time of the crime.

The alibi defense required careful determination of the time of the crime. During the 1956 trial the prosecution did not commit itself on the issue. (It did so later, in 1963, when it fixed the time at 4:00 P.M.) Mr. and Mrs. May, however, testified that they left home about 2:30 in the afternoon, leaving Janice and the boys doing the dishes. At 4:32 P.M. the police received their first call. The crime, therefore, must have been committed at some time during this period of two hours and two minutes. Actually, we can narrow the time span still further because the boys did not leave the house immediately after their parents left, and when they did leave, Janice was still at home. Further, the crime must have been committed at some time before the sounding of the first alarm.

The opening move of the defense was to ask the court to call Mrs. Alice Baxter, Lloyd's landlady, as a court's witness. Malmgren's reason was that Mrs. Baxter was "somewhat hostile" but he added, categorically, that he would not say she was unreliable. Judge Bardens ruled that, like June Lang, she could not be called as a court's witness, but if she was hostile, Malmgren could ask leading questions. He decided not to call her.

What lay behind Malmgren's cryptic statement that Mrs. Baxter was "somewhat hostile"? Not until 1963 was the whole story put before an official body. Malmgren wanted to show the truth of Lloyd's testimony that at 4:30 P.M. he had left Mrs. Baxter's with a prescription to be filled for her. In 1963, before the Parole Board, the full story came out with a powerful assist from a prosecution witness.

It was a singular fact that Mrs. Baxter was called by neither the prosecution nor the defense at the 1956 trial. The defendant worked the night shift, finishing work in the early hours of the morning. According to his testimony and according to the confession, he had been in his room at Mrs. Baxter's residence during the Saturday morning preceding the crime and during the early afternoon. According to the confession, he had left his room sometime before 2:30 P.M. and had returned to his room sometime before 5:45 P.M. following the crime and had stayed there until 5:45 P.M., when he left for work. Lloyd's testimony was that he was asleep in his room until four o'clock on the afternoon of the crime, spent the half-hour from four to four-thirty getting dressed, left Mrs. Baxter's residence at four-thirty, went out for supper, had a prescription filled for her, returned to Mrs. Baxter's house, gave her the prescription and the change, and left for work. It followed, therefore, that whether one accepts the theory of the prosecution or the theory of the defense, Mrs. Baxter or someone else in her residence should have seen the defendant that Saturday afternoon during his comings and his goings.

In early 1963, we learned that early on that Sunday morning, August 27, the police came to see Mrs. Baxter. She was interviewed but never signed a statement and presumably was never asked to do so. The police wanted to go to Lloyd's room; "So," she said, "of course I showed them his room immediately. And they checked everything in the room and everywhere and in the bathroom, and there was three towels in the room. And I heard them remark that there was no blood stains on the towels or anything in his room. There was no evidence of any sort."

Early in its case, the defense called three alibi witnesses. One was Mrs. Gertrude Gates, a sales clerk at the J. C. Penney Store in Canton. She testified that she called Lloyd at his room at 3:35 P.M. on Saturday, November 26. Before the 26th, he came into Penney's, selected a topcoat, and asked to have it put aside for him until Friday or Saturday. One of the other salesgirls had a chance to sell the coat. Mrs. Gates called Lloyd to ask whether he still wanted it. She called once at 3:25, but received no answer. When she called again in ten minutes, the phone was answered immediately.

Another alibi witness was Ruth Langford, a waitress at the Maid Rite Restaurant. According to Mrs. Langford, Lloyd came into the restaurant about five o'clock and ordered a fruit bowl and coffee. Lloyd was wearing a dark green jacket and a cab cap.

The testimony of Mrs. Langford was not alibi testimony in the strict sense, since it concerned a period after the crime. But it was relevant and highly relevant, nonetheless, because the confession purported to cover Lloyd's movements until 5:45 P.M. The confession was silent about the meal at the Maid Rite and, hence, if Lloyd did eat there, it was false or incomplete in this one particular, at least.

Lloyd's third alibi witness was his employer, Lawrence ("Teke") Johns. Teke related that Lloyd started to work for him September 16, 1955, and at the time of the crime was working on the 6:00 P.M. to 6:00 A.M. shift. Lloyd had left a "time call" for 2:30 P.M. on the Saturday afternoon of the murder. Teke said that he missed the time by fifteen minutes and actually put the call in at 2:45 P.M. The phone rang several times before it was answered, and when it was answered, Lloyd himself answered the phone.

The prosecution reaction to Malmgren's question to Teke revealed one of its principal strategies to counter the defense: a determined effort to keep out of the record and away from the jury every bit of possible defense evidence that was not actually helpful to the prosecution in one way or another. This effort largely succeeded and seriously hampered the defense. After Teke testified that Lloyd answered the telephone, Malmgren asked Johns what he said after the phone was answered. Hayes objected to the conversation unless the defense could show it was material to the case. Malmgren sought to justify the conversation on the basis that it was material whether Lloyd was in bed and asleep and in a sleepy state at the time the phone was answered. Hayes rejoined that "You could not tell that over the telephone." Judge Bardens sustained the objection.

The rule excluding evidence as "immaterial" is intended to prevent courts from wasting time on evidence that has no reasonable relevancy to the matter at hand. Since Lloyd was on trial for his life and since his whereabouts at every moment from 2:30 P.M. to 4:32 P.M. on the afternoon of the crime was certainly relevant, one could scarcely say that the conversation between Lloyd and Teke was irrelevant. Unfortunately, after the objection was sustained, Malmgren did not inquire even directly of Teke, as his remarks to the judge suggest he could have, whether Lloyd sounded sleepy.

Teke related also that about ten-thirty that night June Lang visited the cab stand to hire Lloyd for the ride to St. David. Teke was allowed to add, over a series of objections, that he "didn't see nothing unusual about him [Lloyd]. Not any more than he was any other night that he worked for me."

Now Malmgren moved to a new area, an attack on the Hugh Max testimony about seeing Lloyd waving to a little girl near the Kellogg school just after four o'clock on September 23. Through Teke, Malmgren sought to introduce into evidence the cab dispatcher's sheet for September 23 to show that Lloyd was not in the vicinity of the Kellogg school at that time. At the same time, Malmgren asked that the sheet for November 26 be admitted.

This request led to a lengthy wrangle between Malmgren and Hayes. The battle over the dispatcher's records centered on whether they were admissible as a record kept "in the ordinary course of business." As a general rule, a document is not admissible in evidence unless the witness can testify as to its accuracy. This general rule, however, would exclude from evidence most business records, because they frequently represent an accumulation of data prepared from a variety of sources and by many individuals. Hence, the courts have developed a rule which permits the introduction into evidence of records maintained in the ordinary course of business. For such records to be admissible, it is sufficient to have the person under whose supervision the records are kept testify as to the manner in which the records are compiled and to testify that they are kept in the ordinary course of business.

Although the dispatcher's records seem to qualify under the customary rules of law respecting records maintained in the ordinary course of business, Judge Bardens was initially hostile to them and he indicated that he believed the records for both September 23 and

November 26 were inadmissible. After further argument and further evidence, however, the judge admitted the dispatcher sheet for November 26 but refused admission to the September 23 sheet.

There can be little question that the latter ruling handicapped the defense. The dispatcher's sheet lists in order all the calls made by Miller and other drivers during that day. Hugh Max was very precise as to time. He placed the waving incident at exactly 4:02–½ to 4:05 P.M., timing it by the whistle at the International Harvester plant.

The sheet shows that between 3:55 and 4:05 P.M. Lloyd took a fare from downtown Canton to Quality Hill, about ten blocks southwest. The Kellogg school was some twelve blocks southeast of downtown. Moreover, Lloyd's next fare went from the downtown A & P due north six blocks to east Birch Street.

Thus, the documentary evidence directly contradicted Max's story of Miller waving at a blond girl at 4:02–½ to 4:05 P.M. on September 23, and yet the defense was not allowed to put it into evidence. The evidence respecting the September 23 incident was highly prejudicial to begin with, and so the exclusion of a document that showed that it was not true seems most regrettable.

Immediately after the testimony of Teke Johns, the defense received an even more serious setback. Once again, key documents that the jury might have studied at their leisure when they retired to consider their verdict were excluded from evidence. On this occasion, oral evidence was received and the jury did hear it, but they heard it in an attenuated and ineffective fashion.

According to the confession, after the crime Lloyd picked up clean clothes at Carver and Denny Cleaners. (The clerk there said the time was 5:15 P.M.) He went home, changed clothes, went back to the Flats where he had previously abandoned bloody clothing, was scared away by a car, and went down Second Avenue, south to Maple, and east on Maple "to the railroad where a train was going by." He threw a bundle of bloody clothing in a passing boxcar and returned to his room where he stayed until 5:45 P.M.

If one goes to Maple Avenue and Second in Canton (see map page oo) and then east along Maple, one reaches the tracks of the Chicago, Burlington and Quincy Railroad which passes north and south through Canton. A key question, therefore, one which affected vitally the truth of the confession, was this: Was there a train passing along those tracks at any time between 5:15 and 5:45 P.M. on November 26, 1955? On this issue the defense produced Wendall L. Logsdon, chief train dispatcher for the CB&Q. Logsdon had with him the official records of train movements through Canton on November 26. They showed that exactly four trains passed through Canton on the CB&Q on the day of the murder.

We can exclude two south bound trains and one north bound train because they passed through Canton before the murder. The other north bound train did not leave a point south of Canton until 6:10 P.M. That train, Logsdon said, passed through Canton about 6:17 or 6:18 P.M.

There is one inescapable conclusion: there was no CB&Q train passing through Canton into which Lloyd could have thrown garments at the time stated in the confession. In light of the confession, it would be difficult to find documents more relevant to the case. Yet Judge Bardens excluded them. Logsdon was permitted to state their contents, but the driving force of the documents the jury could study in the jury room was lost.

One more point: Lloyd reportedly left Mrs. Baxter's house at 5:45 P.M. to go to work. According to the taxi company dispatcher's record, at 6:15 P.M. he was driving a customer (his first for the shift) from the Maid Rite Restaurant to West Walnut Street. Thus, at the time the only possible train did pass through Canton, Lloyd was taking a fare from the center of town to a destination west, away from the CB&Q tracks.

Next for the defense was Russell Esslinger, Superintendent of the Toledo, Peoria and Western Railroad Company. The TP&W cuts across central Illinois and Canton from east to west. Esslinger too brought official railroad records for November 26. We need consider only the TP&W train 104 which arrived at Canton at 5:15 P.M. and left at 5:20 P.M. (Judge Bardens allowed into evidence the record on this train.) It is the only train that fits the confession timetable.

But there is solid proof that Lloyd could not have thrown garments into train 104. The facts were not produced in 1956, but came out seven years later at the Parole Board hearing on Lloyd's plea for clemency. Then we learned through a prosecution witness that almost at the minute he would have had to be at Eleventh and Maple where the TP&W tracks cross (see map, page 11), he was in downtown Canton at a pharmacy getting a prescription filled for his landlady. We shall relate the full story of this matter later.

The rest of Tuesday and early Wednesday were devoted to testimony by members of Lloyd's family. Lloyd's father gave the location of various places mentioned during the course of the trial, such as the International Harvester plant, the Maid Rite Cafe, etc., but it is questionable whether the jury was able to follow his testimony, which related to a city they probably knew only slightly, and they did not have a map in front of them.

The pair of shorts found in the Van Buren Flats and introduced into evidence by the prosecution were jockey-type. One of the major efforts of the defense was to convince the jury that Lloyd did not wear jockey-type shorts but boxer-type. The defense began with the testimony of Miller's father that Mrs. Miller did Lloyd's washing on Monday. Mr. Miller said that he knew his son wore boxer shorts because he saw Lloyd's shorts when his wife was ironing them. Moreover, he often delivered the clean clothes to Lloyd.

Mr. Miller concluded his testimony on Tuesday by describing the visit to the Tazewell County jail on the evening of December 1 (that is, on the day following the night of the confession). "I asked him if he done this and he couldn't hardly talk. He was so hoarse that he couldn't hardly talk and he said no." Judge Bardens ordered the jury to disregard the answer on Hayes' objection that the answer was "self-serving" and on the ground that Lloyd was in effect testifying through his father. But Malmgren was able to get in a question as to Lloyd's condition: "Well, he was—his eyes was all swollen. He looked pretty bad to me."

Mr. Miller was followed by Lloyd's sister, Margaret Isaak. She said that she and Lloyd's mother did the laundry for Lloyd on Mondays. Mrs. Isaak insisted that her brother wore only boxer shorts. In addition, she related a conversation with Lloyd showing that his departure from Canton was planned before the crime: Mrs. Isaak testified that she spoke to her brother at four-thirty on the Friday afternoon before the murder to tell him that she was leaving Canton to rejoin her husband and to ask Lloyd to come with her. But, said

Mrs. Isaak, "He says, 'No' he says, I am going to leave this weekend to go to Detroit or thereabouts for a job because, he said, he wanted to quit the cab stand because he wasn't making enough money." On cross-examination Mrs. Isaak told the prosecutor that she had not told any of the authorities about the conversation. The reason was that they did not ask: "Had they asked me, I would have told them."

The last of the family to testify was Lloyd's mother, Mrs. Jewel Miller. Bernadine Martin reported that Mrs. Miller walked to the stand with a worn Bible in her hands. Mrs. Miller wanted desperately to help her son. Yet there was little about which she could testify. Her testimony, moreover (that Lloyd wore boxer shorts, etc.), was interrupted by a barrage of prosecution objections.

Tuesday ended with Malmgren's testimony about June Lang, previously related.

On Wednesday morning Curtis C. Mason, Executive Vice President and Cashier of Canton State Bank, produced a bank ledger sheet for savings account No. 2053 in the name of Lloyd E. Miller, 28 East Walnut Street, Canton. There were precisely two entries on the account. It showed that on Wednesday, November 23, Lloyd opened an account and deposited $3.00. The following Friday, November 25, he withdrew the $3.00 and closed the account.

Later that day, before a crowded courtroom, Lloyd himself took the stand. So far as appears, there was never a question whether Lloyd would do so. It seemed obvious to all that unless he did so, conviction was a certainty.

Lloyd began his testimony by saying that he understood that he did not have to testify unless he wanted to, but that it was his desire to testify. To the question whether he had ever admitted the killing of Janice May, he answered "Absolutely not." He denied that the jacket and jockey shorts were his and added that he wore only boxer shorts.

There followed Lloyd's lengthy history from birth and the whole tale of his wanderings as set out in chapter two. Lloyd was allowed to give his entire history up to the day preceding the day of the murder without interruption or objection by the prosecution. As soon as he came to the time of the murder, however, the prosecution fired a barrage of objections.

After working Friday night he went home Saturday morning and was in bed from 9:00 A.M. until 4:00 P.M. He remembered receiving the call from Teke Johns and the call from Mrs. Gertrude Gates. At four, he arose, dressed, and went out to the Maid Rite Restaurant on South Main where he had supper. "I had a fruit bowl, two Maid Rites, two cups of coffee, and a cigarette with my coffee." Mrs. Ruth Langford waited on him. He was in the Maid Rite from 4:45 until 5:15 and from there he went to the Lewis Pharmacy, where he had a prescription filled for Mrs. Baxter. He was in the pharmacy from 5:15 to 5:30. He then returned to Mrs. Baxter's home. He continued with a description of his movements during the Saturday evening following the murder.

When he left Mrs. Baxter's residence a second time after giving her the prescription, he packed his suitcase. He had reason to go by the scene at Hickory and the CB&Q crossing that evening in his cab on three occasions and he talked to Officer Lingenfelter while there. Once he had a passenger with him, Leonard Vaughn. He stopped at the police station to inquire whether they had "any more news for us." "I mean by that there was policeman down there at the cab stand who told us about it. We had strict orders to be on the lookout for any suspicious persons." Then came the trip to St. David with June Lang and after that, more taxicab runs until 3:45 Sunday morning. At that time, Lloyd picked up his suitcase, presumably at Mrs. Baxter's, put it in the cab, stopped for coffee at Mac's Coffee Shop, and left Canton.

Next he told the story of abandoning the taxicab and travelling by bus from Pekin to Champaign and from Champaign to Danville, where he registered at the Grier Lincoln Hotel in Danville under his own name. He told of the day spent in the hotel room at the Grier Lincoln, Monday afternoon at the movie, and finally the arrest about 8:30 P.M. at the bus station. Then came Miller's lengthy account of his arrest, the taking of physical specimens from him (including samples of his pubic hair), the interrogations, and the lie detector test.

At 5:20 P.M., Miller was still on the stand. But Judge Bardens did not adjourn the court for the day. Instead, he declared a recess until seven o'clock that evening. After supper, Lloyd took up his story at the point during the second interrogation when the two lie detector men retired from the scene and turned the interrogation over to Superintendent Christensen.

When court adjourned for the day, Malmgren tendered Lloyd to Hayes for cross-examination.

The trial resumed Thursday, September 27, at 9:00 A.M. The first order of business was the cross-examination of Lloyd by Roger Hayes.

It is a truism among judges and attorneys that the cold typed transcript of a court proceedings does not convey its full import. The tone, the gestures, the manner—all are lost in the translation from the spoken word at the actual scene to the reporter's transcript. An excellent illustration of this point is given by a part of Hayes' opening cross-examination of Lloyd:

Q. Lloyd, do you realize it is still best to tell the truth?

BY MR. MALMGREN: I object, your Honor.

BY THE WITNESS: I am telling the truth.

BY MR. MALMGREN: I object as to this manner of approach.

BY THE COURT: Objection sustained.

BY MR. HAYES: Did you assault Janice May?

A. No, sir.

Q. Did you push her down on the rocks between those cars?

BY MR. MALMGREN: Now, your Honor, I object to this manner of approach. If he wishes to ask the witness questions, let him do it in a not badgering manner.

BY THE COURT: Objection sustained, Mr. Hayes.

Q. Mr. Miller, did you push Janice May down on the rock between the car?

A. I told you where I was at.

MR. HAYES: May the court direct the witness to answer the question by the court.

BY THE COURT: Answer the question.

A. No, sir.

Q. Did you strike Janice May, Mr. Miller?

A. No, sir.

Q. Did you assault Janice May, Mr. Miller?

A. No, sir.

Q. Did you kill Janice May, Mr. Miller?

A. No, sir.

Q. Isn't it so that nobody in Springfield talked to you in a worse way than I have started to talk to you this morning?

A. A lot worse way down in Springfield.

Now let us consider a portion of the same testimony as reported by Bernadine Martin on Friday, September 28:

> Hayes began his cross-examination by walking to within a few feet of the witness stand and asking: "Lloyd, do you realize it is still best to tell the truth?"
> An objection by defense attorney, William Malmgren, cut the answer short.
> Hayes walked near, leaned toward Miller and said: "Mr. Miller, did you assault Janice May?" Janice May is the eight-year-old Canton school girl Miller is accused of murdering.
> Miller said emphatically, "No, sir."
> Hayes, in a louder voice said, "Mr. Miller, did you push Janice May down between those railroad cars?" Miller's "No, sir" was heard at the same time his attorney objected to the "badgering" manner of questioning the defendant.
> Hayes then turned, walked back about twelve feet to the railing which divides the courtroom, turned and repeated in a low, polite tone, "Mr. Miller, did you push Janice May down between those railroad cars?" Miller, appearing angered, answered "No, sir."
> Still speaking quietly, Hayes put another question: "Mr. Miller, did you strike Janice May?" He got an emphatic denial.
> Then Hayes boomed at the defendant: "Mr. Miller, did you *kill* Janice May?" Miller snapped, "No, sir."

Hayes then asked, "Isn't it true that no one in Springfield talked to you in a worse way than I have talked to you
here, Mr. Miller?" Miller is claiming that he was mistreated there and pressured into the confession of a crime.

Miller's answer was "No, in Springfield, it was much
worse."

After this dramatic display, Hayes was ready for serious cross-
examination. His first point of attack was on Lloyd's explanation of
his departure from Canton early on Sunday, November 27. He had
said that he left because of fear that Sue Ann, the mother of his son,
Steve, would institute proceedings against him for failure to provide child support. The defense sought to support Lloyd's testimony
by presenting a letter written by Sue Ann to Lloyd just before the
crime. There was a storm of prosecution objection and the letter
was not accepted in evidence.

Hayes began his cross-examination by asking Miller why he left
Canton Sunday morning.

Lloyd replied, "I received a letter from my former wife, Sue Ann
Williams—ex-wife—she was going to have a warrant out for me for
child abandonment." Hayes had Lloyd admit that Sue Ann did not
state expressly in the letter that she intended to swear out a warrant.
The best Lloyd was able to do was to say, "I can understand her
letters the way she writes."

Between the battle of Tuesday over the letter and the cross-examination of Wednesday, Hayes had had an opportunity to read the
letter and had decided that it helped rather than hurt the prosecution because it did not contain an out and out threat of legal proceedings. Consequently Hayes presented the letter to the court.

Now Malmgren objected. But Judge Bardens admitted the letter
on the basis that it had been tendered in evidence by both the prosecution and the defense.

Hayes immediately read Sue Ann's letter to the jury. It read in
part:

Dalton, Georgia.

Dear Junior.
I am only getting two days a week and I want you to send
Steve some money. It is your place to keep your son up and

you better get some money down here for him. Junior, you know yourself, do let you by on keeping Stevie up longer than any other girl would. Have—but I am tired of it and I mean you have better take this to heart because you know it is a law for a man to keep his kid up.

Next, Hayes turned to an assault on Lloyd's character. Lloyd, having taken the witness stand voluntarily, exposed himself to this sort of attack.

The defense strategy was to reveal to the jury Lloyd as he was, as part of the effort to explain the confession and the Sunday morning departure. This strategy necessarily revealed a man of flaws. Hayes made the most of every one. First, he reviewed with Lloyd the fact that he had enlisted in the military service on the last occasion without revealing two previous enlistments that had terminated with bad conduct discharges. This in itself would not constitute perjury because one essential element was missing: proof that on the enlistment papers Lloyd was asked about and lied about his previous service. The enlistment papers were not in court. Hayes asked Lloyd whether the enlistment papers were under oath and Lloyd answered, "Not to my knowledge. I signed papers and then I was sworn in." By one or two questions Hayes depicted the swearing-in ceremony as an oath as to the truth of the facts stated in the enlistment papers. The crucial question, whether there was a specific inquiry about previous service, was never raised.

The next point of attack was the GI training Lloyd took in Dalton about July 1950. After Lloyd stated he received a bad conduct discharge in late 1948 or early 1949 and a dishonorable discharge in July 1950, Hayes asked:

Q. So immediately as you got your dishonorable discharge in July 1950 you started the GI training?

A. Yes, sir.

Q. Does the government give that GI training to people who have had a dishonorable discharge?

A. I don't know that.

Q. Does the government?

A. I don't believe so.

Q. But they gave it to you?

A. Well, they accepted my records and accepted my GI training, so I went ahead and took it.

Q. Even though you know yourself that they usually don't give it to people that have a dishonorable discharge, they gave it to you. Is that correct?

A. Well, I needed the money, Mr. Hayes.

By this series of questions, Hayes made it appear that Lloyd had been dishonest by taking GI benefits following his dishonorable discharge. The fact is that under the "GI Bill of Rights," a veteran became eligible upon ninety days' service during the Second World War and on honorable discharge. That Lloyd had. Lloyd did *not* lose his right to benefits by his subsequent difficulties in the service.

Malmgren should have objected to all questions about Lloyd's right to benefits. These are legal matters that Lloyd was not qualified to testify about. But Hayes had no business going into the subject, blackening Lloyd unjustly.

After reviewing with Lloyd the taxi ride with June Lang, Hayes began an extended inquiry about Lloyd's residence in Kansas City. When relating his life history, Lloyd had said that he spent about two weeks in Kansas City in July 1955.

A few minutes later Hayes asked Lloyd whether he had ever been in Sioux City, Iowa. Lloyd said he had not. Moments later Hayes asked this question:

Q. Where were you on August 8, 1955? Now, take plenty of time to think about that.

Malmgren immediately objected to the line of questioning "because it isn't apparently going any place." Judge Bardens said, "I confess I don't at the present time see the materiality of it." But Hayes promised "to tie it up," a lawyer's shorthand phrase for saying that testimony that appears at the moment to be irrelevant in fact is relevant and that the lawyer subsequently will demonstrate its relevancy. Lloyd's answer to the question was that on August 8,

1955, he was in Rock Island with his wife, Lynn. (Hayes was not allowed in the end to present evidence on the point and the jury was instructed to disregard the Sioux City and August 8 questions. We will return later to the significance of Sioux City, Iowa, and of August 8, 1955.)

Hayes' final line of attack was to isolate, and then exploit to the full, every discrepancy between Miller's testimony given in the absence of the jury on the question of the admissibility of the confession and the testimony that he had just given to the jury.

Since his version of his interrogation and the signing of the confession was related twice in considerable detail, separated by an interval of several days, inevitably there were differences between the two accounts. Hayes probably was aided by having before him the typed transcript of the initial telling before the judge.

Thus, for example, Hayes exploited a conflict between Lloyd's statement before the jury on Wednesday and his statement to the judge the preceding Thursday as to whether he did or did not show his parents the bruise from the blow on the shoulder given him by Virgil Ball. There was a similar quibble over the question whether the lie detector apparatus did or did not hurt him.

The ordeal of cross-examination ended shortly before lunchtime on Thursday.

The last witness for the defense was Dr. Donald L. Sweezey, a Peoria psychiatrist, who was called as an expert to establish that, based upon his psychiatric examination of Lloyd Miller, he believed that Lloyd would have signed any paper, regardless of its truth or falsity, in order to escape from the circumstances in which he found himself while in the Armory building in Springfield, Illinois. The Court refused to permit such testimony to be introduced.

Late in the afternoon of September 27 the defense rested.

The evidence was now in, but before the jury could retire to consider its verdict, important business remained. The rest of Friday was spent in a conference among the judge, the prosecuting attorneys, and the defense attorneys regarding the instructions to be given to the jury. These instructions, in Illinois state courts, customarily are read to the jury by the judge and then are kept by the jury while it considers the verdict.

At nine o'clock on Saturday morning the first order of business was an agreement to admit into evidence a plat of the City of Canton. This was not, unfortunately, an official plat showing the entire community drawn to scale. It was simply a small sketch showing only the portion of the city from Chestnut Street on the north to Hickory Street on the south and from Main Street on the west to the CB&Q right of way on the east. It came too late in the trial to offer any real help to the jury. The location of the various places mentioned in the testimony was not marked on it.

The time had come for closing arguments to the jury. Blaine Ramsey stressed the confession, Betty Ellis's testimony about the visit to Mac's Coffee Shop at 2:30 P.M., Joyce Hardy's testimony about the cleaners, the early Sunday morning departure from Canton, and the admission to June Lang. Midway in his speech he spoke of the jockey shorts, uttering words destined to be thrown back at him by another court in 1967: "Those shorts were found in the Van Buren flats, with blood. What type of blood? What type of blood? Not 'O' blood as the defendant, but 'A'—type 'A'."

Once more there was a reference to blood types and once again came language that was destined to be thrown back at Ramsey over a decade later: "And, if you will recall, it has never been contradicted the blood type of Janice May was blood type 'A' positive. Blood type 'A.' Blood type 'A' on these shorts. It wasn't 'O' type as the defendant has. It is 'A' type, what the little girl had."

As Ramsey drew toward his conclusion, his oratory grew more passionate: "They brought the little girl in and the mother saw her little girl in the hospital for the first time, lying on the cot, a crushed head, a bad cut on the right side, a gash across the chin, two teeth knocked out, and bleeding."

At the very last Ramsey said: "Now, when you were brought in this courtroom the first day you were here, the court asked you a question. Do you have any conscientious scruples against capital punishment in a proper case? We, the People, asked you the same question because we wanted you to think about it. We wanted you to understand the statement I am going to make now. We think this is the proper case to return a verdict of death."

Harold Haley of the Quincy *Herald Whig* reported, "At this

point of the summation, Miller's parents quietly left the courtroom. Mrs. Miller, who was carrying a Bible, was sobbing as her husband assisted her to the door."

Malmgren, on behalf of Lloyd, began in his customary, reflective manner: "I confess that I have long thought of what I would say to you as I open an argument for Mr. Miller." He began by reading the confession, pointing out inconsistencies. Why, for example, would a man take off bloody pants to abandon bloody shorts and then put back on the bloody pants?

The visit to Carver and Denny Cleaners is inexplicable. "Now, he had a change of clothes in his room by the language of this confession. But, nevertheless, according to this confession, he went out to get more clothes up to the cleaners."

The details set out in the confession were not really corroborative because they were known to the police when the confession was signed. The confession itself should be disregarded because of Lloyd's instability.

Ramsey made a brief rebuttal. The judge read his instruction to the jury. The jury was ready to consider its verdict.

The jury was given a choice of four verdicts: "Not Guilty," "Guilty" with a punishment of death, and "Guilty" with a punishment of life imprisonment, and "Guilty" with a punishment of imprisonment for a set number of years to be fixed by the jury. At the time, there was a peculiarity of great practical significance in Illinois sentencing procedure, the implications of which were never spelled out to the jury. Under the law as it then stood, a sentence of life imprisonment rendered a prisoner eligible for parole after he had served twenty years, less time off for good behavior. Under the good behavior rules, a prisoner serving a life sentence became eligible for parole (but was not necessarily paroled) after he had served eleven years and three months. A prisoner sentenced to a fixed term of years became eligible for parole (but was not necessarily paroled) after he had served one-third of the fixed term. Thus a sentence of fourteen years, the minimum sentence for murder, would make a man eligible for parole after serving four and two-thirds years. The one-third rule applied no matter how many years the jury fixed as the term of imprisonment. The number of years fixed, moreover, did not have to bear a relationship to the length of human life. In consequence, if the jury wished to fix a punishment that substantially reduced the possibilities of parole, it could fix a term of 199 years. Parole then would be possible only if the Governor reduced the sentence by executive action and thus shortened the parole-eligible period. For decades 199-year sentences were imposed in Illinois. (Ramsey had these considerations in mind in the abortive bargaining regarding a possible plea of guilty. See p. 00.)

In recent years the anomalies and hardships of Illinois law have been substantially modified. Under present law, every prisoner, no matter what his sentence, becomes eligible for parole after he has served twenty years less time off for good behavior. Thus every prisoner is eligible for parole after serving eleven years and three months. The rule that a prisoner serving a fixed term must serve one-third of his sentence to be eligible for parole has been abolished. Under current regulations, a prisoner who receives the minimum punishment for murder, fourteen years, may be paroled after serving eight years and three months.

At the Miller trial, the jury was not informed of the consequences of a life term, a term of years, or of their power to impose a 199-year sentence. Thus the jury was compelled to choose between the various forms of punishment without knowing their implications.

At two-twelve on Saturday afternoon the jury began its deliberations. At 5:45 P.M. the six men and six women reported to T. Bluford Stewart, Circuit Clerk of Hancock County, that they had reached a verdict. The news spread quickly. Lloyd, handcuffed, was led into the courtroom at 6:19 P.M. by Sheriff Ivan Latherow. Judge Bardens arrived at 6:20. At 6:23 P.M. the jury returned to the box. One of the women jurors was weeping.

Fay Davis, the foreman, informed the judge the jury had a verdict, but asked that it be read by someone else because of his poor eyesight. Accordingly, the verdict was read by Circuit Clerk Stewart: "We, the jury, find the defendant, Lloyd Eldon Miller, Junior, also known as Jack Franklin Warner, guilty of murder in the manner and form as charged in the indictment and we fix his punishment at death."

Malmgren asked that the jury be polled. Clerk Stewart called the name of each juror and asked whether the verdict was his decision in the case. Each replied, "Yes, sir."

According to Bernadine Martin in the *Journal Star*, "Miller showed no emotion as the verdict was read, nor as the jury was polled, but as he left the courtroom he protested, 'I'm an innocent man.' En route to the jail Lloyd told the officers 'I'm telling you that's one crime I did not commit, and you'll find it out in the years to come.' When they reached the county jail Miller, still sobbing, said, 'I don't know what I'm crying about, you guys are the ones that will get punished.' "

Later the jurors informed the press that there had been two ballots taken on the question of guilt or innocence. On the first, the count was eleven to one in favor of guilty. On the second ballot, the vote was unanimous. Two ballots were cast also on the matter of the death sentence. On the first ballot the count was seven for death and five for life imprisonment. On the second the vote was unanimous for the death sentence.

The next effort of the defense was to convince Judge Bardens that substantial errors had occurred and that Lloyd was entitled to a new trial. Malmgren and Meuth quickly filed papers to that effect.

Judge Bardens heard oral argument on the new trial motion on November 15. As soon as the arguments were over, Judge Bardens, after delivering an oral opinion, denied the motion.

The court was ready to pronounce sentence. The court record notes tersely: "Whereupon the People moved for judgment on the verdict. Ordered that mittimus and death warrant issue." (The "mittimus," from the Latin "we send," is a court order directing the prisoner to be conveyed to the state penitentiary.)

According to Bernadine Martin in the *Journal Star* on Friday, November 16, "Miller, who had sat passively during his long trial in Carthage in September, turned from the bench with tears in his eyes after Judge Bardens pronounced sentence. Only his mother, Mrs. Lloyd Miller, Senior, was in the courtroom. Neither of the May child's parents were present." The story appeared under the main headline, "Lloyd Miller Sentenced to Die in Chair Jan. 18."

Opposite the masthead of the *Journal Star* for that day was a quotation from Byron:

> Nor ear can hear nor tongue can tell
> The tortures of that inward hell!

On the same day, Martin had another story on the case in the *Journal Star*. The headline was, "Jury Could Have Given Miller Life If It Knew . . ." It began, "Would Lloyd E. Miller, Jr., be facing death today if a Hancock County jury had known how to sentence him to prison for the rest of his life? One juror believes not."

The story was told in more detail three days later on November 19.

It was startling news to the defense—and possibly to the prosecution—that, according to Bernardine Martin, the jury had asked to see the judge and had asked him how to fix a sentence which would keep Miller in prison for life. Defense counsel promptly made inquiries. On December 9, Juror Mrs. Evelyn Lovell gave an affidavit to the defense, stating that after the jury had retired for deliberation, she requested Mrs. Hoyt, a bailiff, to "tell the judge we want more information on the life sentence." Shortly thereafter, Mrs. Hoyt returned and stated that "the judge said he could not give any information in answer." The Lovell affidavit did not say clearly what information was requested, nor was it pinpointed to the parole question, as was Bernadine Martin's story. The defense, on December 12, asked Judge Bardens to upset the verdict, because of the information in the Lovell affidavit. This effort failed.

At eleven-thirty on Saturday morning, November 18, 1956, Lloyd entered death row at Joliet's Stateville Prison. His hope lay with the Supreme Court of Illinois.

7

APPEAL

Miller's death date of January 18, 1957, was purely nominal. Lloyd had a right of appeal to the Supreme Court of Illinois. Malmgren and Meuth filed an appeal[1] and the Supreme Court on November 28 automatically issued a stay of execution order.

A *right* of appeal in death cases to the Supreme Court of Illinois did not exist until 1953. Before that time, all persons convicted in criminal cases had a right of appeal, but in death cases the defendant had to obtain leave from the Illinois Supreme Court to appeal. In recent years two men were executed without appellate review of their cases. One, Willard Truelove, did not try to appeal. The other, Harry Williams, was denied permission to appeal. A private attorney stepped in voluntarily and asked the Supreme Court of the United States to review the case. He contended that requiring only death cases to ask permission to appeal was an unconstitutional discrimination. The Supreme Court refused to consider the case and the condemned man was executed in 1952. The very next year the law was changed, too late to benefit Williams, but in time to help Lloyd.

The name of private counsel who volunteered to help Williams was George N. Leighton. We shall meet him again.

At Stateville, Lloyd Miller received the number 39426 and it remained with him throughout his stay in that prison. On December 11, Lloyd was interviewed by two staff sociologists, William M. Meeks and Arthur V. Huffman, who prepared an extended "socio-

---

1. Technically, the review was by "writ or error." For convenience it is referred to above as an "appeal."

logical history." Their report set out Lloyd's version of the case and Lloyd's account of his four marriages. He was unable to recall the last name of any of the four girls he had married, but he gave reasons for each breakup. "Sally [Abbott] didn't tell me until after we were married that she couldn't have any children." Sue Ann [Williams] would not leave her parents and Georgia home to go with him to greener pastures. "There was no work down there (in Dalton) and I kept trying to get her up here but she didn't want to come so I filed for divorce." The marriage to Nan [James] failed because "I couldn't keep a job because I would always oversleep." He separated from Lynn [Marin] in August 1955 because "I came home from a trip once and she told me 'You have been too slow a husband for me.' That was our only trouble, though I had trouble keeping a job."

While Lloyd sat in his cell, Malmgren and Meuth worked on the appeal: the trial testimony had to be converted to a running narrative.

Next, they had to write a printed argument or brief summarizing the facts and advancing arguments of law that the conviction should be set aside. The Supreme Court of Illinois (and other courts which considered the case later) did not consider the question of Lloyd's guilt or innocence as such. The purpose essentially was to determine whether errors of law (e.g., in admitting or excluding evidence) had occurred in the trial.

Approximately fourteen months after conviction came disappointing news. The Supreme Court of Illinois, on January 24, 1958, affirmed the conviction. It declared that the confession was voluntary and corroborated by the facts. The Court upheld Judge Bardens' refusal to permit Dr. Sweezey, the psychiatrist, to testify that Lloyd had been overwhelmed by his interrogation. The testimony by Hugh Max regarding the alleged incident at Kellogg school was at most harmless error. Miller was not prejudiced by the contempt proceedings against Malmgren instituted by Ramsey shortly before trial. Near the end of the opinion, the Court upheld Judge Bardens' refusal to permit a scientific examination of the physical evidence.

The Court set Friday, April 11, 1958, as the execution date. The

Court granted a stay, however, pending an application to the United States Supreme Court. The request was made but denied on June 30.

With the denial of Supreme Court review, Malmgren and Meuth had somehow to stave off a prosecution request to the Illinois Supreme Court to fix a new death date.

During the next few years, many complex legal actions were undertaken on Lloyd's behalf. Over a five-year period, Lloyd was to face seven dates with the electric chair. There were to be six unsuccessful applications to the United States Supreme Court for review, and he was to receive ten stays of execution.

Late in 1958, Lloyd abruptly discharged Malmgren as his attorney.

William Malmgren recognized that he was dismissed by a man who had been laboring for many years under a serious emotional handicap, a man who had faced for two years the prospect of imminent death in the electric chair. Malmgren remained concerned for Miller's welfare and the welfare of his family. Whenever he was able to help (and we who later took up Miller's defense called on him for assistance on countless occasions), he did all he could for his former client, giving freely of his time without compensation.

Malmgren deserves tribute. Shortly after he began the practice of law in a small town, he was asked to take up an unpopular cause, perhaps the most thankless task any attorney was ever called upon to assume in the history of Fulton County.

After Malmgren's discharge, Meuth carried on alone from 1958 to 1960 seeking relief in the Illinois courts. These efforts failed.

Late in 1960 came the request by the Illinois Attorney General, long feared by the defense, that asked the Illinois Supreme Court to set a death date. On November 17, the Supreme Court set a third date for execution, December 16, 1960. Meuth had only twenty-nine days to secure a stay. Within a few days he was before Judge Bardens in Carthage with a petition to set aside the judgment of conviction. The day after, Meuth asked the Supreme Court of Illniois for another stay. The petition was denied. He filed an application for a stay with Supreme Court Justice Tom Clark. It was refused on December 7.

Only nine days were left to Lloyd Miller unless a stay was obtained from one source or another.

George Meuth and the Miller family turned for assistance to a young attorney, Donald Page Moore, then staff counsel of the Illinois Division of the American Civil Liberties Union in Chicago.

Moore turned to the Federal Court in Chicago. On December 9, one week before the scheduled execution, Moore filed a petition for habeas corpus.

Habeas corpus ("You shall have the body") is an order issued by a court to the custodian of a prisoner, commanding him to produce the prisoner ("the body") in court and to explain his authority for holding him. If the explanation proves inadequate, a second order issues directing the prisoner's discharge. The Magna Carta of 1215 declares that the writ shall not be refused. In the United States, it has become the principal means for state prisoners to seek release in federal courts on the ground that their rights under the Constitution have been violated.

The principal ground raised by Moore in the habeas corpus petition was that Miller had been denied a fair hearing at the 1956 trial on the voluntary nature of the confession because of the refusal of the trial judge to permit Malmgren and Meuth to present a full picture of Lloyd's emotional makeup.

The case was assigned to Judge Michael Igoe. The judge had been on the court for many years and was nearing retirement. The choice was favorable for Lloyd Miller. Judge Igoe was a decent, humane man. That same day, Don Moore appeared before Judge Igoe and obtained a stay of execution pending further order of court. Lloyd Miller's life was spared, for the moment.

After hearing argument in March 1961, Judge Igoe took the matter under consideration. While awaiting his decision, Miller and his attorneys suffered another defeat. On March 29, four days after the argument before Judge Igoe, Judge Bardens in Carthage dismissed the petition pending before him. This meant that the time permitted for an appeal from that ruling had started to run, and Moore and Meuth, in addition to whatever work remained before Judge Igoe, had also to appeal Judge Bardens' decision to the Supreme Court of Illinois.

Judge Igoe considered the matter for over two months but, on June 7, ruled for the state and dismissed the petition for a writ of habeas corpus. At the same time he vacated the stay of execution that had been in effect since the preceding December, but at Moore's request granted another stay until July 27 so that Moore could take an appeal. It was stay number four.

Now Meuth and Moore were faced with taking two appeals simultaneously. Meuth had received no fees following the initial decision of the Supreme Court of Illinois. Moore had been paid a fee by Lloyd's parents for handling the case before Judge Igoe, but that again had exhausted their financial resources. George Meuth and Donald Page Moore continued to represent Lloyd without charge.

Clearly the appeal to the Federal Court of Appeals could not be disposed of by July 27, when the stay granted by Judge Igoe was to expire, and therefore the first order of business was to obtain a fifth stay of execution from the Court of Appeals. It was granted on July 17. Then came the task of preparing the records in the two appeals and the more exhausting task of doing the legal research and writing the briefs.

On November 30, 1961, the defense suffered another setback. The Supreme Court of Illinois affirmed the adverse decision growing out of the new proceeding filed in Carthage in November 1960. The Court was testy about the case, commenting that the new proceedings had been filed more than four years after the original judgment sentencing Miller to death.

The following February another hope disappeared. The Court of Appeals in Chicago affirmed Judge Igoe's decision dismissing Lloyd's habeas corpus action. The sixteen-page opinion by Judge Elmer Schnackenberg began with a misapprehension of the argument advanced by Lloyd's attorneys. The court assumed that there was "no denial" that Lloyd committed the crime charged or that the evidence aside from the confession so proved. At no time did Moore and Meuth make such admissions.

The Court of Appeals devoted most of its opinion to Lloyd's contention that the court should have permitted the psychiatrist, Dr. Sweezey, to testify. It is well established in Anglo-American law that a person is not held criminally responsible for acts committed while "insane." It is well established also that one cannot be compelled to stand trial at the time he is unable to cooperate intelligently with his attorney.

But at the Carthage trial in 1956 Malmgren and Meuth sought to introduce psychiatric testimony for neither of these purposes. Rather, they sought to have a psychiatrist testify about the relationship between Lloyd's emotional makeup and his signing of the confession.

In considering whether a confession is voluntary or coerced the courts have always considered the background of a defendant. They have always considered factors like his age, his education, and his previous experience with the criminal law. Moore and Meuth were asking the court to take a next step and to hold that such an important issue need not be decided only in the light of such simple objective criteria, but that a psychiatrist might testify to subjective factors involved as well.

There can be no question that Lloyd's attorneys posed a substantial, serious constitutional question to the court. The court, however, chose not to grapple with the constitutional issue. It avoided doing so by applying various technical rules that need not concern us.

The Court of Appeals rendered its decision on February 15, 1962. Moore and Meuth then faced an important question of strategy. They had ninety days to apply to the Supreme Court for review ("certiorari"). Should they apply immediately or should they first ask the Court of Appeals to reconsider?

It is the custom of the Supreme Court to grant review if four of the nine justices agree to do so. Previous opinions by Justice Felix Frankfurter gave hope that the legal issues in the Miller case might catch his interest; and his vote might sway some other justices. Frankfurter was eighty and the term of the Court would end in June. To be sure of his participation the defense would have to apply right away.

On the other hand, time was precious. A petition for reconsideration to the Court of Appeals stood little chance of success but it would delay the start of the ninety-day period to apply for Supreme Court review. The longer Lloyd was kept alive, the longer was the time to search for ways to save his life altogether.

Moore and Meuth filed the petition for reconsideration. As they anticipated, it was not disposed of for some time, not until April 9. As they were again wondering whether to hurry the application to the Supreme Court or make the most of the ninety-day period, fate took a hand. Justice Frankfurter suffered a stroke and seemed unlikely to return to the bench. Accordingly, they waited the full period and applied for review on July 9.

Under the rules of the Supreme Court a petitioner who files *in forma pauperis* is excused from the usual requirement of filing a printed petition. An individual can even submit a single copy written in longhand. An attorney, however, would be expected to file at least a neatly typed document with enough copies for each member of the court. Moore asked Mrs. June Rosner, who had been active for several years in the Illinois Committee to Abolish Capital Punishment, to conduct a small scale solicitation to meet the expense. She raised several hundred dollars, enough to multilith the petition and provide the Court with the usual forty copies of a clear, legible document.

A few weeks after filing the petition for certiorari, Lloyd abruptly discharged George Meuth. Meuth's letter to Moore on August 6, 1962, tells the story.

> It now appears that you have inherited a 100% interest in a client who is a candidate for the chair. I drove to Joliet Saturday, in response to a request by Warden Pate, to see Miller. It would seem that they had been having some difficulty with Miller which Pate thought I could help smooth over. Upon seeing Miller, I was informed that I am fired. As nearly as I could follow the reasoning for that action, Miller is not wholly unappreciative of what I have done, but what I have done is not enough. There is also some suggestion that I am without sufficient experience to participate further in representation. All of this crap should reach me by way of a letter within the next few days, at which time I will take appropriate action to have my name withdrawn as one of Miller's attorneys in the pending case. . . . The whole thing is simply a repetition of the circumstances which compelled Bill Malmgren to withdraw in the latter part of 1958. I can't say that the prospect does not afford a substantial basis for relief, but, at the same time, the feeling of relief is tempered with a sense of loss.

Like Malmgren before him, Meuth deserves much credit for his efforts on Lloyd's behalf. He continued to follow the case and aided us many times when we needed him, all without compensation.

On September 17, Moore informed Lloyd that he would continue to represent him only in the Supreme Court of the United States. He concluded his letter, "I am not willing to undertake the responsibility of representing you in a proceeding for commutation of sentence before Governor Kerner, if we should lose in the United States Supreme Court."

Only a few weeks before Don wrote, he had successfully concluded clemency proceedings on behalf of Paul Crump.[1] In August 1962, Governor Otto Kerner, in a dramatic press conference before a forest of television cameras and microphones, announced that the life of Paul Crump would be spared because he had rehabilitated himself in the interval following his sentencing. The effort to save Crump had taken an enormous financial and emotional toll of Don Moore. He had received no fees whatever. He had devoted weeks and months to the matter, and had been unable to attend to the affairs of his law office. He decided that he could not undertake another commutation effort.

When the Supreme Court reopened in October, there was an encouraging development. The Supreme Court, acting on its own motion, requested the State of Illinois to file an answer to the petition for certiorari.

In most civil litigation where a petition for certiorari is filed, the party who won the case in the court below is anxious to preserve his victory. He therefore customarily files an answer to the petition explaining why he believes that the case is not worthy of Supreme Court review. In criminal matters, however, the filing of an answer to a petition for certiorari is the exception, because properly done, drafting it is a time consuming, expensive matter requiring the attention of an attorney for several days. Because of the substantial number of such petitions which are filed, it is the custom of the office of the Attorney General of Illinois and other Attorneys General to file an answer in criminal cases only in rare instances or where requested specifically by the Court to do so. Hence the court's in-

1. See Nizer, *The Jury Returns,* pp. 1–138 (Doubleday, 1966) for the full story.

vitation to the Attorney General to file an answer was a most encouraging sign. But the filing of the answer gave Don Moore a right to file a reply. In order to overlook no opportunity, Don Moore filed a reply and filed it rapidly. Under the rules of the court, no specific time is provided for filing of such a reply, but all of the papers in the case are distributed to the judges immediately after the filing of the answer, and therefore the reply, if it is to be effective, must be in the hands of the clerk of the Supreme Court within a few days after the answer. Moore thus had to devote at once additional days of concentrated effort to the Miller case.

Once again, however, hopes proved unfounded. On November 5, the Court again refused review. Moore and Meuth received only a small crumb of comfort for their enormous efforts. The order denying review stated that Mr. Justice Douglas thought that certiorari should be granted. On November 19, the Court of Appeals released its official order (the "mandate") affirming Judge's Igoe's decision. Issuance of this order removed the last legal bar to the setting of another death date. Don Moore did file an application for rehearing in the Supreme Court but it was turned down on December 17.

Two days later Moore wrote to Lloyd, informing him that the petition for rehearing had been denied. Moore said he assumed that the Attorney General would shortly request the Illinois Supreme Court to set an execution date. Moore promised to ask the Court to set the date at "as distant a time as I think that we would have any reasonable chance of securing." Moore also informed Lloyd of his right to request clemency and informed him of the steps that he should take to petition to Governor to commute his sentence.

Moore, as a further service to Miller, informed the Illinois State Bar Association that he was forced to withdraw from the case and that Miller was therefore without counsel. He concluded with a request that the Association find representation for him if possible. Meuth was informed of this further step. Meuth promised that if the Illinois State Bar Association did not succeed in finding an attorney he would call the matter to the attention of Fulton County Bar Association in order to insure that Miller would have adequate representation upon a petition for clemency.

Moore's efforts to invoke the aid of the Illinois State Bar Association were unsuccessful.[1] Similar efforts to obtain counsel through the Chicago Bar Association, the Office of the Governor of Illinois, and, informally, through the Supreme Court of Illinois likewise were unavailing. The courts and the organized bar were prepared to see Miller go to his death without even legal assistance for a commutation petition.

Finally in March 1963, the Attorney General filed the long-awaited petition in the Illinois Supreme Court for the setting of a new death date. On March 26, the Court granted the request of the Attorney General and, in accordance with its usual practice, the Clerk informed Don Moore of the Court's action. The last letter in Moore's file is the letter from the Clerk:

> Dear Mr. Moore:
> The Supreme Court today . . . ordered that the judgment of sentence of death to Lloyd Eldon Miller, Jr., be executed on May 17, 1963.
> Very truly yours,
> Mrs. Earle Benjamin Searcy,
> CLERK OF THE SUPREME COURT

1. The refusal of the Illinois State Bar Association was ironic in view of later developments.

8

SANITY HEARING—
PLEA FOR CLEMENCY

Donald Moore continued his efforts to obtain representation for Lloyd. On Wednesday, May 8, 1963, he spoke to Jean Erkes, administrative assistant, and to Seymour Bucholz, staff counsel of the Illinois Division of the American Civil Liberties Union, in Chicago. Moore explained Lloyd's situation. Bucholz turned first to a leading Chicago criminal lawyer, George N. Leighton, a black who had a distinguished record of public service. Leighton agreed to serve. At Bucholz's request, George Pontikes, a young attorney building a reputation in criminal law, also agreed to serve. So did Edwin H. Conger, another young attorney associated with a respected Chicago law firm. Ted Conger had little experience in criminal law but had an excellent background in trial preparation and legal research.

Bucholz also enlisted Arthur G. Greenberg of Peoria. He was much closer to Canton and Carthage and therefore was able to confer readily with witnesses, Lloyd's parents, Meuth and Malmgren.

Bucholz asked me to serve with the others and I agreed. I had almost no experience in criminal matters but did have substantial experience in civil trials and appeals.

When George Leighton entered the Miller case, he interested his law partner, William R. Ming, Jr., also a black attorney with a lengthy record of public service. Through Ming, another attorney became committed to the case, Maurice Rosenfield. Rosenfield, in addition to practicing law, owned radio station WAIT in Chicago and for many years had been one of the leading members in the Illinois Committee to Abolish Capital Punishment.

All of us knew that having entered the case, we would have to stay with it until Miller was executed or until his life was somehow spared. However, I am sure none of us anticipated that the case would require such an outpouring of time, money, effort, and emotion.

The need for money came rapidly to the fore. Although the attorneys were serving without fee, funds were necessary for inescapable expenses. Jean Erkes undertook to raise them. She called or wrote to a small circle of friends, acquaintances, and persons who might be sympathetic. In this way a few hundred dollars were raised.

Ultimately, however, not hundreds but thousands were required to carry on the battle.[1]

After agreeing to serve, I read the opinion of the Illinois Supreme Court affirming the original conviction. My initial shocked reaction was that the proof of guilt was strong and that the crime was cold-blooded and brutal. Next, I read the abstract of the testimony from cover to cover. This document first caused me to question the fairness of the trial and raised doubts about Lloyd's guilt. The prosecution was abrasive and driving. Counsel for the defense seemed to be sincere, quiet-mannered, hard-working gentlemen who were almost wholly inexperienced and who were overmatched by the prosecutors.

Again and again as I read it seemed to me that the prosecution pressed too hard to get into the record this or that bit of evidence, even though it seemed prejudicial and objectionable. Again and again it sought, often successfully, to bar defense evidence that seemed fair and legitimate. Those of us who have practiced for years sometimes sense that lawyers are pushing more than they should. Law at bottom is combative; yet, a certain restraint is expected of counsel. The lack of such restraint in the Miller prosecution made me feel uneasy.

But those thoughts came later. When the new team of lawyers stepped into the case on May 8, we had to act immediately to save Miller from death on May 17, the date set for his execution. In Illinois it is customary to carry out a death sentence at one minute

1. Miller's situation was desperate, but it did not then appear to present a civil liberties issue. Accordingly, the American Civil Liberties Union did not take on the case or reimburse counsel for disbursements. It did pay for the printing of its briefs on appeal when it appeared as *amicus curiae* (friend of the court) .

past midnight on the designated date, so we had only eight days to work in, including a weekend.

At the time, we knew little about the case—only that our client was in the psychiatric division of the state prison at Menard, near Chester, Illinois. He had been taken from his regular cell at Stateville to the detention hospital, in August 1962, apparently because of bizarre behavior. He was moved to Menard at the beginning of December.

There has always been something ghastly to me about efforts to keep a condemned man healthy and sane so that he can be legally executed. Medicine in general and psychiatry in particular demands a rapport between doctor and patient that is rendered obscene when it is used to restore a man to health so that he can be sent to death. The Peoria *Journal Star* drew attention to the irony in an unsigned article on December 4:

> The law says an insane man can't be executed.
>
> The legal yardstick, translated into lay language, is whether a man would realize what was happening to him and why he was strapped in the electric chair.
>
> If he is found too ill to be executed, doctors will try to cure him so that he can suffer the fate which a jury set for him in 1956.

Nevertheless, the action of prison officials in sending Lloyd Miller to the psychiatric division suggested that a basis might exist for a court proceedings to determine Miller's sanity. On May 14, three days before Miller was scheduled to die, we obtained from the Illinois Supreme Court a stay to June 21.

William G. Clark, then the Illinois Attorney General, allowed us to examine the reports of Lloyd's mental and emotional condition kept since he entered prison on November 17, 1956. A striking aspect of the reports was that from the first, Lloyd had denied his guilt.

A petition for a sanity hearing was filed on May 22. Under the law, the hearing was to be held in Carthage, where Miller had been convicted seven years before. Because Judge Bardens was no longer on the bench, the case was to be heard by Judge Keith F. Scott, who set the hearing for June 17. On our application, the Illinois Supreme Court, four days before the execution date, granted a stay to July 26.

On June 17, Miller returned again to the large, old-fashioned courtroom on the third floor of the County Courthouse at Carthage where he had been sentenced to death seven years before.

A jury of nine men and three women heard the case. On Lloyd's behalf the contention was made that the long years of imprisonment, the many dates with the chair, and the many postponements had affected his sanity. The reports of the state's own psychiatrists were introduced to show that the authorities themselves considered Lloyd no longer sane.

A prison psychiatrist appeared, but as a witness for the state. He testified that he had indeed considered Miller mentally ill the preceding September, when he had declared that Miller's condition would require treatment of a "prolonged nature" but he did not consider him mentally ill in April.

The state called two prison guards to testify. One was Sergeant Elmer Schardt, who said that all Miller talked about was "hunting, fishing, and the Bible." The other was Lt. James A. Sharp, supervisor of guards at Menard. He said that during the past six weeks he had "passed the time of day with Miller" and as a result he believed that the prisoner was sane. The only witnesses for Lloyd were his parents and sister. On Thursday, the hearing ended. After brief deliberation, the jury found Lloyd sane.

With Miller declared sane, hope of relief from the courts seemed ended. It appeared that only commutation by the Governor could save Lloyd.

Leighton and Greenberg, who had handled the proceedings, left Carthage in separate cars late in the afternoon of June 20. Leighton decided that since he had to pass through Canton, he would stop to speak to Alice Baxter, Miller's former landlady. That decision was to have momentous consequences.

Later Leighton told me that upon arriving in Canton, he visited the Millers and asked Mrs. Miller and Margaret to accompany him to Mrs. Baxter's. It was early evening when he arrived at Mrs. Baxter's home on Walnut Street. When Mrs. Baxter came to the door, he introduced himself as one of the attorneys for Lloyd. Mrs. Baxter agreed to answer a few questions and the interview took place with

Leighton standing on the porch and Mrs. Baxter just inside the door. The prime question was this: "Do you know where Lloyd was on the afternoon of November 26, 1955?" Mrs. Baxter answered that he had been in his room until four o'clock that afternoon. At four-thirty he came downstairs. Mrs. Baxter asked if he would have a prescription refilled for her at Lewis' Pharmacy. He agreed to do so. He left about four-thirty, returned about five-thirty with the prescription and change from the money Mrs. Baxter had given him, and shortly thereafter left for work. Leighton said, "You have been very kind, Mrs. Baxter," and left.

With those few words Mrs. Baxter gave the case a new dimension. Until that moment our efforts had been devoted primarily to saving Miller's life.

In Chicago, Leighton discussed the matter with Maurice Rosenfield. Rosenfield, intrigued, hired a reporter, Richard Applegate, to make an investigation.

Applegate interviewed Mrs. Baxter and learned that her grandchildren had been at her home on the day of the murder, and could confirm Mrs. Baxter's statement that Lloyd had been home until 4:30 P.M. The grandchildren were Rebecca and Adrian Watters. At the time of the murder Rebecca was eight years old and Adrian seven. In 1963 they were sixteen and fifteen. When interviewed, they remembered that on the afternoon of the murder their grandmother had sent them upstairs at four o'clock to awaken Lloyd.

As Dick Applegate continued his investigations, he began a daily program over WAIT relating his latest analyses of the case and latest findings. The result was a rash of condemnatory articles in the press. From the moment Mrs. Baxter first said that Lloyd was sleeping in his room on the afternoon of the murder, the central Illinois press became hostile to Lloyd's attorneys. During the 1956 trial Lloyd and his counsel were treated somewhat like the villains in a drama. In a drama we do not hate the villain, because he is merely playing his role. So long as Lloyd and his attorneys played their roles in acceptable fashion, the press, while not sympathetic towards them, was not abusive. There were even occasions when the press showed a certain sympathy for the terrible plight of Lloyd and his family. But with the July 1963 revelations the attitude towards Lloyd's counsel was transformed.

On July 17, a Peoria *Journal Star* editorial urged commutation of the death sentence to life imprisonment without parole. The courtroom merry-go-round had:

> inflicted on Lloyd Miller himself a unique and cruel punishment beyond the demands or rightful function of law to the point of deranging him to some extent.

But for the attorneys, the newspapers had only scorn:

> The last act of the sideshow was almost inevitable—this cheap rinkydink about "witnesses" whose testimony is really meaningless and who were available on the scene at the time and place of the investigation and trial—and now pop up via some radio station's hopped up "sensation" nine years later!

The Canton *Ledger* two days later declared, "New Evidence Changes Nothing." It too dismissed the new evidence, but concluded it would be inhuman to proceed with the execution. On July 31, the *Journal Star* condemned Miller's attorneys for "Unprincipled Pursuit of Principle."

Variety, the show business newspaper, on July 24 ran a story, "Chi WAIT One-Man News Dept. Turns Up With Life Saving Scoop." The article told of the WAIT-Rosenfield-Applegate efforts. Major stress was on Applegate's firm belief that Lloyd did not have a fair trial and that he was innocent. At the end Applegate was quoted, "The point is this, even if he did commit the murder, a Chicago radio station says he didn't, and that's news in itself."

The Peoria *Journal Star* pounced on this sentence in an August 1 editorial. It ignored Applegate's claims of Lloyd's innocence. Righteously it proclaimed:

> Applegate and his employer do not consider it very important whether Miller is guilty or not! What is important is that "one radio station says he is innocent."
> Why is that more important than justice?
> In the light of this remark, the material in the publicity blurb we received, and his other public statements, we can

only believe that in addition to the questionable character of this whole propaganda operation, the principals are guilty of duplicity.

They seem to be knowingly, purposely indulging in deceit—at least trying to deceive the public as to their motives—and possibly trying to deceive the public, knowingly, about Miller, himself.

This is inexcusable.

July was a period of extraordinary activity, as the July 26 death date drew near. The Supreme Court of Illinois had recently granted two short reprieves. Rather than go once again to the Court, on July 16 Leighton asked the Governor to grant a reprieve to give opportunity for an application for executive clemency. The following day the Governor granted a stay until August 23. At the same time Governor Kerner summoned an extraordinary meeting of the Illinois Pardon and Parole Board for August 12 to consider a clemency plea. Before the Governor granted the stay, we had begun to prepare for the commutation hearing.

The Illinois statutes contemplated that the views of the trial judge would be ascertained regarding commutation. Ted Conger and I made arrangements to meet the retired Judge Bardens at his vacation home near Traverse City, Michigan, on the following Saturday, July 13. The Judge heard us out, interrupting only occasionally to ask a question or two. I outlined the proceedings that had taken place since the trial before him seven years before and then advanced a number of reasons why we believed that clemency was warranted in the case. I stressed what was to us the most significant development up to that time, Mrs. Baxter's statement that Lloyd had spent the entire Saturday afternoon asleep in his room until he was awakened by her granddaughter and grandson, at 4:00 P.M., and that he had left Mrs. Baxter's house to have a prescription refilled about 4:30 P.M.

After I had finished the presentation, which took about half an hour, Judge Bardens told us that it was his practice not to make any recommendation to the Pardon and Parole Board. In his view, his role ended with the trial. He had nothing further to say for prosecution or defense. We asked Judge Bardens whether he would have imposed the death sentence if the case had been tried before him without a jury. His answer was that he would not have imposed the death sentence because he had strong reservations about the imposition of capital punishment by a single judge.

We put another question: Some time after the Miller case had been tried, there was an important change in Illinois law regarding the death sentence. Under the law at the time Lloyd was tried, the jury fixed punishment in murder cases. Subsequently, the law was changed to provide that if the prosecution sought the death sentence, it was necessary first for the jury to find the defendant guilty and to recommend the death sentence to the judge. After receiving such recommendation, it was in the discretion of the trial judge to impose the death penalty or to impose a sentence of imprisonment as he saw fit. If the law now in effect regarding the death sentence had been in effect at the time of the Miller case, and if the jury had recommended the death sentence, would he have imposed such a sentence? Judge Bardens replied that he would have been reluctant to substitute his judgment for the verdict of the jury. He said that just as he would not have imposed the death sentence in a trial as only one person, so he would have been reluctant to substitute his decision for that of the jury.

The Judge then told us of the talks during the course of the trial regarding a possible plea of guilty. It was the first that Ted and I had heard of this matter. He told us of a conference in his chambers at which the possibility of a plea of guilty was discussed. The question was raised as to what sentence the prosecution would recommend. He did not remember the details, but did recall that the prosecution was asking for a long time. No understanding was reached at the conference and the Judge heard nothing further about the matter. He added that had there been a plea of guilty and a recommendation by the prosecution for a prison sentence, he would have imposed the sentence recommended.

We thanked the Judge for his time and patience and left, in a driving rain. What Judge Bardens said did not come as an unexpected blow. Both of us were fully aware that Judge Bardens was not favorably disposed toward the defense. We thought that perhaps the lapse of time might have had some effect. We felt, too, that the statement of Mrs. Baxter might raise some doubt in the Judge's mind about Lloyd's guilt. We did not approach our interview with Judge

Bardens with high hopes, but we did approach it with hope. We had been graciously received but we were not given the word of mercy that we so much wanted to hear.

As we began to prepare for the clemency hearing before the Pardon and Parole Board, we realized the magnitude of our task. The guilt or innocence of a man is to be determined in the courts. It is the usual function of the Pardon and Parole Board simply to make a recommendation to the Governor whether the guilty man shall be granted mercy. But if we proceeded in orthodox fashion, asking mercy for Lloyd without raising a question as to his guilt or innocence, we could scarcely hope to succeed. It was essential for us to raise a substantial doubt regarding Lloyd's guilt. We knew we could count on the testimony of Mrs. Baxter and the two grandchildren. What else was there? We reviewed the files carefully, considering every fragment of evidence.

Because of our activities, Dick Applegate's broadcasts over WAIT, and the Governor's reprieve there was another flurry of articles about the case and current developments in the central Illinois press, radio, and television. Roger Hayes wrote a letter to Canton Radio Station WYDS on July 24, stating

> ... I am convinced, to a moral certainty, that Justice will be thwarted if I do not, now, speak out on this matter.
>
> The people who are conducting this campaign [to convince the Governor that Miller is innocent] are not merely showing great irresponsibility, but are maliciously attempting to abort justice. They have fabricated what they term evidence. They have ignored the fact that thirty-two witnesses testified at his trial to the material facts showing his guilt. And, that there have been, during the last eight years, at least twenty-one Court Decisions, affirming the legality and morality of his conviction.
>
> ... there was enough evidence without his confession to prove his guilt beyond a reasonable doubt. This evidence is permanently recorded with exacting accuracy in the Official Transcript of the case. . . . The other people [in addition to Applegate] involved in this conspiracy are improperly motivated by considerations known to me,

which, if anyone is interested, I will be willing to discuss and make known.

After criticizing the statements of Mrs. Baxter and the grandchildren, Hayes added "It has been editorially suggested in at least one newspaper, 'The best solution to this comedy of Justice would be a life imprisonment, with no chance of parole.' " Hayes pointed out that the Governor had no power to commute the sentence with a binding "no parole" condition. He concluded by saying

> Unfortunately, the lips of a defenseless, little eight-year-old girl are sealed by death. The Radio, Television and Newspaper statements, of former and present counsel for the convicted defendant can only result in one ultimate conclusion and that is to bring courts, both Federal and State, into ridicule and contempt in the eyes of the public.
>
> I assure you, I speak up with great reluctance, due to my status as a lawyer. But, I sincerely believe that, with non-legal action pending now in this matter, substantial justice demands that I do so. Also, in 1956, after most of the jury was selected, and before the trial commenced, MR. MALMGREN AND MR. MEUTH, MILLER'S ATTORNEYS AND MILLER, PERSONALLY, OFFERED TO PLEAD GUILTY TO MURDERING JANICE MAY, IF THEY COULD MAKE A DEAL THAT MILLER'S SENTENCE WOULD BE NO MORE THAN SIXTY YEARS. This offer was rejected! [emphasis in original]

Two days later Hayes wrote another letter in a similar vein to Governor Kerner, urging him to deny commutation.

As soon as Malmgren learned of Hayes' statements about the discussions regarding the guilty plea, he immediately wrote Leighton to give his version of this matter (see page 57 above).

From time to time as we worked on the Miller case various episodes provided tragicomic relief. The chief one related to Sayre T. Meldon. On October 24, 1962, Don Moore received a letter from Meldon bearing the return address, "Finchly Common No. 7, Charleston, New York." Meldon wrote that he had ascertained the docket number of the petition for certiorari then pending before the Supreme Court and had written a letter regarding the case to Chief Justice Warren and to Associate Justice Arthur Goldberg. Meldon poured out advice to Don as to how best to handle the case and what further legal action might then be undertaken. Meldon explained that he was not in Canton at the time of the crime although he was living there during that period. Moore paid no attention to the advice but was much interested in the question whether Meldon was in Canton at the time of the murder and whether he had information which could be helpful.

But first, Moore was concerned about the possible repercussion of Meldon's letter on the Supreme Court. He and Meuth considered the outlook for Supreme Court review reasonably bright and they did not want to have their chances diminished by a development which might give the case a crackpot flavor. Moore immediately wrote a letter to Chief Justice Warren and to Justice Goldberg informing them that Meldon was acting entirely without his knowledge or consent.

About a month later George Meuth reported, "Meldon was a nut, by commonly accepted standards, who lived in a ramshackle shack which was completely surrounded by accumulated junk and dogs and which was located approximately four blocks north of, and on the street which bordered, the scene of the murder. Rumor hath it that Meldon actually left Canton shortly after this crime [the murder of Janice]. Within a short period of time thereafter, fire destroyed the shack and the junk yard."

Mr. Meldon, after some false starts, managed to get George Leighton's address and began to correspond with him in June 1963. He wrote George pages upon pages of advice and suggestions. He also drafted petitions and other documents himself which he forwarded to the courts. He had sent to the Hancock County Circuit Court at Carthage a petition for a sanity hearing on Miller's behalf and complained with some petulance that it had been summarily denied.

The next day Meldon poured forth another several pages of advice to Leighton, commenting at the end on his own situation:

> I myself am being held as a "ward of the State of New York" at this Finchly Common State Hospital Charleston, N. Y., though there is nothing awry with me, mentally,

physically or morally. If you contemplate sending me a subpoena to appear on June 17, I might possibly get permission from the Acting Director here for leave to attend the hearing, upon written request from you.

The rain of letters to Moore and to Leighton and Meldon's flood of "legal documents" to the various courts again raised a question whether Meldon might actually know something important about the case. His letters did not reveal a detailed knowledge of the facts of the crime and actually contained many errors, but it was an aspect of the case that had to be checked out. Accordingly, one day in August 1963, Rosenfield and Leighton visited Meldon at the State Hospital. After spending some hours with him they were convinced that he knew nothing whatever of the case and paid no further attention to him.

On Sunday, August 11, final preparations were made for the Parole Board hearing scheduled to open the following morning at ten o'clock. We had asked a number of witnesses to come up from Canton. Maurice Rosenfield underwrote their accommodations and meals at Executive House in Chicago.

We spent all day Sunday until late in the evening interviewing witnesses, a number of whom we met only that day. The focus of activity was Leighton's Chicago office on the third floor of the office building at 123 West Madison Street. Almost every room and the library were in use for interviewing prospective witnesses. Mrs. Jean Erkes was busy all day shuttling witnesses back and forth and putting them at their ease. When Rebecca Watters arrived, there was a small crisis—traveling in shorts and an old blouse, she had left her dress at home in Canton and had nothing presentable to wear. Somewhere that Sunday we had to buy or borrow a suitable garment, or forego the benefit of her testimony.

The proceedings were held in a large hearing room on the nineteenth floor of the State of Illinois Building at 160 North LaSalle Street. There at 10:00 A.M. on Monday, August 12, 1963, the seven members of the Illinois Pardon and Parole Board assembled to hear a plea on behalf of Lloyd Eldon Miller, Jr. The Chairman, Charles Kinney, presided. All of the attorneys were present for all or a substantial portion of the proceedings: Leighton, Greenberg, Bucholz, Pontikes, Conger, and I. For the prosecution there were Oral Kost, then State's Attorney of Fulton County, Blaine Ramsey, and Roger Hayes. There were also the witnesses, many newsmen, and members of the public. Everyone was there but Lloyd Miller. He was in a cell in Stateville Prison thirty-five miles away.

Chairman Kinney opened by calling attention to the statute providing that the Board was in no case to act as a court of review to pass upon the correctness, regularity, or legality of the proceedings in the trial court which resulted in conviction, but was to confine itself to clemency matters.

Leighton called Hayes as the first witness. They reviewed the discussions regarding a possible plea of guilty by the defense in exchange for an agreed-on sentence recommendation to the Judge. These discussions have already been described (page oo).

Hayes stated that he had never been directly involved in any of the negotiations. The defense felt that, he said, "I was a driving force towards conviction in this case and they actually set this meeting up, as I understand it, on purpose to exclude me because they figured I would not be susceptible to talk of a plea." [of guilty, in exchange for a prison sentence]. When Ramsey discussed the matter with him, Hayes said to Ramsey that "whatever he did was all right with me, but my opinion was that he should not talk plea to the defense at all."

After Hayes came Blaine Ramsey. He was asked point blank whether he, Ramsey, ever had a conversation personally with Lloyd. His answer was "No." Nor did he ever participate in any discussions with the defense counsel while Lloyd was present. It thus appeared that the testimony of the two chief prosecution attorneys flatly contradicted Hayes' letter to Radio Station WYDS a month previously. In Hayes' letter to the Canton Radio Station WYDS of July 24, Hayes wrote in solid capital letters that "Miller personally" offered to plead guilty if he could make a deal that his sentence would be no more than sixty years.

Before the Parole Board, Ramsey no longer believed that ninety-nine years was an adequate sentence: "The fact that twelve people heard this and made this decision. This is not a one-man decision. It is extremely difficult in your own mind to make this decision, but when you go through the trial and twelve people make this decision, then I believe that, shall we say, the administration of justice and our whole procedure, they determined that should be the punishment. I say that should be upheld."

Mrs. Miller made a brief appearance on the stand to help her son. Speaking softly she explained her husband's absence from the hearing, saying that he was at the hotel, sick. Her plea for the life of her son was almost inarticulate: "Well, I think that my son's sentence should be commuted; that I don't think that he ever did this terrible tragedy. He was always noted as a—I don't think—he was a good citizen in Canton, Illinois. He has never been in any kind of trouble. He grew up in Canton and always got along with all the children and had played with everybody and it seemed to me that he was always well liked and never had any enemies of any kind."

She said once again that her son wore only boxer shorts.

Roger Hayes, on cross-examination, pounced on Mrs. Miller's statement that Lloyd had always been a "good citizen" in Canton and that he had never been in "any kind of trouble." He asked, "You are aware, are you not, that he has been convicted for auto theft previous to the trial in 1956?"

A. That I hadn't remembered.

Q. Are you not further aware of the fact that he served a jail sentence as a result of that conviction?

A. That I don't remember.

Q. Mrs. Miller, if someone had murdered and raped your daughter and your daughter had died, do you feel that person should be granted a commutation after a jury had imposed the death sentence?

A. I wouldn't recommend the death penalty for nobody because in my heart I believe in the Bible.

Lloyd's protestations of innocence to his parents which the defense tried so hard to present in 1956 over prosecution objections finally were heard. Hayes asked about them himself. Mrs. Miller answered, "He has always said he is not guilty—always has. In letters, I have stacks and stacks and stacks of letters from every place he's been—from Lewiston—I save all his letters. I don't throw any of them away."

Lloyd's sister Margaret, the next witness, saw a side to Lloyd that no one else had seen: "I had my girlfriends who would spend the night with me and he was in the house, and he couldn't harm anyone. He wasn't a boisterous person. He liked to read books. As he grew older, he wasn't interested in girls and didn't go out with girls. He was just interested in sports and books. Then he went to service and when he went in service he never smoked or drank, and then when he came out of service and was married—when he went to service he got lonesome and started having girlfriends, and when he came home he had dates with girls but I most always went with him. He always invited me to go along."

After the dates with Margaret as chaperone: "Then he got married. I mean, he was a normal person as far as that goes, but he didn't run around. He didn't get in trouble."

Margaret felt that her brother's sentence should be commuted because, "I knew, I am positive he is innocent. He could never do anything like this. I grew up with him."

Donald Isaak, Miller's brother-in-law, explained to the Parole Board that Mr. Miller, Sr., was not present because he was sick at the hotel in Chicago: "Well, one thing I have never seen a sicker man in all my life as Mr. Lloyd Eldon Miller, Sr. . . . Yes, sir, I don't think I have ever seen a sicker man than Lloyd Eldon Miller, Sr. He is a very nervous man and at times he is so nervous, and he's got a hernia and a bad back and a nervous condition that I have never seen before. And at times he has to come home and sit in that bathtub and he will sit there and just cry. And he misses work continuously all the time."

Oral Kost, State's Attorney of Fulton County, put a few questions to Isaak on cross-examination, but after a few minutes, Roger Hayes took over. His first question was: "Mr. Isaak, you described how sick Mr. Miller, Sr., is. Is he as sick as Dean May and Jean May, the parents of this little girl, have been in the last eight years, do you think?"

Hayes reviewed Lloyd's police and military record with Isaak, asking a number of questions about his convictions and difficulties with the military authorities. But Hayes was not satisfied with this.

His next question to the witness was: "Are you familiar with the fact that prior to his conviction in 1956 an investigation was underway by the Federal authorities, which investigation was terminated by his conviction in this case, for the rape-slaying of a two-year-old child at Sioux City, Iowa? Are you familiar with that?" The witness replied that he knew nothing about it.

This was a second reference to Sioux City, Iowa, and the first prosecution effort to forge a link between a crime there and Lloyd Eldon Miller, Jr. This second reference to Sioux City caused us to do some investigating. What we learned was shocking. We shall relate that story presently.

Next Mrs. Alice Baxter took the stand. Becky and Adrian had been staying with their grandmother because of their mother's illness. On that Saturday Mrs. Baxter first saw Lloyd when he came into the kitchen about nine o'clock. Mrs. Baxter, her husband, Robert, and the two children were having breakfast. Lloyd came to the door and said, "Mrs. Baxter, will you call me at four o'clock. I'm getting in late and probably won't wake up." Mrs. Baxter said that she stepped up, saw who it was, and said, "Yes, Lloyd, I'll be glad to." Lloyd turned and left and Mrs. Baxter heard him walking up the stairs. At 3:30 P.M. Rebecca came to the kitchen and told her grandmother that it was time to call Lloyd. But Mrs. Baxter said, "Rebecca, it's just three-thirty so wait a while. He said four o'clock, so at four o'clock you can call him." A half hour later Rebecca appeared on the scene again and said, "Grandma, it's time to call him." She went upstairs but in a moment was back. She said, "Grandmother he isn't in his bed. The bed is all made. He hasn't slept there." Mrs. Baxter replied, "There is often times he does that. He had done it before. . . . You go into the room. Over at the side of the room there is a studio couch and the telephone is right there and oftentimes he sleeps there. You go back and go in." But, continued Mrs. Baxter, "I guess she was frightened to go in by herself or something so she asked someone to go with her, so she asked her little brother on the way up to go with her and they both went to the door of the room and he was on the studio couch." Rebecca reported back to her grandmother. "She said they went into the room and he raised up suddenly like he was frightened, like they woke him out of a sound sleep."

About four-thirty, Lloyd appeared downstairs. Mrs. Baxter went on, "I said, 'Lloyd are you going to work now? If you are, I want you to get my prescription refilled.' I said 'Here is a ten dollar bill and you can take out for your call.' He said, 'Mrs. Baxter, I am not going to work now. I am going to eat but I will do it for you.' I said 'Fine' and he took the ten dollars and my bottle for the refill and went on his way. He was gone approximately a half-hour to forty-five minutes and he came back and gave me my change and I offered to pay him something for his trouble and he said not at all, he was glad to do it, and he stood there a moment and kind of glanced around and he whirled on his heel a little and said, 'Mrs. Baxter, you won't need to make my bed tonight because it's already made.' Of course, I suppose if he hadn't slept in it it wouldn't have needed to be made."

Mrs. Baxter confirmed that Lloyd wore boxer shorts. She had an opportunity to see his clothing when Mrs. Miller, Sr., brought his clean garments to him. She concluded her testimony by saying that she had never seen Lloyd wearing the "dirty crummy-looking jacket" introduced into evidence at the 1956 trial.

On cross-examination Mrs. Baxter explained why she had not considered the story about the events between 4:00 and 4:30 P.M. important earlier. "I'd always been under the impression that the little girl was killed at 3:15 because when the officers came to my home I asked them 'What time did they set for her death?' They said 3:00 to 3:15, so I thought 4:00 to 4:30 meant nothing to anyone." There was a long wrangle in the hearing about what the 1956 evidence showed as the time of the crime and what Mrs. Baxter thought was the exact time of the crime. In the end, Leighton called the attention of the Board to Hayes' letter to the Governor in which he fixed the time of the murder at 4:00 P.M.

Mrs. Baxter was followed to the witness stand by her granddaughter, Rebecca Watters, wearing a dress hastily borrowed from Mrs. Seymour Bucholz. Becky told the Parole Board that she was sixteen and a junior at Manito High School. At the time of the murder she was eight years old but she did remember the events of that critical Saturday. She could even recall the loss of her father when she was about five or six years old. She vaguely remembered that Lloyd asked Mrs. Baxter to awaken him at four o'clock and she believed that she was then able to tell time. Her testimony regarding waking up Lloyd paralleled that of her grandmother.

Teke Johns for a second time came to appear on behalf of his ex-employee. At the 1956 trial Teke testified that he had phoned Lloyd at 2:45 P.M. to wake him up as he had requested. On this occasion he said that he was asked whether he could identify the jacket found in Big Creek. He told police that it was not Miller's jacket because it was too old. According to Teke, Lloyd was always plainly but neatly dressed. The jacket that was found in the creek was "old and ragged, and I don't believe Miller would ever wear a jacket like that. It was too old, and it looked like it had been fished out of the creek to me.

"And me and my boy laughed. The night they called us to come down to the police station to identify the jacket, and we laughed about the jacket because we didn't think he wore anything like that. I never had seen him in anything like that. It had a big patch on the shoulder, and I know I never seen him in a jacket like that."

Teke was asked to compare Lloyd Miller with his own sons. He said that he couldn't make such a comparison because, "Well, my own sons are a little rough. I mean, they are athletic type boys. But my boys is different. They go to baseball games; they go to fights, and I've known them to get in a few. And Miller was not like that."

Lloyd was not in all respects an ideal employee. "Miller was a hard boy to wake up. There's no doubt about that. You had to go down and pull him by the hair of the head to get him up. I know the night I went down there I had already sent one driver to wake him up. And I went down and got him up."

Furthermore, Teke knew that Miller was planning to leave Canton: "Not for sure, but we figured he was because he had already mentioned he was going to leave. But I had already talked to another driver to take his place." Teke added, "And there are two questions I would like to ask Miller sometime: What he done with the driver's cap and what he done with that last call he took. Of course, I know what he done with the money. He had it on him when they caught him. Whatever he took in that night he owed me. He still does."

After Teke, George Meuth and William Malmgren told of their role in the case. Malmgren emphasized his inexperience and sense of isolation in Canton: "It is something to walk alone in [a rural] community. I think along with that [newspaper hostility] I think there was a thing which transpired which just simply was perhaps inexperience of counsel." Malmgren had had virtually no court experience before the Miller trial. Hayes had tried over forty cases. Ramsey was completing his four-year term as State's Attorney and was running for reelection in the November following the September 1956 trial. "And by inexperience I think what you would mean in that area is perhaps sheer weariness—the inability to go out and talk with any receptivity to witnesses who might know—and the general censure of a small community."

The day's session was long. The Board did not adjourn until 8:30 P.M.

On Tuesday morning at ten o'clock, the first order of business was the brief appearance of Lloyd's father.

Leighton asked Mr. Miller to tell the Board why he thought that the sentence against his son should be commuted. Mr. Miller answered, "Because I don't think he is guilty of it."

The prosecution had no questions, and we closed the case on Lloyd's behalf. It was now the turn of the prosecution.

Hayes began the presentation for the prosecution by informing the Board that he had spoken to the parents and family of Janice May. They had told him that they were unable to talk about this matter, but they were present and were asked to stand.

The first prosecution witness was Edward R. Lewis, Jr., proprietor of Lewis Pharmacy where, Lloyd testified, he had brought the prescription given to him by Mrs. Baxter for a refill. To the astonishment of the defense attorneys Ed Lewis did not contradict Lloyd's story about refilling the prescription; rather, he corroborated it in minute detail. Both prosecution and defense were aware of the need to check the truth of Lloyd's claim; it was vital also to determine, if possible, the exact time he was in the pharmacy. The visit was not an alibi in the strict sense of the term because it clearly took place after the crime. Nevertheless, it was important to both prosecution and defense for at least two reasons. First, it was not mentioned in the confession, which presumably was an exact account of Lloyd's movements throughout the afternoon. If a significant event took place that was not mentioned in the confession, the confession was to that extent erroneous, and might also be wrong in other respects.

Second, according to Joyce Hardy, the clerk in Carver and Denny

Cleaners, Lloyd was there about 5:15 P.M. According to the confession, by 5:45 P.M. he had left Mrs. Baxter's home to report for work at the cab company. In the interval, according to the confession, he had done much. He had gone back to Mrs. Baxter's, changed his clothes, gone to the Van Buren flats in the unsuccessful effort to retrieve the shorts, and disposed of the bloody garments by throwing them in the car of a passing train. If we crowd into that half hour a trip to Lewis Pharmacy—not to make a simple purchase but to have a prescription refilled, a more time-consuming transaction—we crowd too much into the half hour. Moreover, according to the view of the prosecution, Lloyd Eldon Miller, Jr., had committed a heinous crime sometime shortly before 4:32 P.M. If, within an hour he was known to be in a drugstore calmly doing a simple favor for his landlady, the picture of the brutal criminal becomes difficult to hold in mind. The quiet, everyday, simple, friendly character of the act becomes inconsistent with the picture of a brutal murderer.

Malmgren learned from Mrs. Baxter the prescription number and patient's name. From Ed Lewis he learned that that prescription had been filled about 5:25 or 5:30 that Saturday, but Lewis told Malmgren that he had no personal knowledge that Lloyd was in the store.

With that much established from Lewis, it is too bad in retrospect that the defense did not call Lewis to testify. It would have bolstered Lloyd's testimony about the prescription. Lloyd might even have remembered that the prescription was in the name of Mrs. Fidler. If so, the truth of Lloyd's testimony would have been established beyond question and a serious blow struck at the confession's timetable. As it was, the vital corroboration came seven years after the trial.

Lewis began his testimony by reading to the Board a prepared statement that on November 26, 1955, he filled prescription numbered 493889 issued to Mrs. Everett Fidler by Dr. H. C. Putnam. "This prescription was presented to a clerk in my pharmacy at approximately 5:25 P.M. this date for a refill by Lloyd Miller, Jr., a taxi driver. [The defense gasped.] The clerk, Mrs. Ruby Groff, brought the prescription bottle to the prescription department, and obtained the original prescription from our files. As I counted the tablets necessary to fill this prescription, I found there were not enough tablets in stock. Knowing that Mrs. Groff was to leave our store at

5:30 P.M. I glanced at the clock to see if there was sufficient time for her to go to a drugstore just two doors away and borrow the necessary number of tablets to fill the prescription. This she did, and returned in a matter of a few minutes. I filled and recorded this prescription refill in our prescription refill book, and Mrs. Groff took the prescription out to Lloyd Miller, Jr., and he then left our store."

The affidavit concluded: "The above affidavit records testimony and events that were investigated by attorneys and law officers within a few days after November 26, 1955." So the prosecution had known from the first the truth about the pharmacy visit.

Ed Lewis told how he came to reconstruct the story. Mr. Miller, Sr., first called to his attention the importance of the prescription. "He came into my store one morning and asked me if his son had had a prescription filled in there on this particular day, the Saturday afternoon of November 26, and I said, 'Well, Mr. Miller, I don't know, because I honestly don't know your son.'" Lewis checked his records for a prescription under the name of Miller but found none. "So later on that day, or it possibly could have been the next day— I believe it was the Sheriff, Virgil Ball, or it could have been the Chief of Police, came in with this prescription. They had obtained this from Mrs. Baxter. We looked in our books and immediately we found it, and then, calling my attention to the time, it dawned on me who I had waited on and when."

Lewis amplified on his affidavit: he had very little conversation with Lloyd because he was busy at the time waiting on other customers. When he realized he was short of the full quantity he stepped out and said to Lloyd, "It will be just a couple of minutes, if you will wait."

One of the Parole Board members, Louis Zahn, asked a pointed question:

Q. Do you think Miller, Junior, was distressed? Do you think he was acting unnatural, or do you recall?
A. No, I was much too busy to even—he was just like any other customer that would come in and would look like anyone else.

But Mrs. Hardy had said that the man who came into the cleaners at 5:15 P.M. had a jacket streaked and spattered a bright red from the waist up. Yet Lewis noticed none of this. Shortly after, Ramsey told the Parole Board that Joyce Hardy was unable to identify Lloyd immediately after the crime when she was taken to Springfield to view him. She first identified him at the Grand Jury session about January 10, 1956, five or six weeks later.

So far as we know, neither the prosecution nor the defense actually spoke to Mrs. Groff, the clerk who actually waited on Lloyd and who presumably had more contact with him than did Ed Lewis. But the defense did not know the crucial detail of Joyce Hardy's description of the stains on Miller's garments until the actual moment she testified at the trial. By then, nearly a year had gone by. Malmgren and Meuth were in the midst of trial and it would have been difficult if not impossible in September 1956 to do what could have been done easily early in December 1955.

We have always been grateful to Ed Lewis for his 1963 testimony. The prosecution case was shaken by Mrs. Baxter, but it was Ed Lewis who gave prosecution testimony undermining the confession. Without that testimony we might not have been able to obtain a stay of execution at a crucial moment.

James Christensen for a third time related his interrogation of Lloyd on the night of November 30, 1955, at the Bureau of Criminal Identification in Springfield. His testimony was that his memory of the crucial scene was excellent and his treatment of the suspect exemplary. Christensen made both these points in a few brief words: "I was sitting close to him, I recall very well. How could I ever forget it! I never raised my voice. I never threatened this boy. I never treated any individual any finer than I treated Lloyd Eldon Miller, Jr."

Regarding June Lang, Jim Christensen had his own view of the reliability of her testimony. "June Lang may not be a Sunday School teacher, and she may have some skeletons in her closet, but I have respect for June Lang, that when she knew that she had information concerning the death of Janice May, that she was mighty honorable to come to the authorities and give that information."

In cross-examination, Leighton inquired closely whether the words used in the confession were the words of Lloyd Eldon Miller, Jr., or the words of James Christensen. Christensen answered in some detail.

"I'm glad you brought something up there. No, I'm quite sure defense counsel and possibly you, Mr. Leighton, and any other ones connected with the case, might have said all of that statement is not in the exact words of Lloyd Eldon Miller. They are not in the exact words of Lloyd Eldon Miller. There were times when Lloyd Eldon Miller, it was difficult for him to say what he wanted to say."

Leighton complimented the witness for his replies saying, "Mr. Christensen, you have answered my question perfectly."

At the conclusion of his testimony, Christensen volunteered, "There is just one thing that I would like to add before I leave this stand. I don't hold any malice toward Lloyd Eldon Miller, and I have the deepest sympathy for the parents of Janice May as well as Lloyd Eldon Miller's parents. I did the only thing in this case that I should have done as a law enforcement officer, and I believe that everything that I did was done honestly and with no malice toward no one."

Next came Kenneth M. Lindzey. He added little to his testimony at the 1956 trial. He described his participation in the interrogation of Lloyd, expressing his delight at the opportunity to work with Mr. Christensen: "I was thrilled to think that a small town police officer was going to have the opportunity to sit in with a man that was known in police investigative work. I admired his actions in every way. I can assure you gentlemen and everyone in this room that never at any time was this man mistreated. He was treated with absolute kindness."

A minute later the Parole Board heard the real reason for calling Chief Lindzey to the stand. Once again Hayes was to mention Sioux City, Iowa. Chief Lindzey told the Board that during the time between Miller's arrest and the trial he was contacted by federal authorities in connection with the sex slaying of a two-year-old girl in Sioux City, Iowa, and that FBI men had attended a portion of the trial in Carthage.

What was the link between Lloyd Eldon Miller, Jr., and the slaying of a two-year-old child in Sioux City, Iowa? Immediately after the Parole Board hearing, I put in a phone call to Wayne Shaw, City Editor of the Sioux City *Journal,* who quickly sketched the story for me. On August 8, 1955, a two-year-old child, Donna Sue Davis, of Sioux City, Iowa, on the east bank of the Mississippi River, was found dead in South Sioux City, Nebraska, a community on the west bank. The crime was never solved.

On a previous occasion the prosecution had seriously prejudiced Lloyd Eldon Miller by intimating that he was responsible for the death of Donna Sue Davis. We have already noted the first occasion, causing perhaps the most prejudice to Lloyd. It came during Hayes' cross-examination of Miller during the 1956 trial, when Hayes asked whether Miller was ever in Sioux City, Iowa, and shortly afterwards asked "Where were you on August 8, 1955? Now, take plenty of time to think about that." Malmgren objected, but the Judge overruled the objection on Hayes' promise to show its relevancy. Lloyd answered that he was in Rock Island with his wife, Lynn Marin.

At no time during the trial did Hayes or any member of the prosecution mention the name of Donna Sue Davis. Perhaps they feared that if they did, the Supreme Court of Illinois might reverse the conviction for prejudicial error. They may have thought it might be enough to mention the date in the hope that the jurors who lived in Western Illinois would recall the crime which took place a little over a year before and would themselves draw the inference.

Now for a second time and on this occasion without subtlety the prosecution was openly mentioning the Sioux City crime. Again, it did not mention the name of the child or the date. Lloyd might have been guilty of that crime, because, according to Hayes, "investigation showed . . . that at the time this slaying occurred in Sioux City, Miller was on one of his traveling periods of time and he was in that general vicinity. . . ." Moreover, according to Ramsey, the description of the man who committed the crime in Sioux City was "very similar" to the characteristics of Mr. Miller. Finally, there were cigarette burns on the body of Donna Davis. The link here was an incident between Chief Lindzey and June Lang. Hayes put the matter to Chief Lindzey with delicacy:

Q. Now did June Lang at any time show you any part of her body or voluntarily show you any part of her body that is not normally apparent in street clothes?

A. Yes, sir.

Q. And would you describe what took place on that occasion?

A. She opened the bosom of her dress and showed her breasts and it
looked to me as if there had been cigarette burns on her
breasts and her upper bosom.

As Chief Lindzey related the story, June Lang told him that (and
now it was Chief Lindzey's turn to speak with delicacy) "during the
height of Lloyd Miller's emotions that he had burned her with
cigarette butts."

There were other reasons, according to Hayes, for the Parole
Board to recommend a denial of clemency for Miller. It had to do
with Mrs. Baxter's residence. The defense had referred to it as a
"private little rooming house" but Hayes asked Chief Lindzey
whether it was true that one Whitey Simms was pulled out of that
room and charged with murder, tried for murder, and acquitted on
the grounds of self defense. Moreover, a Whit Burns was pulled out
of that room, indicted, and sent to the penitentiary for burglary.

On cross-examination Leighton explored at some length with
Chief Lindzey the Sioux City matter. The Chief acknowledged that
the Sioux City police did not send a man to see Lindzey. They did
write him a letter which he did not answer because about the time
it was received FBI agents interviewed him. The Chief did not know
when the crime was committed in Sioux City and did not know the
name of the victim. Leighton ended his cross-examination asking for
enlightenment:

Q. Now, Chief Lindzey, I would like to ask you one last question.
This is more for my enlightenment than anything else. Of
what materiality or relevancy would this be to know about
something you know nothing about in connection with the
plea for clemency when you don't know the name of the
person or anything else? Why do you think Mr. Hayes
asked you that question?

A. I have no idea why he asked it.

After lunch Blaine Ramsey took the stand. His testimony was
largely an oral argument, devoted to defending the truth of the confession and finding corroboration for it. He told the Board that he

had spoken to Alice Baxter shortly after the crime. According to Ramsey, Mrs. Baxter told him when interviewed in the company of Roger Hayes that she had no knowledge what Lloyd Miller did the crucial day or afternoon until about 5:30 P.M. when she asked him to take the prescription to the drugstore for her. If we accept Ramsey's statement, we are then faced with an unexplained contradiction in the prosecution testimony. Ed Lewis put Lloyd in the drugstore at 5:25 that afternoon. There can be no question that Mrs. Baxter must have spoken to Lloyd before the trip to the drugstore, and therefore there can be no question that she must have spoken to him substantially before 5:30.

It was nearly six o'clock Tuesday afternoon when Roger Hayes appeared before the Board as a witness for the prosecution. Hayes' testimony was a combination of testimony and argument, similar to the statement of Blaine Ramsey. When he finished, Oral Kost, the State's Attorney of Fulton County, related a telephone conversation that he had had the preceding Thursday with Judge Bardens. Kost had put to Judge Bardens some of the same questions that Ted Conger and I had, most importantly, whether he would have imposed the death penalty if there had been a trial before him without a jury. Judge Bardens informed us that he would not have done so. According to Oral Kost, Judge Bardens told him that he would have imposed the death sentence.

It was 6:15 P.M. when the last witness left the stand. The Board took a fifteen-minute recess and at 6:30, without supper, began to listen to final arguments. Leighton spoke first, summarizing the case for Lloyd. He was followed by Oral Kost and Kost was followed by Roger Hayes.

Hayes felt that Miller's attorneys were doing him a great disservice. "Lloyd Eldon Miller, no matter who he is, no matter what he has been convicted of, has rights. He has a right to be treated fairly. But what has happened? Counsel, and it is right here in the newspaper—two columns—'Rosenfield and Leighton decided that Mr. Rosenfield, who owns a radio station, shall withdraw as his attorney and go out and publicize this case'—publicize this case by hiring a ringmaster to run this circus. . . . Why did this circus commence? I say to you it is obvious because of the connection of Mr.

Rosenfield and Mr. Leighton with The Committee to Abolish Capital Punishment. . . . Maybe it is a great cause to abolish capital punishment. I don't know. But there is no cause great enough to deprive a man, even a vicious criminal, of his right to have his prayer for clemency considered in a proper climate when the climate that has resulted is from a three ring circus. . . ."

Leighton made a brief statement in reply and then at 7:30 P.M. the session adjourned. But the members of the Parole Board were not finished with their day's work. They left the hearing, ate supper, and, by agreement between the prosecution and the attorneys for Lloyd, immediately went to Stateville to interview the prisoner.

At ten o'clock that night the Parole Board resumed its session at the prison. The first witness was Dr. Julius Venckus, the prison physician. Dr. Venckus reported that Dr. Kruglik had suggested to Warden Pate on the preceding July 30 that it would be best to put Lloyd in the detention hospital at Stateville where he could be observed and treated. Lloyd was complaining that he was having difficulty sleeping. He was admitted to the detention hospital that same day and received thorazine, three times a day.

The first report was dated August 9, four days before the night session at the prison. After some initial comments, Dr. Kruglik's recommendaiton was "Continued observation." There were precisely ten days left to carry out that recommendation.

Let us anticipate our narrative: On August 16, three days after the hearing, Dr. Kruglik saw Lloyd again and again submitted a report. Among the observations:

> He has cloaked himself with a "Faith" that is conditional upon God doing his (the inmate's) will, and is perhaps only today beginning to entertain the possibility that true faith, of the nature he has said he professes, is not conditional. But his "faith" is still not strong and offers no bulwark to his fright.
>
> We do not profess any knowledge as to Mr. Miller's specific guilt or innocence. We have reviewed the voluminous data and material available in the record of the Criminologist and can only say that Mr. Miller possesses the personality structure not inconsistent with the nature of his offense.

IMPRESSION: Without mental illness or mental defi-
ciency. Emotionally immature, emotionally unstable personality structure.

We return to the night session at the prison after Dr. Venckus.
Lloyd was invited into the room and offered a chair. The Board
asked Lloyd a number of questions about his childhood and his
wanderings over the country preceding the day of the murder.
Prime questioning centered on the events of Saturday, November
26. They asked him whether he recalled being awakened during the
afternoon. He recalled the telephone call from Teke Johns and then
he said, "And I no sooner got in bed than the telephone rung again
and some woman called me. I can't recall her name." He didn't
know who it was or what she had to say. Then he recalled someone
else disturbing his slumber: "Well, someone called me about around
four o'clock but I just, like I said, I heard someone call me but I am
not—what I am—I heard someone call me but again I just rolled
over and then I finally woke up. I would say it would be about ten
minutes to four, or something like that. I am not sure whether it was
about that time or not." The someone who called did not call on the
telephone but opened the door, it sounded like a woman's voice but
Lloyd did not see who it was. The voice said 'Lloyd it's time to get
up,' 'You are oversleeping,' or something like that, or 'Did you hear
your telephone?' "

It could have been Mrs. Baxter who woke him up but he was not
sure. He had never seen any children in the house and as far as he
knew no children ever visited there. After leaving the house with the
prescription, he went first to get a bite of supper, then had the prescription filled, returned to Mrs. Baxter's, and went to work at the
cab stand.

Lloyd remembered the taxi ride to St. David with June Lang and
remembered that they had discussed the crime.

Early Sunday morning he left with the cab, taking it as far as
Pekin where he abandoned it and took the bus to Danville.

Mr. Zahn asked Lloyd what made him go off with Mr. Johns' cab
and leave it in Pekin. What made him do that? Lloyd answered, "It's
just one of those things. I mean, I know I have straightened up now,
but in fact in those days, that's the way I was living—more of a wild

life and I made too many quick decisions, which if I stopped I would be better off today."

After a fairly quick review by the Board of the events following Lloyd's arrest, Board member Zahn asked Lloyd whether he was ever intimate sexually with June Lang. He answered, "No, sir."

Q. Think very hard now. Are you sure you were never sexually intimate with her?

A. No, sir.

Mr. Zahn asked why Lloyd never had sex relations with June. Lloyd gave the best answer of all: "Well, I just—I just didn't care for the woman."

The Board inquired about Mr. Baxter. Lloyd did not know what kind of work he did and did not see him at home during the week preceding the crime. (During the evening session Lloyd did dispose of Teke Johns' question about what had happened to the cab driver's cap. Lloyd told the Board that he had disposed of it near Bartonville, a small community almost due south of Peoria. Teke was concerned about it because the drivers owned their own uniform but the cap belonged to the company.)

The rest of the interrogation was devoted to the details of Miller's life in Canton and his work habits in the eight months preceding the crime. At the end, Mr. Zahn asked Lloyd whether he would like to make a statement "something we haven't asked you or something you could think of?" Lloyd answered, "Well, I mean what I would like to ask is what does an innocent man have to do to prove his innocence to get home?" Mr. Zahn answered, "I wish I knew."

Lloyd was excused. The hearing was finally concluded. The attorneys had done all they could for the moment. It was now the duty of the Pardon and Parole Board to prepare its report to the Governor and for the Governor to make his decision.

Late on August 15, I made the first of many trips to Stateville to see our client. I visited Lloyd each time there was a significant development in his case. During the entire period, from August 1963 to my last visit in March 1967, the routine hardly varied. Almost always another attorney drove with me—usually Ted Conger, Harry

Golter, or George Pontikes. We drove out from the Loop, taking a highway through Romeoville. It was one of the minor amusements of the case that our drive to see a man married so often and in such deep trouble, at least in part because of a woman, should take us through a town so named.

Another minor amusement was the Stateville parking lot. Opposite each parking space stood a small sign on a post: "Lock your car." If there is any validity to the deterrent theory of punishment, surely it should operate with maximum force within the very shadow of the institution which is its physical embodiment. For me those small signs epitomized the essential failure of the criminal law.

After we had parked the car (and locked it), we went to the reception building where we signed in. We made it a fixed practice to call the warden's office in advance and make arrangements for a convenient time. Through all of the years, Warden Frank J. Pate found it convenient for us to come at the time we wished to come. Our waits in the visitors' room generally were not long. We think, although I never inquired specifically on this point, that the warden saw to it that Lloyd was spruced up for our coming. We understand that the prisoners are shaved only two or three times a week and that opportunities for showering are somewhat limited. Nevertheless, when we arrived Lloyd was always freshly shaven, appeared to have had a fresh shower, and wore a clean and neat prison uniform.

The visitors' waiting room was the most depressing part of our visit. What we saw of the prison as a whole, had a certain bustle. The guards, prisoners, and visitors were coming and going. But the visitors' waiting room had a peculiar atmosphere of despair. Long, plain wooden benches were provided for those waiting to see the inmates. Along one side were doors to toilets for men and for women. The men's room lacked the customary privacy of a door on the booth. The depersonalization and lack of privacy characteristic of a prison had permeated even to visitors' facilities.

On the benches in the waiting room were scattered copies of the monthly inmate magazine, *Time,* which contained short articles about prison events, short stories, poetry, photographs of events in the prison, and pictures of inmates. The articles usually were of the uplift sort, presumably written by experienced prisoners seeking to advise their newer colleagues how best to adjust to life within the walls. The short stories, and the poems particularly, were sad and wistful.

The prisoners, needless to say, did not enjoy their lot, but they had to make the best of it. The very mechanics of living, the routine of prison, made it difficult to be constantly depressed. As far as I could see, it was a prison run without brutality or harshness. The guard at the reception desk in the main administration building usually had one or two prisoner assistants: their relationship, at least on the surface, seemed that of superior and subordinate. The prisoners were respectful without being fawning or cringing. The ordinary business of every-day life put an overlay on the deep hurt and pain of confinement.

But for the visitors, the very act of coming to the prison caused the keenest feelings of anxiety and grief. A visit to the prison re-called the unhappy experiences of arrest, trial, and sentencing. Bright hopes of earlier and happier periods had been dimmed, if not extinguished, by the sentence to the penitentiary.

For a visit with a son or husband or other family member, ordi-nary visitors are ushered into a long room. A long table running the entire length of the room is partitioned into small cubicles. Visitors sit on one side, prisoners sit on the other. Guards watch constantly. Opportunities for a meaningful and happy visit are not great.

We never interviewed Lloyd in the general visitors' room. Almost always we saw him in a small office near the warden's office. Usually he was waiting for us when we stepped in. We were always greeted with a smile and a handshake. Then we would settle down to the serious business at hand.

We soon learned that we could stop at a visitors' commissary on the way out and order a few commissary items to be sent up to Lloyd. The maximum we were permitted to order was about $2.50. At first we relied on the commissary clerk to select items for us, usually fruit, candy, and a pint of ice cream. During the last six months Lloyd was in Stateville, he would say as we rose to leave, "If you fel-lows are going to stop at the commissary, would you mind getting me—" and he would hand us a small slip of paper with his order written out.

I had read in articles about life in prisons and other "total insti-tutions" that the little amenities of every-day living take on enor-

mous significance in the eyes of the inmates. There for the first time
I saw it in actuality. A man nearly forty years of age was totally
without income and totally dependent for the amenities of life on
the small sums sent to him from time to time by his parents, his
lawyers, and others. He was reduced to asking for candy, fruit, and
ice cream, like a small child.

The first time I met Lloyd he was eight days away from the electric chair. I called on him to find out what had happened the preceding Tuesday evening when he had been interviewed by the Parole
Board, since at that time we did not have a transcript. Considering
the circumstances he seemed incredibly composed and was able to
give us a fairly coherent account. When I looked back over my notes
of that first interview and compared it with the transcript, I was
impressed with the relative completeness of the substance of the
interview as relayed to me by Lloyd. He was able, at least on that
occasion, to put aside the spectre of death then hanging close to him
and relate to his attorneys facts which might be of use in staving
off the execution.

Five days later, and only three days before the execution, a telegram came to Leighton from the Governor dated August 20, 1963,
11:28 A.M. It read, "I have this day denied the petition of Lloyd
Eldon Miller Jr. otherwise known as Jack Franklin Warner for commutation of sentence of death. S/Otto Kerner Governor." Word was
relayed immediately from the Governor's office by telephone to
Leighton of the Governor's decision. Leighton immediately wired
back to the Governor at eleven-forty asking for a reprieve to present
the case to the courts and for an interview with the Governor.

Leighton was unable to arrange the interview. The Governor's
formal response to Leighton's telegram came in a letter, dated August 27, from Thomas G. O'Connell, Superintendent of the Pardon
and Parole Board. The letter said in part: "Please be advised that
the Governor is aware of all the testimony given by additional witnesses, since a transcript of their testimony was presented to him,
but their testimony did not materially alter the facts in the case."
Our sole hope of saving the life of our client lay in the courts.

9

HABEAS
CORPUS

Because the Governor denied clemency, only the most energetic action could save our client's life. Only sixty hours remained before the scheduled execution. There were few means left to secure a stay. They would have to be used vigorously.

One possibility was an application to the Supreme Court of Illinois. Because it was late summer the Court was not in session. We did have the right, however, to request a stay from Justice Walter V. Schaefer, a former professor of law at Northwestern Law School. He had been on the Supreme Court for a number of years and was one of its most eminent judges.

Another possibility was a second habeas corpus petition in the United States District Court in Chicago. It also was not in regular session. A habeas corpus petition would be heard, not by the judge to whom the case was assigned, but by Judge Bernard M. Decker, the Judge sitting that week to hear emergency matters.

If Judge Decker denied a stay, our next step would be to request a stay from a judge of the United States Court of Appeals—also on vacation. The problem would be to find a judge of that court, also located in Chicago, and to explain the matter to him within the hours available. We were not free to present the matter to a judge of the Court of Appeals until the matter had been heard and ruled upon by Judge Decker.

If we were refused by a Court of Appeals judge, our very last hope would be a stay from a justice of the United States Supreme Court. The reality, however, was that if we did not secure a stay from Justice Schaefer or Judge Decker, our chances were very slim indeed.

We would go before a judge of the Court of Appeals or a justice of the Supreme Court having been refused twice. There would hardly be time left to make an adequate explanation of the grounds for a stay. The effort would appear just to be another frantic appeal by attorneys desperately advancing insubstantial grounds to obtain a last-minute reprieve.

We felt that we had solid grounds and that a serious injustice had been done to Lloyd Miller. A court should have an opportunity to consider the testimony of Mrs. Baxter and Ed Lewis. We had seriously undermined the post-murder timetable outlined in the confession and thus had cast serious doubt on the truth of the confession.

We decided to pursue simultaneously the Schaefer and Decker openings. All of us worked on August 20 until late in the evening preparing the necessary documents. The trained help of our secretaries—Frances Zukerman, Hazel West Blair, Diane Reichenberger, Harriet Kopsian Pontikes, and Eleanor Kopsian—was invaluable.

We also had to ascertain by telephone whether the judges would be sitting and to find out when we could come in. Justice Schaefer informed us that he would receive the petition at ten o'clock on the morning of August 22. Early the day before, we hurried over to the District Court in the old post office building at Clark and Adams Streets. We presented our petition to the clerk, together with Lloyd's affidavit that he had no funds. We were allowed to file *in forma pauperis* and were not required to pay the fifteen dollar filing fees or the other fees customarily charged litigants. The clerk received the petition, picked up his rubber stamp, and stamped the case number, No. 63 C 1496. We were ready for assignment of a judge.

At the District Court in Chicago, judges are not assigned in rotation. If they were, it would be simple for a litigant to wait until a favorite judge appeared on the rota. Permitting assignment by a clerk could easily lead to charges of partiality or favoritism. Hence for many years cases have been assigned by judicial lottery. Small cards about two inches square are printed with the name of one of the active judges in the district on each. The cards are thoroughly mixed and made into pads, printed side down, and sealed on all four sides, with a blank card on the bottom. To learn the judge for a case, the clerk stamps the case number on the top card and pries it off with a letter opener. We drew Judge J. Sam Perry. He would hear the case that fall—if Lloyd was still alive.

Leighton and I immediately informed Judge Decker's clerk that the suit had been filed. Judge Decker at once issued a formal notice to the Attorney General requiring him to "show cause" why a writ of habeas corpus should not be issued and set a hearing for two o'clock the next afternoon, August 22, ten hours before the execution.

We returned to Leighton's office where we met the other attorneys to plan the strategy for the next day. The two o'clock hearing time meant that the judge would be free from the press of routine business customarily handled in the morning. Setting it so late in the day, however, posed a grave problem for us. The hearing probably would last an hour-and-a-half or two hours, and that would push the time to 3:30 or 4:00 P.M. or possibly even later. There would then only be about eight hours before the execution in which to take further legal action. If we were to have an opportunity to present an application for a stay to another judge, plans had to be laid immediately to facilitate such an application. We decided our last effort would be an application to a Supreme Court justice. Bob Ming called the office of the clerk of the Supreme Court and explained the situation. The clerk's office made arrangements with Justice Tom Clark. Justice Clark agreed to make himself available for an emergency hearing at his home on the evening of August 22 if necessary. This arrangement required a lawyer and papers on the case in Washington.

On the morning of August 21, Bob Ming called William B. Bryant, a Washington attorney, and asked him to stand by. We assembled a packet of papers and mailed them air mail special delivery to Bryant. The difficulty was that Bryant knew nothing about the case. He did not have the complete records which would make clear the full significance of all the facts which had come to light in recent weeks. Thus it would be very difficult for him to make a forceful presentation to Justice Clark. Moreover, there were serious tactical difficulties. Ordinarily when an emergency application is presented to a Justice of the Supreme Court (or to the judge of any reviewing court), it is customary to present certified copies of the order of denial of the lower court and the other papers. It would be nearly impossible to obtain the necessary certification and get them to Washington in time. There was, moreover, a serious technical difficulty in this approach. It meant bypassing the Court of Appeals. We had no idea whether the law permitted this bypass. We had no time to do research on this question, or any other question.

On the morning of August 21, we took one other step to expedite certifying the record if Judge Decker turned us down. George Pontikes handled the matter. He went to the office of the District Court clerk and explained the urgency to the young clerk in charge of certifying records for appellate review. The clerk was Greek and she and Pontikes exchanged a few words of greeting in that language. She put aside her other tasks, assembled the papers for certification in case No. 63 C 1496, and placed them on one corner of her desk. She promised Pontikes that if there were a denial of the stay by Judge Decker, she would do the necessary work the moment that order was brought to her and have a complete certified record in Pontikes' hands within sixty seconds.

That morning the attorneys were split into two teams. One team, Bob Ming and Maury Rosenfield, went to the chambers of Judge Schaefer, then located at 30 North Michigan Avenue. The other team, Leighton, the other attorneys, and I, prepared for the two o'clock hearing before Judge Decker. About nine-thirty that morning I called Bryant's office to make sure that he had received the papers sent air mail special the preceding day. He had not![1]

Shortly before the two o'clock hearing before Judge Decker, we re-

---

1. Throughout the day I put in calls to Bryant's office in Washington to see if the papers had arrived. As the day wore on we became more and more alarmed. Early in the afternoon we decided upon a shift in strategy. We realized it was unrealistic to expect Bryant to make an effective plea to Justice Clark as he knew nothing about the case. Therefore, early in the afternoon, Bob Ming and Maury Rosenfield took a copy of the habeas corpus petition and all the other documents they felt would be helpful and went to O'Hare Field, the Chicago airport. From there they would check with Leighton's office from time to time and if the stay were denied they would leave immediately for Washington. They wouldn't have with them a certified copy of the order of denial but would have all other documents. By this arrangement the hour or possibly two that would be lost going from the Loop to O'Hare during the rush hour would be saved. As soon as Judge Decker granted a stay, we paged them at the airport and they returned home. The papers sent to Bryant never arrived. By some strange chance they were lost in the mail and never turned up.

ceived word from Bob and Maury that Justice Schaefer had refused
the stay. It was a blow. Everything now depended upon obtaining
the stay from Judge Decker. Failing that, our chances of obtaining a stay from any other judge were remote. At two o'clock there
was a substantial crowd in Judge Decker's court. The central Illinois
press had a substantial contingent of photographers and reporters.
There were the attorneys for the state, for the Attorney General, the
Chicago press, and members of the general public. Leighton reviewed the facts we had recently learned, such as the testimony of
Mrs. Baxter and Ed Lewis. The State responded briefly. At about
4:30 P.M., when the lawyers had finished, Judge Decker announced
his decision. He said that the matter appeared to be complex. He
had no time to evaluate the facts that had come to light in recent
weeks. The case ought to be heard in due course by Judge Perry.
Therefore, he said, he had decided to grant a stay of execution and
would sign an appropriate order immediately. He did so at once.
It was seven-and-a-half hours before Lloyd was to die in the electric
chair at Stateville. The order was taken immediately to the clerk's
office for certification. We called Warden Pate and told him that a
certified copy was on its way to him. Judge Decker sent it by a United
States Marshal. The life of Lloyd Eldon Miller, Jr., had been saved.

Obtaining a stay meant at the least many months of life for Lloyd.
If we lost in the District Court, we would have a right of appeal to
the Court of Appeals and a right to apply for Supreme Court review.
Meanwhile Lloyd was protected by the stay order.

Preparation for the forthcoming trial demanded many meetings
of the attorneys, generally in the evening after a day's work. Nearly
all were held in Leighton's offices. After George Leighton had related anecdotes of his life and times in court, and Bob Ming had followed suit when he was there, we would consider the next step to be
taken to save the life of our client. The meetings usually concluded
around nine-thirty or ten o'clock, after which we had a late supper.
(I learned early in the case to have a substantial snack beforehand
and thus stave off kwashiokor.)

Despite the seriousness of the case, the spirit at the meetings was
like that in an attorney's office when a client comes in to sign a will.
Every lawyer, I am sure, will recognize the mood. The matter at
hand is very serious. The client is about to sign a document that will

become effective only after he sleeps in the dust. Yet (unless the client knows he is fatally ill) signings are often occasions for levity.

On August 22, the very day George Leighton was most intent on the stay issue, his secretary gave him the following memorandum:

> TO: George N. Leighton
> FROM: Pat Pratt
> RE: Lloyd Eldon Miller, Jr.
> Mrs. B R of T, Illinois, is on her way to see you (left driving about 3:00 P.M., should arrive Chicago about 6:30– 7:00 P.M. this evening.) Her phone number is ————. Do not call this number. Mrs. B R's husband has threatened her and her children if she talks to you. She is to call you on her arrival either at the office or at home. Mrs. B R's sister called. She said Mrs. B R did have a nervous breakdown about two years ago. However, she is perfectly sane. She has information re Miller case. Important. Please listen to what she has to say. She has been thinking about it for a long time. Mrs. B R's sister would not leave her name, address or phone number.

Neither Mrs. B. R. or her sister were ever heard from again.

Our client felt that it was unfair to leave the full burden of the legal work to us. He sent us a memorandum outlining a number of suggestions. The first of many such memoranda we were to receive follows:

Suggestions.

1. Get Governor's executive order, or all necessary Supreme or circuit court orders unto sheriff and his deputies (and state police if expedient) to commence *Fresh Pursuit.*

2. Have them inspect local cabins and haunts of lone and dependent persons, some indicated on map, . . .

3. Consult Illinois Supreme Court justices as to "propriety" of trial charge of "rape and murder" whereas this was no first-class homicide, but a second-class homicide from injuries concomitant to original assault, . . .

Fall of 1963 was an opportunity for us to complete our preparations for trial. Because of other cases on Judge Perry's calendar, Lloyd's hearing was continued from time to time. It was finally set for Wednesday, December 4.

Each attorney had his own pet project. On some, enormous time was spent with inconclusive results. An example:

Carver and Denny's dry cleaning ticket No. 2616 was shown to Malmgren and Meuth at the evidence examination. On it was the name "Miller" and the notation that the ticket was for a pair of brown pants and a plaid shirt. The ticket was never introduced in the evidence. Why not? If it had actually been brought in by Lloyd, it would have been powerful proof that he was in Carver and Denny Cleaners on the day of the murder despite his protestations to the contrary.

Art Greenberg inquired about the Carver and Denny claim check system. When a customer came in to pick up clothing, a yellow ticket pinned to the garment was removed and placed on a spindle. This was intriguing information. If the yellow tickets were spindled, then presumably the tickets from early in the day would be on the bottom and the tickets from later in the day would be on the top. By knowing where ticket 2616 was found on the spindle, one could estimate the time that the ticket was spindled. If the matter had been investigated immediately after the murder, an accurate time assessment might have been possible. Since the names appear on the yellow tickets, the police could have interviewed various customers as to when they were in the store and thus the time when tickets preceding and following No. 2616 were spindled. Thus the time interval for the critical ticket would have narrowed.

On the evening of September 24, Art Greenberg spoke to Mrs. Joyce Hardy (the clerk at the store in November 1955) and her husband. Initially apprehensive and defensive, they discussed events freely after a period of small talk. Joyce Hardy repeated in substance what she had said at the trial, adding that she was alone in the cleaners at the time, as her co-worker, Mrs. Violet Gaskill, had just gone out to supper. But Art was unable to obtain light on the question of the position of ticket 2616 on the spindle.

So far as we know, the authorities never thoroughly explored and carefully noted every detail regarding ticket 2616. The full stock of tickets for November 26 should have been preserved, with the location of ticket No. 2616 precisely noted.

The whole matter demonstrates several lessons:

(1) The crucial importance of speed in a criminal investigation. After a short time, inquiry of the sort mentioned above would have been difficult as memories faded.

(2) The crucial importance, known to every lawyer, of checking witness accounts against positive facts and documentation. Did the position of No. 2616 on the spindle corroborate Mrs. Hardy's testimony as to the time Miller was in the store?

(3) The enormous cost of a complete investigation. To do a thorough job just on the ticket matter would have required days of work by several men. Yet there is no short-cut if the truth is to be learned. To do a real job, the investigation should have included inquiry as to the date the garments were brought in. Since the tickets were issued in numerical order, it might have been possible to learn who was on duty when No. 2616 was issued. That might have thrown light on who brought in the garments for which the ticket was issued.

Another inquiry had, however, profound results. Leighton, Rosenfield, and Greenberg hoped to find and interview June Lang. Clearly there was much she could tell us about her role in the case. How did she come to relate such incredibly varying stories to prosecution and defense? Was her trial testimony against Lloyd true? After a long search, Art Greenberg found the address of June's father and her brother, both in the Canton area. Someone had an inspired thought: why not leave a subpoena for June Lang for the December 4 hearing at her brother's home and see what happened? Such a subpoena was not enforceable because not served personally on June, but our immediate goal was only the opportunity to talk to her before the hearing. A few days after the subpoena was left, June called Art Greenberg. On Sunday morning, November 24, Art put June on a plane for Chicago so that Leighton could interview her that evening at his office. It was planned that one of us would be with her at all times because June was unreliable and we were afraid she would disappear. She was met at the airport by Jean Erkes, Mother Superior of Witnesses, who spent the morning with her. I took her to the art museum in the afternoon since every other public place was closed because of the assassination of President Kennedy two days before.

As we became acquainted, I found that the afternoon was going well. June had remarried since the Miller trial but had then been separated or divorced from her husband and was now June Lang Gross. She looked very much as she did in the pictures taken at the Carthage trial, a pleasing, somewhat chubby woman of about thirty. Her manner was pleasant. When she spoke there was a quiet earnestness in her manner. June and I toured a special exhibition then on display at the Art Institute. At five o'clock when the museum closed we went to Landers' Restaurant on Wabash Avenue for supper. I chose a dish that would take a long time to prepare. I had only one anxious moment. After we had been shown to a table, June left for the ladies room. Her absence began to seem longer than such trips normally take. Just when I was becoming genuinely concerned, June reappeared. After supper we met Leighton and Maury Rosenfield in the office.

Despite our enormous efforts to arrange the interview, it was, on the whole, disappointing to us. In general, June reaffirmed her trial testimony about Lloyd's confession to her in the taxicab. But we learned a few significant facts. First, according to June, when Lloyd first told her that he "done it," she had the impression that his statement was merely an attention-getting device and she did not believe it. Second, she did not immediately report the conversation to the police and had no contact with the authorities until the following day. Third and most important, she told us that at the time of the crime she had known Lloyd only "a matter of weeks." Yet at the trial she had told Judge Bardens and the jury that she had known Lloyd for about two years. This discrepancy, for reasons I shall explain later, was of great moment to us. Meanwhile we turned our attention to other problems.

There is a strange, nearly incredible anomaly in American law which is only now, slowly and fitfully, being erased. Since about 1937 in the federal courts (and later in most state courts) in non-criminal trials, each side has the opportunity to learn in advance of the actual trial the facts in the possession of his adversary. Opposing witnesses can be questioned under oath, premises examined, documents inspected, etc. These rules nearly eliminate surprise in civil trials. But these rules in general apply only in civil cases. Only very recently have they been applied, limitedly, to criminal matters.

In the federal courts, a habeas corpus proceeding, even though its purpose is to upset a criminal conviction, is regarded not as a criminal matter but as a civil proceedings. We assumed that the court rules applicable were the civil rules, including the all-important rules for pretrial discovery. We presented to Judge Perry a request for an order compelling the prosecution to bring its files into court. There was no objection from the prosecution. Judge Perry granted the request.[1] In addition, Judge Perry requested the Illinois Supreme Court to send to his court the exhibits from the 1956 trial.

In late November, the documents and exhibits began to arrive. As each batch came in, I hurried to the judge's chambers to examine them. First to arrive were the trial exhibits.[2]

One of the documents produced was a statement from a man dated November 30, 1955, that at about 11:45 P.M. on Saturday, November 26, 1955, he met June in Canton, drove her to Peoria, stopped at a restaurant, and then drove her back to Canton where they arrived about 5:45 on Sunday morning.

This statement was highly significant. That very November 30, June Lang gave the police a statement that Lloyd had confessed the crime to her during the course of the taxi ride to St. David on the night of November 26. One would think that if June believed Lloyd's story, she would have gone immediately to the police so that he could have been arrested at once. Not so. The police knew they had no contact with her until Sunday morning, the 27th. Further, June's all-night travels were strange behavior for a woman who presumably believed that she had just heard the confession to one of the most brutal crimes in Canton's history. All this tended to con-

1. Six years later, in 1969, the Supreme Court ruled in *Harris* v. *Nelson* that in a habeas corpus case discovery is discretionary with the judge.

2. Judge Perry was exceedingly meticulous in his handling of the evidence. At all times they remained in his chambers under lock and key. Whenever we examined them, we did so only in the presence of some member of his staff, usually his secretary, Mrs. Rosemary Zimmerman.

firm June's recent statement to us that she did not believe Lloyd's confession to her.

A second document sent by Ramsey was June's statement to the authorities of November 30, the one read aloud to Lloyd or at least summarized for his benefit, at the confrontation scene between June and Lloyd in the Springfield Armory late in the afternoon of November 30. The statement in general was similar to her trial testimony, with one crucial difference. At the trial June told Judge Bardens and the jury that she had known Lloyd for about two years. In her statement of November 30, she said that she first met Lloyd "about five weeks ago." That was substantially in accord with her statement at our Sunday evening meeting with her. This was the key-pin as far as defense counsel was concerned, for June's November 30 statement showed conclusively that the prosecution knew that June misstated the fact when she testified to a two-year acquaintance with Miller in Carthage.

The lie known to the prosecution gave us something substantial to work on. Some years before the Supreme Court had overturned a conviction in which a prosecution witness had made a false statement on the witness stand to the positive knowledge of the prosecution. Perhaps we could invoke that case to help Lloyd.

In that case, Henry Napue was convicted of murder during a robbery, largely on the testimony of George Hamer, who said he was a participant in the robbery. Hamer pleaded guilty.

At Napue's trial the Assistant State's Attorney asked Hamer whether anyone had promised him any reduction of sentence. Hamer said, "No, sir."

Napue served seventeen years. Then help came from an unexpected source. Hamer claimed the State reneged on a promise to him of leniency made in exchange for his testimony against Napue. His attorney was the Assistant State's Attorney who had prosecuted Napue, and, said the attorney, he himself had made the promise.

Stateville's walls do not keep out news of the outside world. When Napue learned of the allegations made by Hamer through his new attorney he retained George Leighton to seek relief for him, charging that the State had made known use of perjured evidence. In June 1959, the Supreme Court set aside Napue's conviction.

On December 2, only two days before the hearing was to open, I was back in Judge Perry's chambers to examine documents. One document sent shock waves through me. It was comic, pathetic, and tragic. The document was a memorandum to the file prepared by Supt. Christensen reporting a meeting with June Lang on February 27, 1956, about three months after the murder. The memorandum stated that June came to see him accompanied by one S.T., who lived not far from Urbana, Illinois. June had some vital revelations to make to Christensen. She confessed to him that she was deeply involved in a vast criminal conspiracy in Canton for selling narcotics: she was acting as a sales agent for Lloyd. The conspiracy embraced substantially every well-known person in Canton. The source of supply was Mr. A. B., etc. etc.

June claimed that Janice's parents were involved in the hideous racket. They, however, had stepped out of line and as a result the persons in charge of the entire ring had instructed Lloyd to rough up Janice. But unfortunately Lloyd had gone too far and Janice had been killed. June, Supt. Christensen's memo continued, had reported the matters to the Sheriff and State's Attorney of Fulton County but they did not believe her story. June told Christensen she was desperately afraid someone in the ring would try to take her life. There were other people in the ring besides those already mentioned. William Malmgren himself was one of the chief conspirators. Malmgren had already attempted on three occasions to kill her by running her down with his automobile.

S. T., the man who accompanied June to the conference, had a horrible revelation of his own to make. One conspirator, K. L., a student at a nearby college, was putting a narcotic into the popcorn machine in one of the theatres in the area. Children in their innocence would buy popcorn, unknowingly become addicted, and would become customers of the ring.

It is evident that Supt. Christensen shared the scepticism of the Sheriff of Fulton County and the State's Attorney about this preposterous tale. The authorities arranged for June to take a lie detector test in Lewiston on March 12. A few days later, Bureau Lie Detector Examiner, William Abernathie, submitted a report to Christensen in Case No. 2069, "June Lang—suspected of being untruthful in statement given local authorities regarding delivery and sale of narcotics." The report stated that at the request of Sheriff

Virgil Ball, "subject June Lang was examined regarding the truthfulness of her statement given to local authorities regarding the selling and delivering of narcotics. June Lang was given three polygraph tests. Due to the physical condition and extreme nervousness of this subject it is impossible to accurately interpret her polygrams. Therefore, bar [sic] polygrams would be classed as inconclusive. June Lang was interrogated at length and from the interrogation and observation of this subject, it is my own personal opinion that she is untruthful. However, since June Lang is a material witness in the Lloyd Miller murder case which is now pending, it was agreed by the Fulton County Authorities and our Bureau to not go any further into the case until the Miller murder trial is concluded."

Clearly Christensen's memorandum and Abernathie's report were documents of the gravest import. June's testimony at the trial about a spontaneous confession in the taxicab unquestionably had corroborated the confession to the authorities. But little had been said at the trial about the relationship between June and Lloyd, and absolutely nothing had been said about June's background, character, and emotional state. Malmgren knew a great deal about June's background because of the lengthy statement he had taken from her on March 17 during the all-day central Illinois auto tour, but little of that statement had been produced by the defense at the trial and then only in a watered down, fragmented form. That was not the prosecution's fault. The Christensen and Abernathie memoranda, however, supplied evidence that the prosecution had the gravest reasons for doubting June Lang's reliability. Her story to Christensen on February 27 was so outlandish it was clearly past belief. Abernathie's memorandum showed that he at least thought she was not truthful. And the general tenor of the memorandum indicated that other authorities, too, severely doubted June's veracity.

The two memoranda made it possible for us to make a new contention: because of the clearly fantastic character of the dope ring conspiracy tale, the authorities should have viewed all of June's statements skeptically, including the statement about the taxicab confession. We could now contend that at the trial the prosecution should have revealed to the Court and the jury that vital facts had come to their attention regarding June's veracity.

If we took this line it would be necessary to produce the two documents in court for Judge Perry's consideration. But there was another dimension to the matter. The allegations by June, while they showed up June's infirmities by their wild character, also were allegations against Lloyd and his counsel. It is general policy in the defense of criminal cases to shield from the Court, if possible, knowledge of any previous crime that the defendant has committed or is suspected of committing. The reason is obvious; if the defendant has committed or is thought to have committed other crimes, even an impartial judge may be more apt to come to the conclusion that he is guilty of the crime for which he has been charged. Moreover, the serious allegations against the May family, even though wholly unsupported by evidence, would work serious damage to the case if the court inferred that we were attempting to help Lloyd Miller by defaming the May family.

After long consideration, we decided to use the Abernathie report but not the Christensen memorandum.

Let me jump ahead for a moment to the trial. We called June as a witness. On the morning of December 20, as Hayes was completing his cross-examination, I experienced a joy of anticipation followed almost immediately by a crushing disappointment. Hayes reviewed with June the various occasions when she had discussed the Miller case with Ramsey. June mentioned one occasion when she was there to take a lie detector test on "another matter." Judge Perry showed immediate interest. The "other matter" turned out to be the trip by June and S. T. to Supt. Christensen. In the course of a colloquy on the lie test incident, suddenly Hayes said, "In these files, there is a copy of a two-page, single line, typewritten letter, which is not addressed to anybody; but it is signed by James Christensen. No, that is not the one." (Hayes began to run through his papers.)

While Hayes was searching for a copy of the Christensen memorandum, I felt sure that it would be shown to Judge Perry and received in evidence. This document, I thought, would be the capstone of the case and would provide the final bit of proof, if any were needed, that the prosecution well knew that June's word was not to be trusted. The very next moment my hopes were destroyed for Judge Perry did not ask to see the memorandum.

The trial moved to other topics and the Christensen memo never became part of the record. If it had, the trial might have taken quite a different course and we might have been spared years of anxiety and effort.

The Christensen and Abernathie documents came as a shock but in the course of the document examination in the judge's chambers on December 2, I read another memorandum that was truly stunning in its impact. It was a three-page, single-spaced memorandum dated December 7, 1955, just about two weeks after the crime. The author was Forrest (Jess) Litterly and it was addressed to Superintendent Christensen. The memorandum concerned Lab case No. RA 533-55. Litterly was the State Crime Lab chemist who testified at Carthage. He reported to Christensen that two days after the murder, Officer Dwight Whitlock turned over to him a packet of evidentiary materials, most of which had been found near the scene of the crime. In addition, he had received Carver and Denny claim check No. 2616 from Chief Lindzey, the jockey shorts, and the jacket. The report revealed why there was no expert testimony at the trial as to Janice May's blood type. Litterly stated that among the evidence sent to him was a "small white glass jar" containing a sample of Janice May's blood. But, said Litterly, "when received, the blood deteriorated to the extent that serological examination to determine the blood group was impossible."

It was apparent that the authorities had seriously bungled the job of typing Janice's blood. To begin with, the specimen was labeled November 27; it had been taken the day following her death. Why had it been sent to Litterly's laboratory in Springfield for typing? Certainly Graham Hospital was equipped to do the job.

The dry cleaning check had a slight stain on it which was found to be human blood. According to Litterly, it was insufficient for typing purposes.

A dark grey "Bantamac" brand zipper jacket had two minute blood stains, one on the right sleeve cuff and one on the right inside collar. But the stains were so small that it was not possible to determine whether the blood was human blood.

Litterly discussed the jockey shorts. There was Type A blood on the shorts. Moreover, there were pubic hairs on the shorts. These hairs were compared microscopically with a sample of Miller's pubic hair. While they had similar characteristics, Litterly could form no definite opinion as to whether or not they were the same. There were fibers on the shorts that matched the fibers in Janice's blue jeans.

But there was a real shocker in the report and it had nothing to do with the evidence introduced at the trial. It concerned a wholly new matter, something about which the defense had only a hint previously.

When Lloyd was brought to the state crime lab on the night of November 29, one of the first steps taken by the authorities was to draw a sample of his blood, and to take a sample of his pubic hair to compare with the hairs found on the jockey shorts. But there was another reason. On the night of the 30th, shortly before Lloyd confessed, he had been told that a pubic hair had been found in the body of Janice and that it matched his. Lloyd told how he had demanded a look through the microscope and had declared that the hairs didn't match. This incident was puzzling. It had a ring of truth, and it was never denied by the prosecution. We thought it might have been a hoax perpetrated by the prosecution to weaken Miller's will and induce him to confess. If it was not a hoax, why did not the prosecution put in evidence the finding of a hair in Janice's vagina and introduce expert testimony that the hair found in the vagina matched Lloyd's? Surely such evidence would have been the most conclusive possible that Lloyd was guilty.

Litterly's memorandum cleared up the mystery for us. The story of the pubic hair was not a prosecution fabrication. A hair had in fact been found. Among the evidence turned over to Litterly was item No. 6, "Small, round, clear plastic container, labeled—Janice May 11–26–55, Dr. R.J.M. Box was sealed with white surgical adhesive tape." Miller's hair sample was item No. 15. What did Litterly have to say about items No. 6 and No. 15? "The small, round, clear plastic, container described as #6 contained two rolled Kleenex that has been used to obtain a vaginal smear from Janice May. On one of the Kleenex a hair was found. A surface cast of the hair was made and upon microscopic examination of the cast several characteristics were observed which indicated that the hair was probably of human origin. The hair was then mounted for microscopic examination and compared microscopically with mounted samples of pubic hair from Lloyd Eldon Miller, Jr. (Described as #15). No similar characteristics between the two hair samples were observed and it is the opinion of the examiner that the common origin of the two hair samples is not probable."

At last we were able to put together the whole, unbelievable story. At 6:20 P.M. Dr. Mercey, the county coroner, examined Janice's body while it was still on the operating table at Graham Hospital. Litterly received his packet of exhibits at 2:00 P.M. two days later, including the vial labeled "Janice May 11/26/55—Dr. RJM"—the date of death and Mercey's initials. Inside the vial were "two rolled Kleenex" used to obtain a vaginal smear from Janice May. Presumably Dr. Mercey had taken the vaginal smear to determine if there was semen in the vagina. Presumably unknown to Dr. Mercey a single strand of hair adhered to the Kleenex used for taking the specimen. The Kleenex with a hair clinging to it was placed into the vial. When the vial was examined by Litterly, he immediately realized its significance and compared that single strand of hair with the pubic hair taken from Lloyd, concluding that the two hair samples were probably unrelated. This fact of crucial importance was never revealed to the defense, which knew nothing of it until December 2, 1963, when I first read Litterly's report in Judge Perry's chambers. Yet the prosecuting authorities were well aware of this report. The carbon copy in the files at the state crime lab bears the notation that copies were sent to Sheriff Virgil Ball, State's Attorney Blaine Ramsey, and Chief of Police Lindzey.

What was worse was that the authorities, to induce Lloyd to confess, falsely told him that a strand of hair was found and that it did match his pubic hair.

Lloyd's habeas corpus trial opened before Judge Perry at ten o'clock on Wednesday, December 4. Each morning Lloyd was brought down from Stateville and led manacled to Judge Perry's courtroom. There the manacles were removed. Lloyd sat at the counsel table wearing a neat dark prison suit, shirt, and tie.

In addition to Leighton and me, Sy Bucholz, Art Greenberg from Peoria, and Ted Conger appeared on Lloyd's behalf. For the state there was an Assistant Attorney General, Daniel Kadjan—and Roger W. Hayes. Blaine Ramsey was a witness but was not an attorney of record.

The day produced a few surprises. Blaine Ramsey, called as our first witness, admitted that he was aware of June's statement to the authorities in November, 1955, that she had known Lloyd for "about five weeks" rather than "for about two years" as she had testified.

After lunch Dr. Augustus Caesar Webb, a pathologist, testified that Janice's head wounds could not have been received in the manner described in the confession: the confession stated that Janice "fell and hit her head on a cement block." According to the autopsy, however, there were three skull fractures, one in the frontal bone, one in the temporal bone on the side of the head above the ear, and another in the occipital bone in the rear. Dr. Webb testified that a person could not get three fractures of the skull in three different places in a single fall.

Lloyd's mother told Judge Perry that the grey jacket found in Big Creek off the Walnut Street bridge was not her son's.

When Lloyd was arrested he had a large black suitcase with him. Eventually the prison authorities delivered the suitcase with its garments to the elder Millers. We learned that the Millers still had Lloyd's suitcase intact with the clothes in it. Mrs. Miller identified the suitcase as her son's and then identified two pairs of boxer shorts in the suitcase as his. She knew them because she used to wash them. Her son, as she always maintained, wore boxer shorts and never jockey shorts.

Our next witness was Alexander I. Dunsay, a wholesale salesman of men's clothing. We called him to show that the pair of jockey shorts introduced at the trial were too small for Lloyd. During the investigation in the Miller case and the trial, neither prosecution nor defense ever explored a number of such obvious matters. In 1955–1956 this would have simply required a tape measure. A thorough investigator would have measured also the shorts in the suitcase and the shorts he was wearing, noting the brand of shorts in the suitcase. He would have asked Lloyd to try the jockey shorts on and observed the fit. So far as we can determine no one did any of these things.

In fall 1963, we attempted this sort of investigation. A try-on was meaningless after Lloyd had sat in prison for eight years. But Dunsay was able to testify that the jockey shorts were too small to fit the man who wore the boxers and a man of Lloyd's height and weight when admitted to prison. They would have been too tight in the waist. Moreover, the witness said with delicacy, "if you wear anything too small, being a member of male gender, it would constrict your organ and you would be extremely uncomfortable and you could not wear them. That's the only explanation I could think of, your Honor."

But Dunsay's testimony lacked impact in 1963 because it could have been made in 1956 and because the boxers had been in the hands of the Miller family for many years.

After Dunsay, Robert Baxter, the husband of Alice Baxter, corroborated his wife's testimony that Lloyd was in their home that day until four-thirty in the afternoon. We called Robert Baxter as a witness before Judge Perry because he was not available at the time of the hearing before the Pardon and Parole Board. He was a cook for the Ohio River Company and worked on barges in the central United States. He was on duty for thirty days and then off duty for thirty days. Baxter's testimony closed the day's proceedings.

Late in the morning came the witness that was to win the case for us before Judge Perry—June Anne Lang Gross. Her appearance so far as we knew, was a complete surprise to the prosecution. When we brought her to the courthouse we did not bring her directly to the courtroom, but to a small anteroom near Judge Perry's courtroom. There she waited until she stepped to the stand. She told Judge Perry that because of a recent operation, it was difficult for her to sit for long, and therefore requested permission to stand next to the witness chair. She spoke in slow, even tones, pausing to measure and choose each of her words carefully.

The high point of her testimony came after she had been on the stand about forty-five minutes. Standing by the railing next to the witness chair, in her solemn measured tones, she disavowed her testimony given in Carthage seven years before regarding the events of the taxi ride from Canton to St. David on the night of the crime. She told the judge, prosecution, and defense counsel that her testimony then had been false. How did she explain her terrible lie to the authorities? For seven years the tale of her role in the case had been fragmented—known in part to the prosecution and in part to the defense. Not until 1963 did it stand revealed in full.

Malmgren, because of his lengthy interview with June in the middle of March 1956, knew a great deal of her history: the events of the taxicab ride, the brief visit with her brother in St. David, the gin squirts at the tavern, the speedy return to Canton, the ride to Pekin when she abandoned her escort and rode back with another man. What was put on public record for the first time in Judge Perry's courtroom in December 1963 were the details of June's interrogation by the public authorities immediately following the crime. June told Malmgren that while she was at work at Harriet's Lunch on the Sunday following the crime, she heard for the first time that Lloyd was missing with the taxicab. "The minute I heard it I went to the phone and called the police station. I told them at the police station that Lloyd didn't do it. . . ." As one would expect, the police were intensely interested just then in someone who troubled to tell the authorities that Lloyd hadn't done it. As far as I can piece the story together, what followed was something like this. Immediately after June's phone call, the police sent two officers to the restaurant to talk to her. Apparently they brought June to the police station where she was interrogated by Sgt. Robert Harding, whom, in her testimony in 1963, she called Lieutenant. June described "the Lieutenant" as "tall and blond and blue-eyed," a description prosecution and defense alike thereafter applied to him.

June was interviewed several times by the authorities, sometimes at their request, sometimes at hers. She said nothing to the police about a confession on Tuesday afternoon. She came (or was requested to come) to the police station again that day.

According to June, it was then she changed her version of what Lloyd had told her and the change was not voluntary. It was a version into which she was coerced and tricked. Sgt. Harding interrogated her endlessly about her conversation with Lloyd in the cab, asking her to repeat over and over his words. Harding kept asking her whether Lloyd said "he did it."

> By this time I was very confused and crying, and I said, "I guess he did." . . . And from that moment on, I told lies. (This last sentence the Court ordered stricken as testimony.)

At Harding's request, she signed a statement to this effect.

Later June said she told Sgt. Harding that "maybe" Lloyd said he had done it. But she signed the statement without reading it because she trusted Sgt. Harding. Yet the minute she signed the paper she had a guilty feeling "because I knew the word 'maybe' wasn't in there."

June was arrested (why?) and her room searched.

The next morning, Wednesday, Deputy Fuller and Deputy June Schoonover took June to Springfield. There she was given a lie detector test by Jack Lynch. In addition, she wrote out the statement that was read to Lloyd Wednesday afternoon when he was brought to the armory to be confronted by her. According to June, when they came to the crucial question about Lloyd's admission—"I winked at him and he knew it wasn't true and I knew it wasn't true." She felt a compulsion at the time because of the statements that she had signed. "I did not understand the law and I was afraid of imprisonment because of the lies."

Did June ever make attempts to correct her statements? According to her, she made several attempts, all abortive. The first was on Wednesday night with Chief Lindzey. There was another abortive attempt with State's Attorney Ramsey on Thursday and again on Saturday, again on Sunday and again on Monday.

June Lang's recantation of her 1956 testimony came as a shock to the prosecution. We have related her story as a continuous narrative. But actually after her direct examination on the afternoon of December 5, 1963, Roger Hayes asked for a continuance so that the State could prepare cross-examination. Judge Perry continued the trial to December 19, and stipulated that none of the attorneys were to talk to June Lang until the case was resumed.

June's sense of the dramatic was always superb. After she had finished her direct examination and before Judge Perry had put her under a vow of silence, she passed a note to George Leighton:

> Mr. Leighton,
>   I want to make a public apology to Mr. Miller, Jr. in the court room. If this is not possible, will you give me your comment on this at the time Mr. Miller, Jr. comes out of the court room in your presence also.
>
> (signed)
Mrs. June Gross
> P.S. Am I to wait here in this building or what.

Undoubtedly it would have been a marvelous scene, her public apology to Mr. Miller, Jr., in open court. We regretted that it could not be arranged.

The decision of the prosecution to ask for a continuance no doubt was difficult. By doing so, they magnified the significance of her testimony. The alternative was to proceed immediately with cross-examination. But then the prosecution would have no opportunity to analyze the transcript and to prepare a proper line of cross-examination. A third possibility would have been to ask Judge Perry to adjourn court (it was then the middle of the afternoon) until the following morning. That would have given the prosecution the evening to map its cross-examination strategy. If they requested "daily copy" from the court reporter, they would have a complete transcript in their hands not long after court adjourned for the day. Hayes and the other attorneys, however, had spent the whole day in trial. They felt perhaps the few hours' time they would gain working in the evening would not be adequate for them to analyze June's testimony fully.

June was cross-examined the entire day on December 19 and was to return at 9:00 A.M. on December 20. That morning, June was seen in the federal building shortly before 9 but when court was called to order, she was not on hand. We attorneys were alarmed. True, her testimony on direct examination was in the record. But if June disappeared before her cross-examination had been concluded, the prosecution might well ask Judge Perry to strike all of it. In any event, the effect of her testimony would be seriously diminished. Judge Perry asked the attorneys as well as a woman from the Clerk's office to make a search. Shortly before ten o'clock, June, to our joy, appeared in the courtroom. We didn't bother to ask where she had been.

Late that afternoon the prosecution presented its last witness, Jeff Litterly, the state crime lab chemist who had testified in 1956, concluding the trial for the week. Judge Perry told us to come back to court at ten o'clock on Monday morning, December 23.

The day got off to a slow start with little new testimony being put into the record. One fact of minor interest was added. Sheriff Ball admitted that the authorities obtained a job for June Lang at the Lewistown Nursing Home and reimbursed the home for the salary paid to her. The prosecution at last concluded its case.

We had one final witness—James S. Martin. He was on the stand for only about half an hour. His testimony covered only twenty-seven pages of the printed record. But his testimony ultimately was to prove decisive.

A circuitous road brought Martin to the witness stand. Each of the lawyers had, as I have said, his pet project. Mine was the physical evidence. The question I pursued was this: Was there any way in fall 1963 to determine whether Lloyd Miller had ever worn the jockey shorts? If it could be shown that Lloyd had never worn the shorts, then the confession would be demonstrably false in a very important particular. But, how could one tell after a lapse of eight years whether a person had worn a particular garment? Was it possible that residues of body secretions (perspiration, urine, or feces) adhering to the shorts could be identified as Lloyd's or not Lloyd's? After a number of inquiries, I was referred to Dr. Leon N. Sussman, an internationally-known hematologist in New York City. I called him and stated the problem. He said there was a possibility that something could be learned from perspiration embedded in the garment. To make a thorough study of the question, the shorts would have to be sent to him, or if that was not possible, swatches cut from the garment. He required a blood sample from Miller and two ordinary gummed mailing labels, one of which had been licked by Lloyd.

Dr. Sussman explained that the perspiration of some individuals contains the various factors which appear in the blood. That a person has type A blood can in some individuals be determined not only from the blood but also from perspiration and other body secretions. Such individuals are known as "secretors." Not all individuals, however, are secretors. If Lloyd was one, said Dr. Sussman, it might still be possible to type perspiration residues in the shorts (assuming they were Lloyd's) in much the same manner as blood is typed.

It seemed a promising line of inquiry, but the trial was set for December 4, only about a week off. Speed was essential and nothing could be done without court orders at each step of the way.

Judge Perry, on the afternoon of November 27 and with the consent of the State, allowed us to cut out two swatches from the shorts in his presence and to send them to Dr. Sussman by certified mail that same day. One was near the waistband and the other in the crotch, in an area heavily covered with deep, dark stains. On Friday afternoon, Judge Perry entered another order permitting the drawing of the blood samples.

A few days later, I received a phone call from Dr. Sussman. He had received the swatches and the sample of Lloyd's blood and had subjected the blood sample to exhaustive analysis. Lloyd did have type O blood, but Dr. Sussman in a written report submitted a few days later did not stop merely with the determination that the blood was type O. He determined the numerous sub-groups, too, and reported the blood group as group O, MN Rh_1rh Le $^{(a+b+)}$ (nonsecretor).

The licked label disclosed that Lloyd was not a secretor; his blood group did not appear in his saliva or other body fluids. Moreover, reported Dr. Sussman, it was not possible to analyze perspiration that had soaked into the garment because of the presence of a "hemolyzing contaminant" from previous washings—probably saponin from soap or detergent. Thus the hoped for test could not be completed. This was a blow. Had Dr. Sussman been able to identify a blood group—any blood group—from the perspiration in the garment, it would have been strong evidence that the garment did not belong to Lloyd because it would have meant that the garment had been worn by a secretor.

But Dr. Sussman told me something else of enormous significance: He stated *that the dark stains in the swatch from the crotch* did *not* give a *reaction for blood.* This was truly incredible information. The swatch from the crotch was heavily stained. It had never for a moment occurred to me that the stains were not blood stains. I decided to pursue the subject intensively. What were the stains? My efforts were to have momentous consequences.[1] I called an old friend, Charles Ryant, who was a chemical engineer. I explained that I needed someone qualified to undertake laboratory tests to determine precisely the nature of the staining material on the shorts. He would have to be a person of unquestioned scientific competence and someone whose word would be believed by the Court. A few days later Charles called back to report that he had a chemist willing to undertake the task, James S. Martin, a microanalyst and general

1. Dr. Sussman sent a written report dated December 6. After receiving it, I asked Dr. Sussman about the waistband swatch. He said that it, too, did not give a reaction for blood.

manager of Walter C. McCrone and Associates in Chicago. His firm specialized in research in the physical and biological sciences. We took advantage of the two-week lull in the trial between December 5 and December 19 to explore further the question of the shorts. Shortly before Monday, December 16, I appeared before Judge Perry and obtained a court order from him permitting Martin to remove a large number of small individual threads from various portions of the shorts and to take them to his laboratory for analysis. The actual cutting of the threads was done in Judge Perry's chambers that day. Present were Martin; Charles Ryant; Judge Perry's secretary, Mrs. Rosemary Zimmerman; and I. Speed had now become essential because the trial was set to resume on Thursday, the 19th. If valuable evidence resulted from the tests, the scientific examination would have to be concluded rapidly.

Martin appeared as a witness late on the afternoon of December 23. He was the last witness heard in the case. In all, twelve threads were removed from the shorts, selected to obtain at least one sample from each significantly different degree of coloration on the shorts. (The colors ranged from brownish red to reddish brown.) Each area had been marked on the shorts and recorded. The threads themselves were in twelve small vials. Martin described the tests to which he had subjected the threads: each was put under a microscope and moistened to see whether the staining material on the thread dissolved in water. It did not. It did not dissolve in a saline solution. It was left overnight in a saline solution. No disintegration. Blood would have dissolved. Martin found that the staining material was in the form of "particulates," small individual bits adhering to the threads.

As a further test to see whether the stains behaved like blood, Martin took a sample known to be blood—his own—stained a cloth, removed a thread, and put it under the microscope. At 1,200 diameter magnification, the erythorocytes, the blood corpuscle, measured 7.7 microns. Martin showed the judge a Polaroid color slide. He showed also color Polaroid slides taken through the microscope of the twelve threads. In each case the particulates were much smaller in size, only one-half to two microns in size.

The particulates, moreover, unlike blood, exhibited the property of crystals or crystallites. What were these particulates? They exhibited the characteristic properties of—paint. Of the twelve threads, ten appeared to have paint stains; one had no visible particulates adhering; one appeared to have a carbon particulate. Martin found no trace of blood.

Martin, under direct examination, had been careful to stay within the limit of his professional competence and not to lay himself open to a disastrous and destructive cross-examination. He was almost too scientific for the drama implicit in his revelations. He had prepared himself well.

Martin's testimony undoubtedly came as a surprise and perhaps a shock to the prosecution. The cross-examination did not hurt us. Rather it strengthened our case substantially. After some period of questioning, Hayes, who cross-examined, asked to make Martin his witness for a few questions—that is, instead of examining him as an opposing witness, he was allowed by the Court to call him as a witness for the prosecution. By so doing, by implication, Hayes acknowledged Martin's scientific qualifications and trustworthiness as a witness. During this short period, Hayes asked whether, if the blood were on the shorts in 1955, unless the contrary were shown, it would be presumed that blood residues of some sort would be present either in visible or invisible state.

Martin's answer was, "That is correct." It would degenerate into another product, that is, break down to another chemical substance. He added a few words which later found their way into the Supreme Court opinion: "In the literature, blood substances are detectable over prolonged periods. That is, there are records of researches in which substances extracted from Egyptian mummies have been identified as blood." With this answer Hayes returned to cross-examination.

A few minutes later Hayes asked another question helpful to us: "Wouldn't you have been very much surprised if those stains were blood—I mean just looking at them." Hayes evidently hoped for an answer to the effect that it was obvious by looking at the stains that they were *not* blood. But Martin's answer was, "Not without an examination, I wouldn't be prepared to say what they were. I heard the witness Litterly on Friday testify that when presented, they were heavily stained with blood; and before I made my examination, that same statement which had been made on the record was read to me.

I assumed I was dealing, in the first instance, with a pair of shorts which was heavily stained with blood. Within the ordinary meaning, at least, to my mentality, it would appear to a layman, for example, that what I see before me is a garment heavily stained with blood."

Minutes later Hayes did for us what we had been afraid to do for ourselves. He asked Martin "As to this garment here, have you made any tests whatsoever to determine if there is any blood on what is here in my hand?"

This was a crucial question. Martin's testimony had shown that there was no blood on the twelve threads. But might there be blood elsewhere on the garment? That question was left open. We were keenly aware of this issue. Let me go back from the afternoon of December 23 to the preceding Thursday, the 19th. That morning about eight-thirty, Martin came to my office and reported on his studies of the threads. But the question remained whether there was any blood whatever on the garment, perhaps not as visible stains. Clearly we were nearing the end of the trial. Any day could be its last day. It might be difficult to obtain a recess from Judge Perry in order to complete further scientific investigation. We had to hurry. Sometime Thursday afternoon Martin came up with a suggestion: If the shorts could be removed to the McCrone laboratory in Chicago, it would be possible for him to perform a test for blood on the entire garment.

On Friday morning George Leighton presented the matter to Judge Perry. There was some objection from the prosecution, but soon the Judge signed an order permitting the shorts to be removed to the McCrone laboratory and returned to court by the United States Marshal.

As I look back upon the incident it seems to me that we were running greater risks than we realized at the time. The opportunity given to Martin to test the entire garment meant that if he found blood on the garment he would have to report that finding to the court. Any presence of blood would diminish the effect of his other testimony that all the visible stains on the garment were paint. But we were committed to the examination and proceeded.

After we arrived at Martin's laboratory, it took about forty-five minutes to set up the equipment for the test. The room set for examination was a small one, barely large enough for Martin, the Deputy Marshal, Ryant, and me. A chemical called Luminal had to be prepared in a spray bottle. Then the shorts had to be mounted on a board. A clean handkerchief containing dried blood in one corner was prepared for control purposes. The theory of the luminal test is this: One of the constituent elements of blood is hemoglobin. Blood as such decays rapidly once exposed to the air, but hemoglobin remains. When Luminal is sprayed on a garment containing hemoglobin, the areas containing hemoglobin glow brightly or luminesce for several seconds. The other portions of the garment have a noticeably lesser background luminescence.

The decisive moment had come. The lights were extinguished. Martin sprayed all areas of the shorts with the bottle of Luminal. There was a diffused general luminescence from the shorts except over those areas containing visible stains and in those areas there was no luminescence whatever. Next Martin sprayed the handkerchief. There was a similar diffused background luminescence on all areas of the handkerchief, except the area stained with blood, where we saw an intensely bright glow. The spraying operation was repeated two or three times on each garment. Then the lights were turned on, the shorts removed from the board and turned over. Once again the lights were extinguished and the test repeated. The results were the same.

The Luminal test had failed to reveal the presence of hemoglobin and thus had failed to reveal the presence of any blood on the garment.

Elated as we were by the Luminal test, we were concerned about presenting this test on direct examination. The test took Martin out of his direct area of specialization. It was a visual test and not precise—Martin could not say flatly that it ruled out the presence of any hemoglobin on the garment.

Thus, when on cross-examination Hayes asked Martin whether he had made any tests to determine whether there was blood on the shorts, he opened the door to an area we feared to open. Hayes knew that the shorts had been taken to the McCrone lab for the Luminal test and knew that we had not mentioned this test on direct examination. Doubtless he felt Martin would testify that he found blood. But to answer the question, Martin told Hayes and the Court about the Luminal test and tersely described the nature of his examination. Judge Perry was somewhat confused and asked, "Did you find any traces of blood or not?" Martin replied, "There were not; that would be shown by the Luminal test, for whatever that test is worth." Judge Perry repeated the last words "For whatever the test is worth." But Hayes was not content to let the issue rest, but gave Martin an opportunity to explain his last remark: "All I can say is that I used standard methods in searching for areas worthy of further examination. I was not able to find any such areas. All I found was a uniform background luminescence over all parts of the garment, except those covered with the substance I described as paint."

Hayes asked whether that couldn't indicate "a little blood all over." Martin replied, "Well there again, since the luminescence observed —with the exception of that in the areas covered by paint-like substance—was uniform, the only possible conclusion is either there was none, or if there was any, that it must be extremely uniformly distributed throughout the entire area. I would not want to try to choose between those two alternatives."

We are not quite at the end of the paint-on-the-shorts story. On December 13, during the trial intermission, I made my last trip to Judge Perry's chambers to examine documents. This time the prosecution brought in a memorandum from Sergeant Harding, the tall and blond and blue-eyed, to Chief Lindzey, written shortly after the crime. Evidently attached to the memo were various physical exhibits: No. 1 the jockey shorts, No. 8 three pieces of flooring, and No. 9 three empty paint cans. Harding described No. 1 as jockey shorts stained with blood and brown paint. No. 8, the three pieces of flooring, were smeared with *new* brown paint over old brown paint. There were single and wadded hairs in the *new* paint. No. 9 were two cans of brown paint and one can of mahogany stain. Sergeant Harding had a theory.

#1. Jockey shorts—stained with blood and brown paint.

#8. Three pieces of flooring with *new* brown paint smearing on old brown paint—single and wadded hairs embedded in *new* paint.

#9. Three empty paint cans (two brown—one mahogany stain).

Miller ran into flat at 131 Van Buren Court, took off his blood-stained shorts, poured drippings from the three paint cans on to the old floor and smeared his shorts into the paint in an effort to camouflage the blood stains, and in so doing left some hair, blood, and paint as evidence.

#5. Towel, with similar stain on shorts #1. Miller attempted to wipe blood from jacket and trousers with the towel, then smeared towel in the same paint drippings, then threw towel into basement of next door flat, 123 Van Buren Court.

So, the prosecution knew almost from the first that there was paint on the shorts, yet it said not one word to judge, jury, or defense counsel. Just before Martin testified, while Prosecutor Ramsey was being cross-examined, Leighton asked him:

Q. Let me ask you this, Mr. Ramsey. As a matter of fact, Mr. Ramsey, didn't you know at the time of the trial of Lloyd Eldon Miller, Jr., that these spots on this exhibit were not blood?

A. Oh, I knew that all of them were not blood; yes sir.

Leighton asked Ramsey what the nonblood spots were.

A. I am trying to recollect that. They said there was also paint on it, I think. That is from memory only.

Moreover, Ramsey knew about the Police Department memorandum:

Q. Have you ever seen such a document that contains a theory of how this exhibit contains all the paint on it?

A. Yes, sir. I think there was such a report that came from the Canton Police Department, if I am not mistaken. It was not at my request.

Martin's testimony concluded the evidence on both sides. On Wednesday, December 24, when Court resumed, George Leighton and I made final arguments on behalf of Lloyd Miller and Hayes on behalf of the prosecution. When Hayes discussed the shorts, he took the position that it had been obvious to all in 1956 that the stains on the garment were paint.

Immediately after the final arguments Judge Perry began to read a final order. When he said, "the writ of habeas corpus applied for herein by the relator is ordered to issue . . .", we knew that we had won the case. Judge Perry authorized the state to continue to hold Lloyd for an additional four-month period. The 1956 conviction was set aside. Within four months the State could retry Miller. If the State did not do so then the court would enter some further order, presumably an order of release.

After he had finished reading the formal order, Judge Perry added that his decision rested entirely on the fact that June Lang, who was one of the principal witnesses in this case, has taken the stand and sworn here that she committed perjury in 1956.

"I do not hold that she did commit perjury at that time. I am more inclined to believe that she is now committing perjury. However, the fact remains she is a most unreliable and unbelievable witness and the jury did give consideration to her testimony. The jury did not have before it the type of unreliable person that she is." Even though it was about noon on the day before Christmas, Judge Perry did not close shop. Matter of factly he added, "Call your next matter on trial."

For the first time in eight years, the threat of execution had been lifted from Lloyd. As we left the courtroom we walked down the corridor to the large circular corridor of the old federal building. Over us was an enormous rotunda. Six floors below us in the center of the main floor an enormous Christmas tree had been set up and decorated. A chorus of Federal Building employees were around the tree, singing Christmas carols. Their music filled the building. They seemed to me a message of justice and mercy.

10

THE SUPREME
COURT OF
THE UNITED STATES

The next move was up to our opposition. It had three choices. It could appeal to the Court of Appeals in Chicago, the court which had rejected Lloyd's plea in 1962. It could proceed with a new trial within four months as permitted by Judge Perry's order. Or it could allow the four months to elapse and let Judge Perry enter "such further order" as he might see fit, which presumably would be to discharge Lloyd from Stateville Prison and terminate the case. The latter course would almost certainly have been heavily criticized by the press. The realistic choice, then, was an appeal or a new trial.

A new trial would have presented the corps of defense attorneys with serious problems. We were familiar with the facts of the case, but preparations for presenting them in court would have required extra weeks or months. The trial probably would have been in Carthage, 250 miles from our homes and offices, and probably would have been at least as long as the original three-week trial in 1956. At the time it appeared that all the expense of preparation, presentation, and living near the trial site would have fallen on the attorneys: the nominal sum provided to defense counsel in such cases by Illinois law would not have begun to cover out-of-pocket costs, let alone a fee.[1] It would have been rational for us to withdraw and let local

---

1. Some time after 1967, the Illinois Supreme Court awarded reasonable, not nominal, fees and reimbursement to counsel in a lengthy murder trial held far from their homes.

counsel present the previously suppressed facts that we had un-covered.

We might not have had an option, however. A court has power to appoint counsel in a criminal case where the accused is indigent: the Circuit Court of Hancock County might well have appointed us. But we had far too great an emotional investment in the case by then; had the State decided to retry Lloyd, I'm sure we would have found a way to defend him.

But an immediate retrial posed a serious problem for the State as well. A new trial would mean that the 1956 conviction would be set aside once and for all. The prosecution would have the burden of establishing once again Lloyd's guilt beyond a reasonable doubt— and possibly without the services of Ramsey and Hayes, both of whom were in private life. If they were appointed as special prose-cutors, the county would have to pay their fees. If a new state's at-torney handled the case, he would have a huge task of trial prepara-tion.

The appeal permitted the State in habeas corpus cases must have seemed attractive, particularly since Lloyd could be retried if the appeal were lost. On January 17, 1965, the prosecution filed a notice of appeal.

We were unhappy but perhaps a bit relieved. While the appeal put the victory in jeopardy, it at least postponed a retrial. Generally delay favors the defense. Public view of the crime becomes less im-passioned. Key state witnesses may die or become unavailable. Memories dim. Moreover, the tide of decisions in the courts, in particular in the Supreme Court, was favorable to the defense. New rules were being enunciated during each court term strengthening the constitutional rights of persons accused of crime. Perhaps a new rule important to Lloyd's case would be enunciated.

As the appellate phase of the battle began, George Leighton re-ceived the nomination of the Democratic Party for a vacancy on the Circuit Court of Cook County and was elected in November 1964. The task of leading the defense fell to me. I asked two friends, both Chicago lawyers, to join the defense team—Harry Golter and Robert Grossman, who remained to the end.

On February 8, George Pontikes and I saw Lloyd. He seemed well enough and as rational as ever. About two months later, however, I received a disturbing phone call from Daniel N. Kadjan, the assistant attorney general who represented the State before Judge Perry. Dr. Meyer Kruglik, the consulting psychiatrist for the Department of Public Safety, had reported that Lloyd was suffering from hallucinations and delusions. Kadjan wanted authority to transfer Lloyd from Stateville to the psychiatric unit at Menard.

We were not happy about a transfer because it would be much more difficult for us (and his parents) to visit Lloyd. We no longer needed to interview him to gather evidence, but he needed comfort and reassurance, which could be given best by occasional trips to Stateville.

There was another implication to consider. If the State was successful on its appeal, Lloyd would again be under sentence of death. Our only recourse might be a plea of intervening insanity. Although the Governor had once denied clemency, Lloyd's recurrent psychiatric breakdown might be enough to cause a change of mind.

We decided to seek a psychiatrist willing to go to Stateville and serve without fee. After considerable search we were fortunate to secure Dr. Brahm Baittle of Chicago. Moreover, his wife, Margery Baittle, a psychologist, agreed to serve also. In May 1964, the Baittles sent us their reports. Mrs. Baittle's psychological report was disturbing. In her view, Lloyd's thinking was disorganized. She found that his judgment was erratic at times. He could adequately evaluate reality, but equally, he was often tangential and did not always perceive things as others did. He had lapses in memory indicating that his frame of reference for ordinary events was disturbed.

Dr. Baittle's report also left us worried for the future. We had our first real insight to what had been happening to our client in recent months. According to prison records summarized by Dr. Baittle, he had had several emotional upsets after the August 22 stay of execution.

On May 14, a few weeks after the Baittle visit, George Pontikes and Sy Bucholz saw Lloyd and reported that he was in poor shape. We then decided not to oppose the State's request to transfer Lloyd.

The question of Lloyd's transfer to Menard was only one of the numerous problems that faced us during the case. I mention it because it illustrates the subtle interplay of legal and nonlegal considerations which arise so often in litigation: technical legal questions, attorney–client questions, the problem of securing expert witnesses, and questions about the long-range course of the case if there were a bad outcome on the appeal.

Defending the victory in the Court of Appeals was not easy. Our problem was that Judge Perry had ruled for us on the ground that June Lang had lied, either in 1956 at Carthage or in 1963 in Chicago and he would not send Lloyd Miller to his death in part on the testimony of a perjurer.

To us the ruling made good sense. But, the state insisted in its appeal that this ground was not a proper basis for a federal court to set aside a state court conviction in a habeas corpus proceedings. To set aside a state court conviction, the State claimed, it was necessary to show that Lloyd's constitutional rights had been somehow impaired. June having changed her testimony from 1956 to 1963 did not mean that Lloyd had been deprived of his constitutional right to a fair trial. Her variability, the State said, was not the fault of the prosecution.

Our answer was that the prosecution had known in 1956 that June was an unreliable witness. Neither did we neglect the rest of the story. We told the Court about the hair, the paint on the shorts, and much else.

All of the foregoing was set forth in a printed brief of sixty-seven pages. (The Court of Appeals would have waived the requirement for a printed brief but we felt that the importance of the case demanded one if it were at all possible. We explained our plight to David Scheffer of Scheffer Press in Chicago and managed to raise a small sum, but Scheffer Press absorbed $400 of the remaining cost.)

After oral argument, while we were waiting for the decision late in January 1965, the Supreme Court of Illinois granted a new trial to a Herbert Hoffman because at his trial for murder, the State had denied until the close of its case that a pair of men's shorts had been found at the scene of the crime. The Court held that failure to admit earlier the presence of this garment prejudiced the defendant.

The Hoffman case raised another question of strategy. Should we send a memorandum to the Court of Appeals calling its attention to the Hoffman case? We decided not to do so. Attorneys who handle appellate litigation feel it is risky to ask an appellate court's permission to cite an additional case after oral argument unless the new decision is absolutely in point and comes from an impressive court.

There was another reason for reluctance. If we cited the Hoffman decision, there was some risk that the Court of Appeals would say, "Well, now, gentlemen, there has been a change of view in the Supreme Court of Illinois on a very important question at issue in this case. We will therefore set aside Judge Perry's order since Lloyd has a right to relief in the State courts. If the State courts do not grant any relief, then he may return to the federal courts." We just could not face the prospect of another State court hearing and appeal with the probability of then having to start over again in the federal courts.

On February 15, a reporter from the Chicago *Tribune* called. "What are you going to do now that you have lost the Miller case?" One of our secretaries sped over to the court and picked up the opinion, a small printed pamphlet.

Once again Judge Schnackenberg had written the opinion. Methodically, he reviewed each of our points and refuted them. June Lang? The change in her testimony did not authorize a new trial because the prosecution had no reason to doubt her testimony in 1956. Her false statement that she knew Lloyd for two years? "We see no basis for this contention. One may know a person long prior to the time that they meet. 'Knowing' in ordinary language means to be 'acquainted with.' 'To meet' a person indicates a joining together in some social or other activity temporarily or otherwise." The prosecution effort to insulate June? "It is common knowledge that in capital cases, the prosecution customarily takes steps such as these to prevent its principal witnesses from intimidation or harassment."

The hair?

> The damaged condition of the girl's body when found and the necessary handling thereof by whatever doctors or others who examined it afforded an opportunity for the accidental depositing of the surface hair from the hands, arms or head of any of the examiners. How the hair got there is purely a matter of conjecture. . . . The body was subjected to handling by divers doctors and perhaps police officers.

Our other contentions? Rejected. The order granting Lloyd a new trial was reversed. Immediately after reading the opinion I called the Warden to request him to relay the news to Lloyd. I called

Lloyd's parents in Canton. As usual Mrs. Miller answered the phone. She took the news with a certain flat calm, customary with her. (When we relayed bad news to her, she usually reacted with a brief comment like "Well, I'm very sorry to hear that." Then she would tell me a few of the daily happenings, say how her husband was, and thank me for calling. When the news was good, her reaction was scarcely different. She would say, "Well, that's fine," tell me about her husband and the daily happenings, and again thank me for making the phone call. It was as if the terrible anguish of the 1956 trial had drained from her all surface manifestations of emotion. Her true pain and anguish expressed itself in her heavy, prematurely aged and sagging body and tired voice.)

One possibility still remained in the Court of Appeals. We could, and did, ask for a rehearing. In our petition we hit hard on the Court of Appeals' view that the hair found in Janice's vagina could have come from "divers doctors and perhaps police officers." The court spoke as if the hair were found on the body. We stressed that it was found in the body. Our effort was useless. On April 15, the rehearing was denied.

Our sole remaining hope now was the Supreme Court of the United States.

Shortly after, on April 22, I received a letter from Mrs. Miller. She and her husband had had an unhappy and disturbing visit with Lloyd at Menard. Lloyd "seemed depressed and talked a lot about his inventions he had been drawing out."

About a month later the warden at Menard informed us that Lloyd had been transferred that day to Stateville. This news made us shiver. We feared that the prosecution would contend that Lloyd had recovered from his emotional breakdown. Such prospect, together with the recent defeat in the Court of Appeals, gave us a renewed sense of the importance of the application to the Supreme Court. Unless we could obtain Supreme Court review, Lloyd might be executed after all.

Our petition to the Supreme Court was due July 8. Naturally we wanted to devote every possible moment to preparing it, but we had to recognize that the Supreme Court might not take the case for review. What would we do then?

Our plan was to go back to Carthage, to the court where Lloyd had originally been convicted, and to present there all the evidence presented to Judge Perry. We would have preferred not to take any action in Carthage until after the Supreme Court had ruled on our petition. Unfortunately, there was a possibility that on some phases of our claims, first uncovered in July and August 1963, a two-year statute of limitations might apply.

We put together an eleven-page petition for the Carthage court to which we attached a copy of the three bulky volumes of testimony printed for the use of the Court of Appeals. We did not want or expect any action on our petition until after the Supreme Court had passed on our application.

On July 7, one day before the deadline, we filed our application for Supreme Court review, the "petition for certiorari." The Supreme Court was then in recess for the summer and would not reconvene until October, so no decision could be expected until then. Through the generosity of Maurice Rosenfield, we were able to file a printed petition.

Rosenfield gave other tangible help. He and Professor Harry Kalven of the University of Chicago Law School jointly wrote a "friend of the court" brief on behalf of Radio Station WAIT and the Illinois Division of the American Civil Liberties Union. The brief was confined to a single point, that the finding of the hair excluded Lloyd as the perpetrator of the crime. To our application for certiorari the State of Illinois filed a response and we filed a reply. Once again Maurice Rosenfield paid a printer's bill.

Our chances of obtaining review in the Supreme Court were slim. Numerous previous applications on Lloyd's behalf had been filed and denied, although none of them had presented the dramatic facts unearthed only in 1963. The fact that Lloyd's case was to him a matter of life and death was not a factor in the grant or denial of review. In general it is necessary to show that a case presents a legal question of importance.

The statistics were strongly against us. During 1964–65, the court denied review in over 90 percent of the cases. In criminal cases review was denied in about 98 percent. (These figures are somewhat misleading because most of the criminal cases were filed by the prisoners themselves. Many prisoners, desperate for freedom, no doubt filed applications even though their constitutional rights had not been violated or their cases were not otherwise appropriate for review in the High Court.)

We thought that we would not have long to wait for a decision on our application. We followed the court calendar with care, noting sessions days on which a decision could come. The court sessions begin at ten o'clock Washington time, nine o'clock Chicago time. Shortly after the beginning of each session, the Court hands to the Clerk the list of rulings on certiorari applications. The Clerk immediately sends out collect telegrams to the attorneys which are usually received in Chicago about 1:00 P.M. If we had not received a telegram by that time, we no longer expected to hear that day.

Lloyd managed to keep occupied. I received many letters from him on Stateville Prison stationery. In the box marked "relationship of addressee," he would print underneath my name "My chief attorney." In one of the letters to his chief attorney dated October 20, 1965, despite his years of imprisonment and his unsuccessful ventures into matrimony, he asked me to write to a woman in Chicago of about his age. I was to inform her that "I will win my rightful freedom in the near future. I'm a true Minister of God, I have my own Christian plans in 'blueprint' laying out and I intend to build my own Christian organization belief on the outside, probably in a Big Beautiful Valley, somewhere in the Rocky Mts. out West, with my own legal money-making ideas—."

(About this time Lloyd had become exceedingly religious. He informed me in many letters that he had become a "True Minister of God." He regularly concluded his letters, "In Jesus, our King and Savior." He wrote many letters about establishing his Utopian community, referred to in the letter quoted above. It was to be financed by money from the sale of rights to his story. On many occasions he said that he intended to bring his mother and father to the new community so that they could live in decency and comfort, far from Canton. Almost every letter from Lloyd at this time was equally wistful and pathetic.)

By the end of November, Lloyd's enthusiasm for the Chicago woman had diminished. He wrote Harry Golter asking him to help him correspond with another young woman who made her home in the Indiana Women's Institution (Penal) in Indianapolis. Lloyd intended to take legal procedures to help her in the near future after he was released. Later Lloyd inquired from time to time what we could do for her. We replied that we were not members of the Indiana bar and were unable to assist her.

Lloyd, too, was following the Supreme Court. On December 14, he wrote us about a story in the Chicago *Tribune* that the Supreme Court had accepted six cases challenging the validity of confessions. Lloyd added, "It said that the U.S. Court is now taking a vacation for the holidays, until January 17, 1966—so it looks like that my case is among these six cases." Lloyd was wrong: his case was not one of the six.

Christmas of 1965 was with us. Two years had passed since Judge Perry had granted a new trial "within four months" to Lloyd. He still sat in his prison cell in Stateville. His parents waited at home for word from the Supreme Court, upon which so much depended.

Between Christmas and New Year's, 1966 I received a note from Mrs. Miller. As had happened from time to time over the years, someone had come to her with a wild tale, claiming to have evidence helpful to Lloyd or evidence pointing to the real murderer. Mrs. Miller wrote, "A lady a few miles from here talked to us that she was positive and had proof who killed Janice May."

> The fellow's name is ———, he is married and is thirty-five years old and has two or three children and when this happened he worked at ——— at ———. The lady went to talk to us is Mrs. ——— in ———. She wouldn't talk to us until we identified ourselves. She said she was scared this ——— as he was a convict and killer. He was a suspect here ten years ago when they were questioning the men at the police station.

Since Mrs. Miller's caller advanced no facts to connect the man with the murder, and the authorities had already checked him out, we did not pursue the matter.

The new year came. The Supreme Court reconvened on January 17, 1966, and still there was no word on our certiorari application.

Beginning about March, Lloyd entered an inventing phase and began to have trouble with the authorities about his drawing and patent claims. During the following months we heard a great deal about Lloyd's inventions and his difficulties with the authorities.

The Supreme Court term was nearing its close and still we had not heard.

On Saturday, June 18, 1966, I left Chicago to attend the Biannual Convention of the American Civil Liberties Union at Stony Brook, Long Island. The following Monday, June 20, was to be the last day of the term. All of us felt confident that Monday, June 20, would be the day of decision. A few minutes after 10:00 A.M. I left the ACLU Conference to call the Clerk of the Supreme Court. I didn't have to make a note of the case number. I knew it by heart: "Miscellaneous 387." The Clerk told me that the list was not down yet from the Court. I called back several times during the morning. About noon I received joyful news. "Yes," the Clerk said, "No. 387 Misc. Certiorari has been granted." It was a moment that will live in my memory forever.

I called Stateville at once and left word for the authorities to tell Lloyd and then called my office in Chicago, told them the news, and asked them to proceed according to plan. Months before a list had been prepared of persons to be notified immediately upon hearing from the Supreme Court. There were Lloyd's parents, all of the attorneys who were working on the case, the secretaries who had devoted so much of their time to the matter, our experts like James Martin, Dr. and Mrs. Baittle, and many others. A few hours later, we received a telegram timestamped at Chicago at 1:24 P.M. and sent collect: PETITION FOR CERTIORARI LLOYD MILLER V. PATE GRANTED TODAY. ADVISE ASSOCIATES. JOHN F. DAVIS CLERK.

Summer 1966 should have been happy and peaceful. The grant of certiorari meant that we had before us the task of writing two more briefs, the principal brief "on the merits," and a reply brief. There would be ample time to complete this task.

But the joy of the certiorari grant, the pleasurable anticipation of a vacation trip and the Supreme Court argument, dissolved in a storm of confusion. Within seventeen days after the grant of certiorari our client discharged all his attorneys and began a hunt for new lawyers. Years have passed and yet, as I write, I can still recall vividly the pain of that time. How could Lloyd discharge the team of attorneys who had succeeded in reaching the Supreme Court, where many before had tried and failed? The answer lay both in Lloyd's complex personality and to some extent in our own obtuseness. We were deeply concerned with Lloyd Eldon Miller, the case, and we had overlooked Lloyd Eldon Miller, the man.

The first rumblings of trouble came the very day the Court granted certiorari. Lloyd wrote to Harry Golter protesting a ruling of the Supreme Court handed down on June 20, that certain new rules regarding confessions would apply only to trials begun after June 13, 1966.

We, the lawyers, felt that the evidence of the hair and the "bloody" shorts was so overwhelming that we did not need to rely upon a claim that a confession had been coerced from Lloyd. It didn't matter to us whether the confession rules were retroactive. (Subsequently in another connection we became very much interested in this question.)

The next day the "chief attorney" was summoned by his client for a visit, but I wrote that the attorneys had already held a meeting to discuss the brief. I concluded, "It is difficult to get out to Stateville, but one of us will make it when we can." This casual fobbing off of Lloyd's request for a meeting, in retrospect, was a serious error. On June 29 came another letter from Lloyd. Its tone was demanding, not to say imperious:

> You attorneys have volunteered to represent me in the courts & its you duty to help me restor & protect my rights by legal procedures—In helping me to win my rightful freedom in the near future, as my attorneys—my Faith is based on Facts, which Im Innocent & my constitutional rights is being violated—as my attorneys in representing me, I expect a reversal in the U.S. Supreme Court & be out, at leased on bond, before this Christmas.

So now Lloyd expected us to get him out on bond before Christmas! Nor was that all. Apparently Lloyd felt that his writing to the authorities had been impeded by the prison officials. He wanted us to secure him freedom to write to public officials.

I replied with a note that the matter was in the Supreme Court and letters to senators and other public officials would not help the case. This was a serious error. On July 4 came another long epistle from the client, again complaining about interference with his mail and saying, "If still need be, I will ask you attorneys to seek a court order pertaining to interference with my mail privileges." On July 5 came another request to get him out on bond.

On July 8, the very day Lloyd received my four-line letter of the day before, he responded. In the box where I had customarily been addressed as the "Chief Attorney," the legend read simply, "Legal—Business—My Case." The letter was as follows:

> My Dear Mr. Lassers:
>   I received your recent letter & I appreciate you notifying me of your indifference. So, I, ask you to withdraw from my case. . . . I understand that we will still be friends & be successful in the years to come. In Jesus's name, our King and Saviour. Thanks—
>
>   Lloyd E. Miller, Jr.
>   39426

So, after over three years' work on the case, when we stood on the very brink of success, I was to lose the attorneyship. It was little consolation to know that he and I would still be friends and be successful in the years to come.

On Monday, July 11, the senior Millers saw their son at Stateville. The meeting was brief and unpleasant. Once again we asked the assistance of Dr. Baittle, requesting that he interview Lloyd at the prison to see if he was suffering from another serious emotional disturbance.

We slowly formulated a plan. Our status, as we saw it, was this: I had been discharged but Harry Golter, Ted Conger, George Pontikes, Arthur Greenberg, and Robert Grossman had not. They were therefore qualified to act for Lloyd. The status of Maurice Rosenfield, Harry Kalven, and Bob Ming was not affected because they were representing not Lloyd but Radio Station WAIT and the American Civil Liberties Union.

On Friday, July 22, Harry Golter and I went to Stateville to see Lloyd. When we arrived at the prison, Warden Pate called us to his office and told us of the difficulties he was having with Lloyd. He described Lloyd's insistence upon sending all kinds of documents to

public officials about his case, his inventions, and the like. We saw
Lloyd for about an hour and a half. We tried to talk to him about his
case, but he seemed relatively uninterested in the Supreme Court
and much more concerned about the Warden's holding up his mail
and about his inventions. Miller was primarily concerned with, and
insisted that we assist him, with his struggles with the Warden over
the mail. In the end he told us that unless we were willing to represent him on the mail question and to take legal action in court on
this subject, he did not wish us to represent him any further in the
Supreme Court.

On July 28, Bob Ming and Maury Rosenfield tried to visit Lloyd,
having previously informed him of their intention to come to Stateville. Lloyd refused to see them.

On July 30 Dr. and Mrs. Brahm Baittle went to the prison to see
Lloyd. That interview, too, was unpleasant. Dr. Baittle reported
that Miller was having another emotional episode. Our wait-and-see
strategy received a rude upset early in August. On August 5 came a
short letter from John F. Davis, Clerk of the Supreme Court, saying
that Lloyd had asked for the appointment of new counsel. The clerk
stated that when the court reconvened in October, he would present
the request to the court.

The question now arose, what were our obligations to the client
and to the court? Should we or should we not report to the court Dr.
Baittle's findings? After much deliberation we decided to say nothing about Lloyd's mental status, but simply to write the Court, in
response to Lloyd's letter, that we had represented Lloyd to that
time and that we intended to abide by whatever action the Court
chose to take. The Court, after reading Lloyd's letter, might appoint
other counsel or might conclude from the tone of the letter that his
reasons for changing counsel were frivolous and designate us as the
attorneys to move ahead. There were several reasons for favoring
this approach, even though it would have been unthinkable in the
trial court stage and perhaps wholly inappropriate if we were still
before Judge Perry where testimony was being taken. Lloyd had a
right to be present during each session in court and had a right to
testify. If we thought that Lloyd was mentally in no condition to
testify, or not able to exercise all of his faculties to listen to the testimony for and against him and confer responsibly with his lawyers,

we would have had an obligation to bring these matters to the attention of the Judge.

But in the Supreme Court, indeed in all of the reviewing courts, the cases are decided strictly on the basis of the record compiled in the court below. Briefs are written entirely by the attorneys. Lloyd did not even have a right to be present in the reviewing courts during the argument of his appeal. Our obligation to call to the court's attention Lloyd's mental status was thus diminished. True, copies of the briefs that we wrote and filed without consultation with Lloyd were always sent him. He could read them in his cell and, as long as his mind was clear, he could write us if we had misstated a fact or give us his views on the legal argument. If his mind was impaired, he was unable to do these things.

But there were other aspects of the matter: the Supreme Court might be concerned about hearing a case involving a man's life while the man's mental abilities were impaired.

It might send the case back to Judge Perry instructing him to conduct a hearing on Lloyd's mental health and to take appropriate action, or to hold a hearing and report to the Supreme Court. It might simply hold the case on its docket until Lloyd recovered. If it took any of these courses, disposition of the case would be delayed. In the meantime, there might be unfavorable developments, such as a shift in the membership of the court, or a change in the trend of decisions.

We had to consider another phase of the problem, too. Suppose that the Court granted Lloyd a new trial and the state then contended that Lloyd was not able to cooperate with his counsel and therefore was not able to stand trial again. The state might not have sufficient evidence to convict Lloyd if he were retried, but under the laws of the State of Illinois, a man under indictment for a felony who is not able to stand trial because he is not able to cooperate with counsel may be held in a mental hospital. Thus the practical effect of raising the issue of Lloyd's mental condition might be to change Lloyd's place of confinement from one institution to another.

Faced with these problems we did what lawyers always do. We searched the reported decisions to see what the courts had ruled in similar situations in the past. Hours were spent on this effort, but we were unable to find even a discussion of these questions by a court. Since no satisfactory course of action appeared we decided for the time being to do nothing.

Like Jonah's gourd, the crisis withered as rapidly as it had sprung up. On my return to Chicago from a vacation about the middle of September, I found a letter from our client, dated August 30. Once again the box for "Relationship of addressee" was filled in, "My chief attorney." Lloyd wrote:

> My Dear Attorney Mr. Lassers:
> I reconsidered and requesting you attorneys remain on and proceed on with my case. BE SURE TO VISIT ME IN A FEW DAYS so you attorneys can have a clear understanding of me.

Lloyd mentioned his hope to be free and home before this coming Christmas—if not, anyway out on bailable bond.

On October 1, Harry Golter and I visited Lloyd. He was a changed man, much less aggressive, much more willing to listen to us and much less impatient. He wanted us to file libel suits on his behalf against various publications which had run stories about his case. Lloyd was concerned also about a letter he had written to the *National Geographic Magazine* to inquire about certain islands in the Far East. He wanted to purchase an island after his release for his colony.

With the distractions out of the way, we were able to turn our attention to our brief. The printing of the record was completed and filed in the Supreme Court on October 19.[1] This set the due date of our brief at November 18. When Christmas 1966 came, our brief and the State's brief were on file. All that remained was a short reply by us. It had been three years since Judge Perry had granted a new trial. The final moment was at hand. Just before the close of the year I received word from the Clerk to be in Washington on Wednesday, January 11. We still had to write a reply brief and to plan the oral argument. (Lloyd tried to give us another chore. He urgently needed information about land for sale in Australia and information about Campbell Island, forty-four square miles, in the Central Pa-

1. A separate Supreme Court fund pays for printing the record and briefs in indigent cases. In Lloyd's case these charges totaled $3,183.33. There is no provision for paying for any other expenses, such as trial expenses of attorneys, unless the attorneys are appointed by the Supreme Court.

cific Ocean, part of New Zealand. A few days later, on December 18, I was requested to write a letter to the Prime Minister of Australia informing him that Lloyd would be needing at least several thousand acres—priced right or under $25.00 per acre.)

Saturday, December 31, Harry Golter and I had an uneventful interview with Lloyd at Stateville. We had promised him that we would see him before leaving for Washington. I prepared for oral argument with the fervor and intensity of a Ph.D. candidate preparing for his oral examinations. There are a number of points of similarity. The course work in the form of the lower court proceedings had been completed. The dissertation in the form of the briefs had been filed with the court. What remained were the orals, in the form of argument to the court.

The Miller case was called for argument at two-ten Wednesday afternoon, only twenty minutes before adjournment. I spent the opening minutes outlining the history of the case and then launched into what I regarded as the strongest and the most dramatic ground for reversal, that is, the suppression of the evidence regarding the hair.

Wednesday evening was spent at the home of an old friend and law school classmate, Mozart G. Ratner, and his wife, Shirley. Also invited was another old friend and law school classmate, Robert Hummell. Both men had had extensive appellate experience and both had had experience before the Supreme Court. After dinner, I solicited their advice as to the remainder of the argument to be given the next day. Of the forty-five minutes allotted me, twenty-five minutes remained, of which five minutes had to be saved for rebuttal. So far, I had spoken only about the hair, and hadn't mentioned the painted shorts, Mrs. Baxter, June Lang, etc. I gave Ratner and Hummell a quick survey of the case and asked particularly how to handle the matter of the shorts. Bob Hummell suggested, "Don't hold up the shorts for the justices to see. Hold the shorts in your hand. Perhaps one of the justices will oblige you and ask you to hold them up." It turned out to be priceless advice. The next morning, a few minutes after ten o'clock, the argument resumed. As I spoke, I had the shorts bunched up in my right hand and held my hand on the counsel table. After a few minutes, Chief Justice Warren said to me, "Repulsive as it may be, would you open those shorts up?" There in the majestic setting of the Supreme Court of the United States I opened the shorts and held them up in both hands, gripped at the waistband, as if to pin them on a clothesline—all nine justices saw a small pair of men's jockey shorts heavily stained. For me it was an intense moment, the incredible contrast between the solemnity and magnificence of the setting and the sad and faded and wretched garment I was displaying.

The Chief Justice asked, "Is everything we can see now paint?" My reply was that the examination showed paint but no blood and stressed that the prosecution knew all along that the stains were paint.

On Wednesday afternoon the court had showed interest in the case, but the case really came alive to the court on Thursday morning. Apparently the short argument on Wednesday afternoon had aroused their interest and Wednesday evening they had read over the briefs. By Thursday morning they were clearly familiar with every phase of the case.

After finishing with the shorts, there was very little time left. I told as quickly as possible the story of Alice Baxter. Very summarily, I mentioned the tale of June Lang and some of the other high points of the brief. I did not cite a single legal decision.

Maurice Rosenfield hammered home once again the story of the hair. He began his argument by telling the court of a "ghost" that stalks the legal system, the possibility of an innocent man being executed.

Richard Michael's one-hour argument for the State was an hour of cross-examination. He was scarcely allowed to make a systematic, connected argument. He was hammered with questions throughout. For example, Justice Brennan asked, "Don't you suppose the trial would have been affected by the fact that the hair did not match his?" According to Charles Nicodemus of the Washington Bureau of the Chicago *Daily News,* when the justices weren't peppering Assistant Attorney General Michael with critical questions, most of them sat back shaking their heads in apparent wonder or shaking the legal briefs during whispered conversations on the bench.

> Justice William O. Douglas, the Court's leading advocate of the rights of defendants, did not even bother to ask

questions. He just listened to the arguments with raised eyebrows and could not contain an incredulous smile as Michael sought to explain what had been some of the more controversial maneuvers of Miller's prosecutors.

After the extensive merciless grilling given Michael, I felt that any reply on my part would be anticlimactic. I arose and told the Chief Justice that unless the court had questions, I felt that the matter had been explored in full and would say nothing further. Ratner, who had come to the morning session for the remainder of the oral argument, invited all of us for lunch. We had a slow, leisurely lunch in a downtown Washington club. All of us were euphoric. We had expected a favorable reception from the court but nothing so overwhelmingly sympathetic.

We did not have long to wait for the decision of the Court. About midmorning on Monday, February 13, I received a phone call from an obviously elated Maury Rosenfield. We had won the case. The news had come over the wire service and had been picked up by WAIT-Radio. The station had quickly phoned him and he had called us. He had none of the details. He knew only that the decision was unanimous and that it had been written by Justice Potter Stewart.

A moment later I asked my secretary, Pam Spokes, to put in a call to Mr. and Mrs. Miller in Canton. She reported that there was no answer. I asked her to call Stateville Prison. A few moments later, Pam reported on the office intercom, "There's no answer." I must say that I was prepared for almost any development in the Miller case but to be told that there was no answer at the state prison. Surely the institution was not closed down for lunch. Surely they hadn't taken the day off. Surely Governor Kerner had not proclaimed a general amnesty.

Shortly after we learned why neither call was completed. Monday was wash day in the Miller household and Mr. and Mrs. Miller were in the backyard hanging out clothes. When we did reach them, Mrs. Miller told me that she had already heard the news on the radio. As for the prison, Sunday, February 12, was Lincoln's birthday. The legal holiday was being celebrated on Monday, February 13, and the ordinary switchboard facilities were not operating. After several tries we reached a prison official who promised to deliver the news to Lloyd. As it turned out, he, too, heard the news almost as soon as we did. Some time later he told us that a prisoner in a nearby cell heard about the Supreme Court decision on his radio. He immediately called over to Lloyd to tell him the good news. In the following day's mail we received the full text of the decision. It set aside the conviction because of the concealment of the paint on the shorts. After stating the facts, the court said:

> The record of the petitioner's trial reflects the prosecution's consistent and repeated misrepresentation that People's Exhibit 3 was, indeed, "a garment heavily stained with blood." The prosecution's whole theory with respect to the exhibit depended upon that misrepresentation. For the theory was that the victim's assailant had discarded the shorts *because* they were stained with blood. A pair of paint-stained shorts, found in an abandoned building a mile away from the scene of the crime, was virtually valueless as evidence against the petitioner. The prosecution deliberately misrepresented the truth.
>
> More than 30 years ago this Court held that the Fourteenth Amendment cannot tolerate a state criminal conviction obtained by the knowing use of false evidence. *Mooney* v. *Holohan,* 294 U.S. 103. There has been no deviation from that established principle. *Napue* v. *Illinois,* 360 U.S. 264; *Pyle* v. *Kansas,* 317 U.S. 213; cf. *Alcorta* v. *Texas,* 355 U.S. 28. There can be no retreat from that principle here.

We had won an overwhelming victory.

But one satisfaction was denied us. We had won the case for Lloyd, but the decision would not be a landmark in the law. It was not like *Escobedo* v. *Illinois* and *Miranda* v. *Arizona,* the great 1964 and 1966 cases which had broken important new ground respecting confessions. It was a decision tied to the particular facts of the case which did little more than restate principles already enunciated by the Supreme Court. It was my secret hope that the Supreme Court would use the Miller case as a vehicle to declare that, as a constitutional matter, the defense has a right to examine the physical evidence in the hands of the prosecution. The court might have used the case to denounce the practice of trickery to obtain a confession, using the false statement to Lloyd about the hair and the false statements to him that his parents did not wish to see him as a basis for discussion of this issue. The court might have used June Lang's role as an occasion to discuss the duties of the prosecution when it learns of the emotional instability of a prime witness. It might have considered the propriety of discouraging witnesses from talking to defense counsel. But it did none of these things.

Monday evening the Peoria *Journal Star* ("Serving the best informed readers in Central Illinois for 111 Years") headlined the story on its front page, "High Court Overturns Miller's Conviction in Canton Slaying." It was a lengthy story quoting liberally from the opinion of the Supreme Court. Next to it was an interview: "Attorney Ramsey Denies Facts Falsified." Ramsey was quoted as admitting that the prosecution did not reveal in the trial court that some of the stains on the shorts were paint. "I didn't think we had a duty to show that there was also paint on them," Ramsey said. "Perhaps there was a little negligence, but the old theory was that the defense attorney had some obligations and the fact is they (defense attorneys) didn't go into it."

The decision was favorably regarded in the Chicago papers. *Time* magazine, in its issue of February 24, 1967, summarized the case. Underneath Lloyd's picture was the caption, "The stain was on the state." The Canton *Daily Ledger* on Wednesday, February 15, summarized the holding of court tersely: "When the prosecution waved the shorts before the jury and neglected to reveal that at least part of the stain was caused by paint, it was playing dirty pool in the opinion of the U.S. Supreme Court."

Illinois Attorney General William Clark decided not to seek a rehearing. Accordingly, twenty-five days later the formal order, or "mandate," of the Supreme Court was issued sending the case back to Judge Perry "for further proceedings in conformity with the opinion" of the High Court. Once again Lloyd's attorneys met to plan strategy.

The judgment of the Supreme Court did not free Lloyd from prison. It merely confirmed Judge Perry's 1963 decision setting aside his conviction. After careful assessment of our situation, we decided that the next move would be an application to Judge Perry asking for Lloyd's release and asking also for a court order barring any further legal proceedings against him in the state courts growing out of the death of Janice May. We knew that in the ordinary case such an application would stand no chance of success. A habeas corpus petition in the federal courts ordinarily simply determines the validity of a state court conviction. If the state court conviction is void, then ordinarily the prisoner is entitled to no more than a new trial. In our view, however, it would have been manifestly unjust to hold Lloyd for a new trial after he had been confined for eleven years and suffered all he had suffered. On March 10, we served a notice on the Attorney General of Illinois that ten days later, on Monday, March 20, we would present a petition to Judge Perry asking for Lloyd's immediate release and for a court order barring any further legal proceedings against him.

Suddenly a new crisis arose, destined to cause us anguish, and to prolong the final disposition of the Miller case by years. At the general election in November 1964, Bill Malmgren had been elected State's Attorney of Fulton County, a position held by his old adversary, Ramsey, in 1956. Having represented Lloyd, he was disqualified from acting in any capacity as State's Attorney in Lloyd's case. He adhered rigidly to this requirement. Thus, immediately after the decision of the Supreme Court, one of the newspapers asked him to comment. He said, "Under the circumstances, I must maintain a vociferous silence."

Some time early in the week of March 13, I received a disquieting phone call from Art Greenberg in Peoria. Judge Albert Scott (who had replaced Judge Bardens) was going to appoint Roger Hayes as special attorney in place of Malmgren! Such an appointment, we felt, would mean trouble and I felt it necessary to oppose it strongly. Judge Scott set the matter for hearing at Carthage on Friday, March 17.

It was also my first visit to Carthage. For the first time I saw the old county courthouse and went up to the large, old-fashioned courtroom on the third floor. Shortly before the court opened its session, Roger Hayes came in and took a seat in the jury box. It was obvious that Judge Scott had decided to appoint him, that Hayes had been requested to serve and had indicated his willingness to accept the appointment, and that our argument opposing his appointment would be futile. For me it was an unpleasant task. I felt very strongly that Hayes ought not to be appointed. I told the court that in our opinion both Ramsey and Hayes were responsible for numerous gross violations of the constitutional rights of Lloyd at the original trial. Both Ramsey and Hayes had consistently and vigorously opposed any relief for Lloyd after the original trial. They had opposed clemency before the parole board, even though Hayes was in private practice and had no official position. Hayes had appeared again in the District Court before Judge Perry, opposing habeas corpus relief. I argued that just as a defendant is entitled to an impartial judge, so he is entitled to a fair and impartial prosecution. Indeed, now the first duty of the prosecutor would be to decide whether a new prosecution should be undertaken. Because of the personal involvement of both Ramsey and Hayes, I felt it was most inappropriate to appoint either one of them. It was awkward and unpleasant to say these things with Mr. Hayes sitting in the courtroom. After hearing me out, Judge Scott ruled immediately. He said that he was not too impressed with the argument against Hayes. That very day the judge signed an order appointing Hayes as "special attorney for the State of Illinois for the purpose of representing the People before Judge Perry."

March 20 was a Monday.

Because of the nature of our motion, I anticipated that the state would request several weeks to file briefs and would also ask for oral argument. Thus a decision on our request to release Lloyd and bar a retrial probably was some months off. Not so. There were to be no briefs and no argument at a later date. After the call of one or two cases, the clerk called, "No, 63 C 1496, Lloyd Eldon Miller against Frank J. Pate, Warden." We had sent our petition to the Judge several days in advance and thus he had had an opportunity to familiarize himself with it thoroughly. I said that we were prepared to proceed. Judge Perry responded that he thought the State would want to file an answer and be heard later. Dick Michael told the Judge that the State would not object to Lloyd's immediate release and an order barring a retrial! "Ordinarily," he said, "this is a matter that would lie within the discretion of the State authorities, but," said Michael, "this case, however, does present many unusual factors . . . because of the unusual nature of this case. If Your Honor does feel that such an order is within his jurisdiction and is just, we would not oppose its entry."

Thus the State would not oppose any order Judge Perry thought proper. Hayes, also present, sought delay, to file papers opposing Lloyd's release and a retrial bar. There followed about thirty minutes of colloquy. In the end Judge Perry announced his ruling. He said,

> I am convinced that this defendant should be released forthwith, and that the State—certainly, they did not prosecute him within the time that I indicated, within four months as the law requires. He was not prosecuted within that time. There was not anything to prevent them from doing it and I think that under all of the circumstances, that this is the type of order that should be ordered.

We stepped away from the bench about 11:00 A.M. like men in a dream. Lloyd was to be freed immediately! But there was no time for reflection. Someone, I think it was Ted Conger, called the prison to inform Warden Pate that Judge Perry was releasing Lloyd that very day. Lloyd would have to be prepared for discharge. We lawyers had work to do. I called my office immediately to ask our secretaries, Mia Sumega, Pam Spokes, and Jackie Hozian to stay through the lunch hour to help us with the necessary papers. We had three crucial documents to prepare. One was the formal order of release. This was a terse document and did not present a problem. But the other two documents were important and complex. Federal court rules require that whenever a case is finally disposed of, the court enter "findings of fact" and "conclusions of law." These two documents are supposed to summarize the essential facts relied upon by the court and to state briefly the legal conclusions. Together they indicate the basis for the court's decision. Since we were the prevailing party, it was our duty to prepare these documents. Naturally they would be reviewed carefully by Judge Perry before he signed them because they were his documents and not ours. Because of Hayes' presence in the courtroom that morning, we were afraid that Hayes planned to take an appeal. What went into those findings and conclusions of law could have serious repercussions, for better or for worse, when the case reached the Court of Appeals. Usually when a party prevails and is asked to prepare a draft of the findings and the conclusions, he has weeks, or at least days, to perform this task and to consider carefully the implications of what he is doing. We had three hours. Moreover, we attorneys had not yet given the matter any consideration because none of us had anticipated that a final order would would be entered that very day. All that lunch hour Ted Conger, Harry Golter, Bob Ming, Maury Rosenfield, and I spent at my office drafting and redrafting the findings and conclusions. Shortly before two o'clock we had completed our task and were back in Judge Perry's courtroom. There was a brief colloquy between Judge Perry and the lawyers. With some modifications, Judge Perry accepted the findings of fact and conclusions of law and signed the order. He also signed a duplicate copy of the order which he handed to the clerk for certification, as the original copy would remain permanently in the court files. The certified copy was to be delivered to Warden Pate and would serve as the Warden's authority for releasing Lloyd from custody.

Warden Pate had told us that it would take a while to process Lloyd for release. Judge Perry, at Warden Pate's request, asked the United States Marshal personally to deliver the order of release to the Warden. Harry Golter and I went to Stateville in one car, Maury Rosenfield, Bob Ming and Lloyd's parents in another car. We arrived at the prison gates about three-thirty. An enormous crowd of newsmen, photographers and cameramen had assembled in a small anteroom to the prison just outside the gates. We had to push our way through. After going through the customary procedures to be admitted to the prison, all of us were shown to the Warden's office. Some time later Lloyd stepped through the two steel doors controlled by the interlock which marked his first step on the road to freedom. These were the two doors through which we had passed so often on our way to visit Lloyd in the small room just inside the inner door.

Lloyd was dressed in a dark, prison-made suit, white shirt, tie, civilian shoes. There was a peculiar intenseness about him. I did not sense a feeling of joy or elation, but rather a sense of determination to put the prison past him as rapidly as he could. It was as though, having spent eleven years behind bars, another eleven minutes or eleven seconds was intolerable.

Once Lloyd came through the outer steel door, one of the prison officers asked him to step over to a desk to be given his discharge money. Lloyd had $27.63 in his trust fund at the prison commissary. He was entitled to transportation from Stateville back to Hancock County, the county where he was convicted. That came to $6.25. In addition, the State gives to each discharged prisoner a gratuity of $25. The entire sum came to $58.88, with which Lloyd had to find his way in the world.

Lloyd wanted to take with him all his drawings for his inventions and his books. They were piled into a wheelbarrow. Lloyd grasped the handles of the wheelbarrow and trundled it to a small elevator nearby. We walked down the main staircase and met Lloyd at the bottom. All of us walked the short stretch separating the prison itself from the reception building where Lloyd's parents and the press were waiting. As Lloyd stepped into the reception building, his parents greeted him. The photographers crowded around as his mother embraced and kissed him. There was a quick on-the-spot television interview. Bernadine Martin of the *Journal Star* was there, ready to give her readers a moving account of Lloyd's first moments of freedom since November 26, 1955. Eleven years, three months and twenty-four days had elapsed.

The Miller case did not end at that moment. The subsequent developments, not all fortunate, are part of the tale. What happened to Lloyd after his release? What were the relations with his family? What, if anything, happened to Hayes and Ramsey? What was the reaction of the downstate press? Only when we have dealt with each of these facets of the story will we be able to understand fully the Miller case.

11

AFTERMATH

Maury Rosenfield invited Lloyd and his family to spend a few days at Executive House, a hotel in Chicago's Loop. Monday night was festive. A reporter for The Chicago *Daily News* reported that at the party Mrs. Miller "sat tired, slumped in a chair in a brown and white print dress" while Mr. Miller stood nearby puffing a pipe. " 'We're thankful that it's almost all over,' said the older Miller, a retired factory worker. 'It has been quite an ordeal, and cost us a lot of money, but it was worth it.' " The celebration may have been subdued, but it was peaceful and it was a celebration. That party was the last happy Miller family reunion.

The next evening, Tuesday, Lloyd, his parents, his sister Margaret, and Margaret's husband Don had dinner together at the Executive House at Maury's invitation. At the close of the dinner Lloyd argued with his mother over the size of the tip—a tip which Maury was paying. There was a fierce exchange of words; Lloyd told his parents to leave the hotel immediately; he went to the desk and checked them out. Mr. and Mrs. Miller, crushed, left that evening for Canton. Margaret and Don remained. Maury called me about ten o'clock that evening to discuss the matter. We knew that the incident was a shattering experience for Mr. and Mrs. Miller and the Isaaks but we could do nothing for them. Indeed, we had to be concerned for Lloyd: it would be very bad publicity for him if he were so unruly that the police were called. I consulted Dr. Brahm Baittle, who had examined him in prison, and there was a flurry of calls between Dr. Baittle and Margaret. But before a plan of action could be made, Lloyd was found to have gone to his room and gone to sleep.

Early Wednesday morning Jean Erkes, whom one of us had

called, had an excellent suggestion: to ask the assistance of James Jones, an Episcopal priest in Chicago who formerly had been head of St. Leonard's House. (St. Leonard's is the leading Chicago institution for newly discharged prisoners. It provides a place to stay and a place to eat while men reorient to outside life.) Father Jones is warm and outgoing and has had great experience with newly released prisoners. Jean called Father Jones and made arrangements for him to see Lloyd in the afternoon. Wednesday morning Dr. Baittle went over to Executive House. Lloyd was quite hostile. At first he refused to see Dr. Baittle at all but later did talk to him briefly. That noon George Pontikes, Bob Ming, and I met for lunch. There was an air of futility, perhaps even of unreality, about our discussion. None of us had a firm relationship with Lloyd. None of us could speak to Lloyd with a realistic hope that his words would be heeded. Thus the customary channel of communication between lawyer and client, the channel that we lawyers are accustomed to use and usually use effectively with obstreperous clients, was closed to us. Meanwhile events moved swiftly.

Wednesday afternoon Lloyd began vigorous efforts to sell his life story. He put in calls to both The Chicago *Daily News* and the Chicago *Tribune*. At that moment his case was red hot and very shortly he was waited upon by representatives from both newspapers. Father Jones saw Lloyd sometime that afternoon: somehow or other Jean Erkes arranged it so that Lloyd himself asked to see Father Jones. The priest called me later with a report: Lloyd was off-beat—quite off-beat, but then, there were a lot of people at St. Leonard's House who were quite off-beat and who somehow made the grade. Father Jones thought that Lloyd should just be left alone to make his own way in life.

About the same time Lloyd himself called me. He asked if there were any new developments in his case and specifically whether Hayes had filed a notice of appeal. I told him that I had checked at the District Court that morning and that so far as I knew no notice of appeal had been filed. (We were concerned because the *Chicago Daily Law Bulletin* on Tuesday carried an erroneous story that Hayes had already filed a notice of appeal.) Then Lloyd got down to business. In February, 1964, he and the attorneys had entered into an agreement relating to the story rights. Nevertheless, Lloyd now offered to sell me the rights to his story, either for a lump sum or a monthly payment. He mentioned the sum of $600 per month. I told Lloyd that I was not going to buy the story rights and reminded him of the previous agreement.

During these first several days after Lloyd's release I saw him only once or twice, even though I was devoting almost full time to his affairs. However, I saw many of the people who were in contact with him. During this period he had an extraordinary capacity to create intense apprehension and anxiety in everyone with whom he dealt. Personally, he seemed no more upset or disturbed than he had in Stateville, but somehow he radiated an atmosphere of tumult and worry. An illustration: About ten o'clock Wednesday evening I received a call from a Chicago *Daily News* man. His voice was edgy. He told me that the *Daily News* had been negotiating with Lloyd all day. They felt that they had come to an agreement, but then at the last minute Lloyd had raised the price to an astronomical sum.

Thursday was Margaret's turn to feel the heat of her brother's displeasure. She was undecided whether to stay in Chicago or return to Canton. On Friday I spoke several times to her and to Dr. Baittle. Dr. Baittle concluded that it would be best to let Lloyd alone for the time being and see how things worked out. Some time Thursday afternoon Margaret and Don went back to Canton.

In the end Lloyd entered into a contract with the *Daily News* for his life story, for which he received a cash advance. The balance was to be paid later, after Lloyd had finished his part of the bargain: he was to spend a number of sessions with a *Daily News* reporter and to relate the facts of his story. But Lloyd stayed in Chicago only a few more days and then left. He resumed the life he had led before November 26, 1955, doing more traveling than I have done in my lifetime. His wants are few, his money requirements limited. Somehow he manages to find jobs and earn the few dollars he requires.

Miller was free, but the Miller case was not over.

On April 19, the thirtieth and the last day, Hayes filed a notice of appeal. The notice of appeal did not challenge Lloyd's release as such, only the portion of the order barring a retrial. We saw ahead of us more years of litigation.

The issue on this appeal was precise and narrow. Did or did not Judge Perry properly bar the State of Illinois from trying Lloyd again? But the Court of Appeals did not quickly reach this question. The next four years were consumed with procedural snarls. We will not burden the reader with the details, of interest only to lawyers. Ultimately, the Court of Appeals held that Judge Perry had exceeded his jurisdiction in banning Lloyd's retrial. Would the Fulton County authorities reopen the prosecution?

On September 15, 1971, the Circuit Court of Fulton County, on the request of a new State's Attorney (Malmgren was no longer in office), entered an order dismissing the indictment. The Miller case ended, fifteen years, nine months, and nineteen days after it had begun.

Shortly after Lloyd was freed by Judge Perry on March 20, 1967, the Illinois State Bar Association initiated an investigation of the conduct of Blaine Ramsey and Roger Hayes.

Under Illinois procedure at that time, disciplinary matters were investigated first by the Grievance Committee of the Bar Association. If it found no discipline was warranted, it so reported to the Board of Managers of the Bar Association. If it concurred, the matter ended. If it found discipline was warranted and the Board of Managers concurred, the matter was presented to the State Supreme Court, which made a final determination.

Every phase of the Miller case was in some way convoluted. The Grievance Committee matter was no exception. The Grievance Committee initiated its own investigation; sometime later Lloyd Miller wrote a personal letter of complaint, which apparently was treated as a separate grievance. At some point, the two proceedings were consolidated. Early in the matter I received a request from the Illinois State Bar Association for a Xerox copy of the entire transcript of the 1956 trial, which bulky document we supplied them.

We, as Mr. Miller's lawyers, were never formally participants.

After a year or more, the Grievance Committee announced the results of its deliberations. It determined that there was "no basis for disciplinary action against the prosecutors" and dismissed the charges. Because of the "considerable notoriety" concerning the matter, the Committee determined that an exception should be made to the usual rule prohibiting disclosure of the contents of its records and files. They were therefore released with the consent of the prosecuting attorneys.

The Grievance Committee declared that the Supreme Court had "misapprehended the facts of the case." The prosecution did not misrepresent the shorts to the jury because the State Crime Lab had found blood on them. It was not unethical conduct to fail to disclose the paint because "the presence or absence of paint on the shorts was not a material question in the case." Moreover "the prosecution was under no duty to elaborate upon the dissimilarity" between the hair found on the swab used to take a vaginal specimen from Janice and Lloyd's pubic hair. The prosecution did not act improperly regarding June Lang and Mrs. Baxter.

The Committee added that the Supreme Court opinion "left the impression that a grave injustice had been deliberately perpetrated by a ruthless and unprincipled prosecution. A thorough and objective investigation of the matter has shown that this impression is unfounded."

After the State Bar cleared the prosecutors, *Time* on July 5, 1968, said, "The Illinois Bar Committee seems to be saying that, while a witness is required to tell 'the truth, the whole truth and nothing but the truth', no such restrictions apply to the prosecutors bent on winning a conviction."

On May 17, 1968, two days after the announcement of the Grievance Committee decision, the *Chicago Daily Law Bulletin* reported:

HIGHEST PUBLIC RELATIONS
HONOR PRESENTED TO ISBA

New York—The Illinois State Bar Association last night became the nation's first bar association to receive the Silver Anvil Award of the Public Relations Society of America.

The Anvil is the highest honor in the public relations field.

The bar association was honored, along with its agency, Martin & Punnett, Inc., "for its unique program to explain

the law daily to millions of citizens through regularly pro-
grammed use of mass media."

We have come to the end of Lloyd's story. The Miller Srs. still live
in Canton. Each Christmas I receive a card and occasionally a letter
asking me for the latest news of Junior. Malmgren and Meuth practice law in Canton and Cuba, respectively. Ramsey is a bank trust
officer; Hayes practices law in De Kalb, west of Chicago.

George Leighton is a state appellate court judge. Sy Bucholz practices in New York. Rosenfield, Ming, Conger, Pontikes, Golter,
Grossman, and I practice in Chicago, Art Greenberg in Peoria. We
have had other exciting cases, but none to match Lloyd's.

On two occasions when we were faced with difficult questions regarding Lloyd's mental state, Dr. Baittle gave us skilled professional
advice. He rendered his help willingly, promptly, and at incon-
venience to himself. His early death recently was a loss to his profes-
sion and the community.

Lloyd has continued his nomadic life. Once in 1968, finding himself in Honduras with no money, he telegraphed Rosenfield for $600
for transportation. But he managed to return, even from Honduras,
without Maury's help. From time to time he returns to Chicago and
usually stops in to see us.

In November 1968, the Illinois Division of the American Civil
Liberties Union received Newsletter No. 1 from the Christian Faith
Crusader Association in San Diego. At the top was written, "Please
help . . . Donate what you can. Thanks. Remember your organization helped me win my rightful freedom. 1967. A Illinois case." The
newsletter ran:

> Wherefore by their fruits ye shall know them . . . Matt.
> 7:20
>   Newsletter . . . No. 1 . . . Date 11–22–68.
> As a true minister of our holy Lord God, I put forth . . .
> will President Nixon and his administration, help bring
> this nation and the rest of the world in true peace . . . if it
> wasn't for the true action of the U.S. Supreme Court, our
> constitution wouldn't be stable today, as it was laid out to
> be . . . a true policeman and woman is also a human being,
> give him and her the facilities of true justice and they will

be an asset to it . . . a violator of the law, is a sick person, which is a unlearned human being, and should be maintained for true education only, not for punishment . . . punishment of any form, is the work of the devil.

The newsletter carried Lloyd's picture, and at the bottom the signature, "Pres.-Owner, Lloyd E. Miller, Jr."

During his dark hours, Lloyd acquired an abiding belief in God. He was delivered from death. The newsletter was Lloyd's effort to redeem the commitment he made to himself. Lloyd knows that to him, not an exceptional person, exceptional events occurred.

12

RETROSPECT

The Miller case has a fearful message for twentieth-century America. A man was suspected of a crime. He was apprehended and questioned. He signed a confession on the basis of which he was convicted, sentenced to death, and spent years in prison. Several times he was at the brink of death. Finally he was spared by our highest court.

In obtaining the confession, the authorities told him that his family had rejected him and that critical physical evidence pointed to his guilt. The authorities knew that his family had not rejected him and that the critical physical evidence pointed to innocence. The confession, moreover, was inconsistent with known facts. Yet the prosecutors held to it to the end. Why?

Why Lloyd confessed though innocent, is a problem for the psychiatrist, not the lawyer. But the question of the reliability of confessions is a question for the lawyer and for everyone concerned with criminal justice. One would think that an innocent man would not have confessed, even with the misrepresentations made to him, the duration of the questioning, and the promises made. Yet an innocent man did confess. That such a thing can happen is one of the fascinating and important lessons of the case.

The confession was inconsistent with, and indeed contradicted, known facts. Even convinced as they were of Miller's guilt, one would have expected the authorities to be troubled by this, but they made little or no effort to resolve the inconsistencies or contradictions. When they learned, for example, that the hair found on the vaginal swab did not match Lloyd's, they should (one thinks) have had profound doubts about the confession and bent every effort to study the matter. Yet they did not. On the contrary, at the trial, they misrepresented key evidence and suppressed evidence favorable to the accused. Why did they behave in this fashion?

It is my view that the answers to these questions lie in the nature of the criminal process.

Proving an accused guilty is far more complex than is commonly supposed. Generally it requires proof of objective facts and proof regarding the state of mind of the accused (for example, that he "intended" to do thus and so). Frequently, the prosecution attempts a short cut to its goal by obtaining a confession. It is important to understand how the drive for a confession distorts the criminal process.

1. *The Confession Albatross.*

Too often accused persons are deprived of their liberty on the strength of confessions obtained under circumstances that cast substantial doubt as to their validity or under circumstances that demean the criminal process.

The public generally lays great stress upon a confession. There seems to be an impression that an innocent suspect will not confess under interrogation unless third-degree methods are employed against him. Hence, in this view, unless he is physically abused, the confession is not only reliable but strong proof of guilt. Popular television, motion pictures, and novels reinforce this view. Indeed, in such fictions it is customary for the suspect, after the overwhelming evidence against him is revealed, to confess. Seldom in popular drama and novels is the author content to rest his case upon prosecution evidence. A confession is required as a capstone.

I do not discuss popular fiction lightly. Attitudes about murder and murderers formed through popular fiction have made a deep impression on the general public. In particular, the confession, conceived as a free and voluntary or spontaneous utterance, has colored the public imagination.

This view of confessions is wholly false. Few, few, few confessions are spontaneous. Almost invariably confessions are obtained because pressure, of one kind or another, is applied to the suspect. That pressure may be and has been physical torture or deprivation of food, drink, or sleep. It may be holding incommunicado or threats against the family of the suspect. It may take subtler forms: promise of an easy sentence, an offer of drugs to an addict. It may be the wearing down of the will by a psychiatrist, or interminable questioning by relays of policemen. But pressure there is, sometimes great, sometimes little. The key question, one extraordinarily difficult to answer, is what kind of pressure and upon what sort of man? Under what circumstances was the confession actually given? The effort by the prosecution to introduce a confession into evidence has significant and deplorable consequences. The focus of the trial is immediately shifted from what should be the central questions—What happened at the scene of the crime? Who was in fact responsible for the death of the deceased?—to the question of what happened in the police station and what were the circumstances under which the accused gave his confession. The significant, prime question is slighted and indeed, one feels, is often almost forgotten.

A confession may not be introduced in evidence if it is given under coercion. It follows that if the prosecution is to present its confession it must first prove to the judge (with the jury, if there is one, absent) that the confession was voluntary. If, however, the defense is able to show that the confession was a product of coercion, the court is required to reject it.

Almost no stationhouse confession is voluntary in the sense that the defendant, while sitting in his cell, suddenly was overcome with remorse and asked the turnkey to call the captain, the prosecuting attorney, and a court reporter so that he could dictate his confession. Almost invariably the confession is the result of questioning. There is hence inevitably some measure of pressure put upon the defendant.

These general rules require a confession, as in the Miller case, to be considered twice in a jury trial, first by the judge alone, and, if he rules the confession admissible, then by the jury.

Typically, prosecution evidence concerning the confession consists of a parade of witnesses, usually police officers and prosecutors, who testify in effect that the defendant was treated with the punctilio observed by participants in a Japanese sumo wrestling match.

Counsel for the defense may closely cross-examine the witnesses for the prosecution. Sometimes he is able to find inconsistencies and weaknesses in their stories. Usually, however, his chief witness must be the defendant himself, who in most cases, is not as imposing or as self-assured as the prosecution witnesses. On a murder charge the defendant may have been in jail from the moment of his arrest until the day of the trial. One's appearance, confidence, and sangfroid do not improve in prison. Upon taking the stand the defendant must relate his version of the events leading up to the confession. Sometimes he will have a tale of physical cruelty. Sometimes more subtle means (some of them described below) will have been employed against him.

In deciding the all-important question of what went on in the stationhouse, judge and jury are deprived of the benefit of independent witnesses not beholden to either party. The sole witnesses to the circumstances of the confession are those who have a stake in the outcome. Thus, when called upon to decide whether the confession represents a free act of the accused, judge and jury must decide upon the basis of biased witnesses who tell sharply conflicting stories. Frequently the versions related by prosecution and defense will differ so widely that it is difficult to believe that the same set of circumstances underlie the accounts of the two parties.

Nor is this all. Imagine a case where there is substantially no dispute about what took place from the moment of the arrest of the accused person to the moment of signing the confession. Would judge and jury then be in a position to determine whether the confession was voluntary? I submit that they would not.

Neither judge nor jury knows the defendant nor have they met him before the trial. They may know some of the elementary facts of his life, such as his age, his nationality, the extent of his education, and the nature of his work, but they know nothing of the defendant as a person. They heard him when he took the witness stand to testify in his own behalf, if he did so. If he is fortunate to have a pleasing personality, a gift for self-expression, and a good memory for what happened at the time he confessed, his cause is aided. If he lacks these qualities and if in addition he has a previous criminal record, his cause is harmed. If he is the sort of person able to withstand cross-examination successfully, his cause may be aided substantially. If, however, he becomes rattled, confused, or intimidated upon cross-examination, he may be ruined.

Another important factor is that the quiet atmosphere of the courtroom simply does not offer a suitable medium to recreate the atmosphere that prevailed during the interrogation of the accused. Just as judge and jury are unacquainted with the personality of the accused, so are they unacquainted with the personality of the interrogators. Both the interrogators and the accused are seen only and speak only in the artificial atmosphere of the courtroom, subject to its solemnities, its restraints, and its rules. They are then required to make one of the most difficult decisions of all—a subjective judgment regarding the will of a human being whom they do not know under circumstances they cannot be sure of because they have been given two sharply different versions of what happened.

But what seems particularly unfortunate about the confession problem is this: confessions have become part of the American police way of life. We have institutionalized a procedure that is inherently wrong and we impose upon courts and juries tasks which are in their nature impossible. We do this not in isolated cases, but as routine.

There is a worse evil: The police have developed more subtle methods of obtaining confessions than the old-fashioned third degree. Indeed as long as the police rely chiefly upon interrogation and confession, they are encouraged to develop increasingly subtle methods which are less likely to be rejected in court as coerced. Some of these methods are set out in *Criminal Interrogation and Confessions* by Fred E. Inbau and John E. Reid, published in 1967. Professor Inbau is considered a leading authority in the field of criminal law and for many years has been on the faculty of Northwestern University Law School in Evanston, Illinois. John E. Reid is the director of one of the leading firms specializing in polygraph examinations.

They mention the following techniques. In interrogating a murder suspect, the questioners are advised (p. 43) to suggest to him that they think he acted in self-defense and that perhaps the homicide was not criminal. After obtaining an admission of the killing, the authors say the police can then more easily establish murder by showing that the circumstances are incompatible with self-defense.

Another device suggested (p. 62) is the "friendly–unfriendly" act. "Interrogator A, after having employed a sympathetic, understanding approach throughout his interrogation, expresses his regret over the subject's continued lying. A then leaves the room. Interrogator

B enters and he proceeds to berate the subject, by referring to him as a rather despicable character. . . . After Interrogator B (the unfriendly one) has been in the interrogation room for a while, Interrogatory A (the friendly one) reenters and scolds B for his unfriendly conduct. A asks B to leave and B goes out of the door with the pretended feeling of disgust toward both the subject and A. A then resumes his friendly, sympathetic approach. . . ."[1]

Reid and Inbau warn (p. 63): "In the employment of the friendly–unfriendly act, the second (unfriendly) investigator should resort only to verbal condemnation of the subject; under no circumstances should he ever employ physical abuse or threats of abuse or other mistreatment."

To the extent, however, that the friendly–unfriendly act is well done, a cloud of violence overhangs the suspect. Perhaps it would be insufficient to cause most people to confess falsely, but can we say that no one will be intimidated?

Another trick: where there are two suspects, Inbau and Reid recommend that "Subject No. 1" be led (by skillful artifices) to think that "Subject No. 2" has confessed (p. 84). But suppose the tricked suspect knows he is innocent. What does he think then? That his companion was tortured to confess? That his turn is next?

Or let us suppose that the two subjects are in fact the men responsible for a robbery and that one of them did fire a fatal shot. Justice, it seems to us, demands that the police and the prosecution make every diligent effort to ascertain who fired the gun. Yet playing one suspect against the other if successful may well lead to a deal, express or implied, between one of the suspects and the police. Both men are playing for high stakes. The prosecution's presentation of the case in court may hinge not upon the discovered actual facts, but upon the sequence of events in the interrogation room. Suppose suspect No. 1, who actually pulled the trigger, realizing that suspect No. 2 may confess first regarding the robbery and murder, may decide that he should confess the robbery but accuse his partner of the murder.

---

1. Consider the following nice touch (p. 63) : "As the captain leaves the room after playing his unfriendly role, the detective may say, 'Joe, I'm glad you didn't tell him a damn thing. He treats everybody that way—persons like you, as well as men like me within his own department. I'd like to show him up by having you tell me the truth. It's time he learns a lesson or two about decent human behavior.' "

The device of playing off one suspect against another, recommended by Inbau-Reid, can be a fountainhead of injustice.

If the police and the prosecution simply confined themselves within the four corners of Inbau and Reid, the results would be bad enough. The harsh fact is, however, that the police have resorted to stratagems far more coercive in their effect upon the accused. What is even worse, many of these stratagems have received judicial approval. In many cases where the devices were disapproved, it took the highest court of the state to reverse a conviction. In other cases harsh stratagems received the stamp of approval of a state's highest court and it took the Supreme Court of the United States to reverse a conviction.

Consider the following. Trial courts have accepted confessions of ill or wounded men made shortly after they received pain-killing medication. In New Jersey, the Supreme Court accepted the murder confession of Nathaniel Wade.[1] Wade had just received 100 milligrams of demerol to ease the pain of a broken leg. He claimed that the injection put him "in a fog" and he did not remember the interrogation or signing the confession.

Joe Reddish in Florida[2] was more fortunate. He attempted suicide by firing a bullet near his heart after allegedly killing two persons. He was sentenced to death on the basis of an oral confession taken that night after he had received demerol and codeine. The Supreme Court of Florida granted him a new trial.

In New York the courts upheld a murder confession taken from a 14-year-old boy, Carl DeFlumer[3] shortly after he had been arrested at his home at 9:00 P.M. On the advice of a court-appointed attorney, he pleaded guilty. Years later, the New York courts refused a new trial because of the guilty plea. They declined to recognize that it might have been induced by fear that the prosecution might seek the death penalty if DeFlumer had repudiated his confession at trial.

In Maryland, a murder and robbery confession by Walter Wiggins[4] was upheld. Yet, a day after the confession, he was sent to a state hospital where a diagnosis was made of "acute (temporary) brain

1. See *Wade* v. *Yeager*, 245 F. Supp. 62 (1964)
2. *Reddish* v. *Florida*, 167 S. 2d 858 (Fla., 1964)
3. *People* v. *DeFlumer, Jr.*, 16 NYS 2d 20, 209 N.E. 2d 93 (1965)
4. *Wiggins* v. *Maryland*, 235 Md. 97 (1964)

syndrome, induced by excessive indulgence in alcohol." There is further the bizarre fact that the same judges who heard the case of Wiggins also heard the cases of men named James and Stewart, both of whom had confessed. The girl friend of Wiggins said that Wiggins told her only one person was involved (presumably Wiggins). Thus the police had three confessions to a crime committed by a single individual. James and, apparently, Stewart were acquitted. If the police could obtain confessions ruled involuntary from these men, what confidence should we put in the confession obtained from Wiggins?

The authorities have not hesitated to obtain confessions by deception. For Charles Everett[1] it was a five-year struggle to obtain a new trial. He confessed to hitting and robbing one Finocchio after the police told him that Finocchio was "not hurt bad" but was only a little angry. In fact, Finocchio was dead. Everett was charged with murder.

An unusual mode of achieving a confession was utilized in *Leyra* v. *Denno*.[2] The suspect, accused of the murder of his parents, was subjected to relentless questioning. While in custody, he complained of a bad sinus condition. The police brought in a Dr. Helfond, supposedly to give the suspect medical relief. In fact, the doctor was a psychiatrist who by subtle and suggestive questions simply continued police efforts to induce a confession. Only in the U.S. Supreme Court were the confession to the psychiatrist and subsequent confessions to others ultimately rejected.

State courts have upheld confessions obtained after unrelenting questioning, deprivation of food, or deprivation of sleep. Only in the United States Supreme Court did many defendants secure new trials. A few examples: A 1944 case set aside a conviction after a confession had been secured by thirty-six hours of nearly continuous questioning under powerful lights by relays of police, investigators and attorneys (*Ashcraft* v. *Tennessee*).[3] In 1942, the Supreme Court disallowed a confession secured after nearly three days of continuous questioning, while the suspect, an uneducated Negro, was driven

1. See U.S. ex rel. *Everett v. Murphy*, 329 F. 2d 68 (1964)
2. 347 U.S. 556 (1954)
3. 322 U.S. 143 (1944)

from county to county. (*Ward* v. *Texas*)[1] Questioning from 8 A.M. to 6 P.M. while being held incommunicado and stripped for several hours was enough to upset the confession in *Malinski* v. *New York*.[2] In 1949 a confession secured after denial of opportunity for sleep and food, holding for two days in solitary confinement, and five night interrogation sessions resulted in a reversal of a conviction in *Watts* v. *Indiana*.[3] Four consecutive days of interrogation, while cut off from friends or relatives, rendered a confession involuntary in *Turner* v. *Penna.*, decided in 1949.[4]

Interrogating an illiterate man for two days by five officers working in relays while the suspect was held in a cubicle in stifling heat resulted in an involuntary confession. (*Harris* v. *South Carolina*, 1949).[5]

It was necessary to go to the Supreme Court to upset the conviction of a fifteen-year-old black boy who had been first held incommunicado for three days before confessing (*Haly* v. *Ohio*).[6]

State courts have upheld confessions from the mentally ill. In 1960, the Supreme Court reversed the Alabama conviction of Jesse Blackburn[7] based on a confession. Blackburn had been discharged from the army as "permanently ill with psychosis" and treated for years in a mental hospital. He committed the alleged crime while AWOL from the hospital.

The problem does not lie with the confession rules as enunciated by the Supreme Court. They lay down civilized standards. It is the trial courts which in recent case after case have applied harsh confession rules against criminal defendants. In some of these cases state appellate courts have set aside convictions. In others they have not. United States Supreme Court holdings have proved relatively ineffective in curbing abuses. Why?

Not every contested confession reviewed by the Supreme Court has been set aside. The rule that an involuntary coerced confession will be set aside has a corollary: a voluntary uncoerced confession

1. 316 U.S. 547 (1942)
2. 324 U.S. 401 (1945)
3. 338 U.S. 49 (1949)
4. 338 U.S. 62 (1949)
5. 338 U.S. 68 (1949)
6. 332 U.S. 596 (1948)
7. *Blackburn* v. *Alabama,* 361 U.S. 199 (1960)

will not be set aside. There are numerous cases where the Supreme Court has upheld confessions. Some are shocking. A confession was upheld in a capital case involving a twenty-seven-year-old itinerant laborer in Arizona, Arthur Thomas,[1] even though he confessed to a murder after arrest by a posse, and at one point a rope was put around his neck and he was jerked in the direction of the nearest trees.

It is possible for state courts, from a collection of over forty Supreme Court cases, to find authority for almost any action they choose to take in a given case. The result has been that the courts have permitted confessions to be used in many appalling circumstances. By and large their decisions are immune from reversal because the Supreme Court can review only a tiny fraction of all cases.

In 1964 and again in 1966 the Supreme Court decided to make a break with the past.

The 1964 case was the *Escobedo*[2] holding that once the police process shifts from "investigatory to accusatory," an accused person is entitled to consult with his attorney.

The *Escobedo* case was a forerunner to the even more famous *Miranda*[3] case, requiring the police to warn a suspect of his right to remain silent and his right to the presence of an attorney during his interrogation. The reaction was a storm of criticism. Even though the decision rested on the Constitution, Congress enacted a statute (18 USC §3501) purporting to restrict its applicability in the federal courts and, essentially, to return to the old rules. Moreover, in 1971, the Supreme Court retreated from the *Miranda* rules, permitting confessions to be used for some purpose even though they were taken in violation of *Miranda* requirements.

Yet the *Escobedo* and *Miranda* rules even if fully observed would not really solve the confession problem. The questions would still remain: did the suspect receive the required warning? Did he ask for a lawyer? Moreover, if a suspect talks after being warned or waives his right to an attorney, his confession is valid only if "voluntary"— that is, we are thrown back to inquiring what went on in the stationhouse during interrogation.

1. *Thomas* v. *Arizona*, 356 U.S. 390 (1958)
2. *Escobedo* v. *Ill.*, c78 U.S. 478
3. *Miranda* v. *Arizona*, 384 U.S. 436

A number of suggestions have been advanced for possible reform. It has been proposed that all interrogation of suspects should be taken down verbatim by a court reporter. Another suggestion is to tape record, or even video tape, all interrogation. These suggestions have merit but it seems to me that they fail to come to grips with the underlying problem. One difficulty is that voice tapes, video tapes, and transcripts are subject to ready editing. The defendant perhaps will charge that the crucial few minutes where he was taken out in the hall and given a rabbit punch to loosen his tongue are not on the film or in the transcript. Thus the record would convey to the court and jury a false sense of reliability. The reader of this book should not think for one moment that all public authorities are above such practices. In this very chapter, we have seen many of the tricks resorted to by the prosecution, specific instances of deplorable practices. It seems most unwise to embark upon a course whose main effect, I fear, would be to strengthen the hand of the prosecution without providing any genuinely sure guarantee of protection to the defendant.

These suggestions fall short in another way: no film, no tape, and no transcript can convey the mood of the stationhouse during the critical period of interrogation. They are fundamentally a step in the wrong direction. Our efforts should be directed not to improving the quality of confessions presented in courts of law but in eliminating police dependence upon them.

The core of the problem lies in prosecution reliance upon confessions as such. It tends to corrode our system of criminal justice. The Supreme Court and other courts of review write elegant essays defining voluntary confessions. The authorities have strong inducement to invent devices that will obtain confessions that will pass court approval.

There is a graver evil: supposedly, the aim of the criminal law is to reform. Every confession obtained by force, fraud, deceit, or evasion undermines that goal. Every such confession demeans society, and lessens us. We permit our agents, in our name, to engage in practices that cheapen them and us.

Must we continue to use police-obtained confessions?

Suppose we had a statute which read as follows: "No confession made to a police officer shall be proved as against a person accused of any offence." This statute is Section 25 of the Indian Evidence Act, in force since 1872. It is the law not only of India but also of Pakistan, Burma, and Ceylon. (My discussion centers on India and Pakistan. The law of Burma and Ceylon appears similar.) It should come as a melancholy surprise to us who pride ourselves on enlightened codes of criminal procedures, on constitutional guarantees embedded in the Bill of Rights, to learn that practices which are today an accepted part of the American way of life have been forbidden for a century in four major Far Eastern countries. These four countries all have been deeply influenced by British law and British legal traditions as we have, yet with respect to the law of confessions they have developed positive rules of law which put us to shame. From the law of these four countries we will have a new appreciation of the tragic shortcomings of our system of criminal justice. It is a tragedy that we, with our wealth and our power and our undoubted capacity to utilize modern science, nonetheless remain backward in this area of criminal justice.

India and Pakistan have simply outlawed confessions to police officers regardless whether the "confessor" is in custody or not. Moreover, another section of their law provides that a confession by a person in custody must be made in the immediate presence of a Magistrate. A confession by one in custody made to a prosecuting official, or any other person in authority, or even to a friend or relative may not be used against the accused.

Another key provision outlaws confessions induced by promises or threats. In Pakistan, moreover, after an individual has made a confession, he is not to be returned to the custody of the police but is to be held in the "judicial lockup" where the police do not have access to him. To return an individual to police custody after making a confession is "highly improper" according to Pakistan text writers (M. Q. A. Kahn and S. A. A. Kahn, p. 115 *The Law of Confessions* [1960]). Further, the accused person should be told before he confesses that, having once been brought before the magistrate, he will not be returned to police custody but will be sent to judicial custody regardless whether he confesses or not.

It is important to observe that the mere requirement that a confession be made before a magistrate could easily be subverted unless it was hedged about by a number of other requirements to make certain that an individual, when brought before the magistrate, was still not effectively subject to threats and inducements resulting from police custody. Without such subsidiary rules, the requirement that a confession be recorded before a magistrate could speedily be reduced to mere window dressing to legitimize confessions that were in fact the product of inducements, threats, or other unlawful practices.

The law of India and Pakistan does permit the following. If an accused states, while in custody, that stolen merchandise is hidden under the floor of his tent and if the police find it where the accused says he hid it, the merchandise and the statement may be admitted into evidence. (This was the procedure used by Joshua respecting a goodly Babylonish garment—Joshua 7:16-26.) The problem with this approach is the difficulty of being sure that the statement led to the evidence and not vice versa.

Let us quote from Messrs. Khan and Khan (pp. 1–3) on confessions. Their words are quaint to our ears; their message packed with truth:

> To start with, a confession is always open to suspicion, for it is in human nature to save one's life and one's liberty. . . .
>
> It is next a matter of common experience and observation that agencies at work in the detection of crimes try, more often than not, to find a short cut, for a successful result of their labours, in the confessions of suspects. Induced by a promise, or frightened by a threat, wanderings, in other words, in the region of hope and fear, thus entangled in a web of deceit, persons accused of offenses come out with confessions—which, however, have a short life to live, for, as a rule, they are retracted sooner or later. Stories of ill-treatment and torture by the police, honied words of zemindars, are profusely related, sometimes to the prejudice of the police, but several times to serve the confessor no purpose useful. (p. 1)
>
> . . . it may be taken as a word with meaning that a confes-

sion is, after all, a weak link in the chain of the case for the Crown or State.

Chief Judge Straight in 1884, in *Queen Empress* v. *Babi Lal* explained why confessions are unreliable. His words have force today:

> It requires not a very vivid imagination to picture what too often takes place when two or three of these, not very intelligent or highly-paid police officers, are called away to a village to investigate a grave crime. Naturally, it is a much easier way for them to begin by endeavouring to obtain confession from a suspected person . . . instead of searching out the clues to the evidence from independent sources and seeing what extraneous proof there is. It continually happens that, while the Police have been occupying themselves in getting the confession, many of the traces of the crime, which, if at once followed up, would have produced valuable proof, have disappeared.

An Indian police officer, Sir Edmund Cox, in his work *Police and Crime in India,* p. 173, after mentioning Joshua 7:16–23, advocates a ban on all confessions, saying:

> I state with all the force and conviction at my command that it will be infinitely for the advantage of the Police and consequently the people at large to make it illegal for any one Police or Magistrate to record a confession of any accused person before he has actually put upon his trial. If when he is being tried, he chooses to plead guilty and confess what he has done, let him do so. It will not occur often. If the police cannot obtain sufficient evidence against an accused person to send him up for trial apart from the confession he ought not to be sent up for trial at all. . . . Our laws are so much more designed for the protection of the innocent and for bringing home their guilt to the guilty and so many undoubted criminals are daily acquitted that to add a few to the number of improper acquittals would be of no great consequence.
>
> Besides the effect would be only temporary. In a short time, the Police would realise the necessity of supporting a charge with evidence which frequently exists but is com-

monly overlooked and the statements of Police Officers in court often ultimately carry weight which they will never command so long as they are handicapped by the prejudice inseparable from confessions.

The Indian authorities are particularly critical about confessions allegedly made by defendants to friends, relatives, and the like. According to an Indian judge, such a confession, called a "nonjudicial" confession, is usually "the second string in the bow of the prosecution."

It is easy to see why. Such testimony offers an easy opportunity for the spiteful, the mentally unbalanced, and the limelight hunters. Yet the weakness of such confessions is almost totally ignored in the United States.

A nonjudicial confession poses a special problem for the defendant. The witness to the alleged confession may be testifying falsely but the motives and unconscious factors underlying his testimony are often difficult to discern. Life is not long enough to subject every witness to an extensive emotional examination. Only where the witness is blatantly psychotic or obviously bears ill will is the falsity of the testimony likely to be exposed.

I do not purport to be an expert on the law of Pakistan and India. Every lawyer knows how tricky it is to try to understand the statutes or court decisions of another country without ever having practiced in that country and knowing the practical circumstances to which the statutes and court decisions apply. It may be that war and unrest have in practice eroded some of the above rules. Nevertheless, there can be little question that these statutes and court decisions do represent an official expression of a policy that we have yet to attain.

But reliance on confession is not the sole defect of the criminal law. The adversary system and the rules of evidence designed to promote justice can in fact work injustice. That is our next topic.

2. *Trial by Battle.*

In England, beginning with William the Conqueror, legal disputes between Normans were decided on the field of battle. Not until 1818 was the last vestige of trial by battle finally abolished in England.

Today we like to think that the criminal trial is a dispassionate inquiry into the guilt or innocence of the accused. Anyone slightly acquainted with the criminal process knows that this is not the case. I do not mean to imply that our system purposely and with malice works to convict the innocent. Our failures are not failures of evil intent but rather of institutional organization.

If, after criminal proceedings have begun, evidence favorable to the accused comes to the attention of the authorities, the further they have proceeded in the prosecution, the less likely it is that prosecution will be dropped on the basis of such evidence. This is not due to an inherently vicious attitude on the part of prosecutors. It is due to a trait common to all of us. Once the State's Attorney takes a position on a case, he becomes an advocate for that position. People tend to be slow to admit that they are wrong and, once they take a position on an issue, they are slow to change sides. Imperceptibly they come to see the evidence in their possession as confirming their view of the case. Evidence to the contrary tends to be played down or forgotten. Thus, while the prosecution has a legal and ethical duty to be fair and to prosecute only those whom it believes to be guilty, these duties are extremely difficult to observe in practice. An attorney representing a client speedily becomes convinced, and I mean truly convinced, of the rightness of the cause he is espousing. He is not playacting for a jury; he is genuinely and truly convinced. So powerful is this force that it is sometimes difficult for an attorney to take a dispassionate view of a case and thus serve his client by advising him when the time has come to settle, rather than to proceed with litigation.

Once the trial begins, the analogy of the criminal trial to trial by battle becomes more pronounced. The judge and the jury sit primarily to hear the evidence brought before them by the contending factions. Only in rare instances will a judge request that a witness be brought before him. Indeed, his power to order such a step to be taken is largely circumscribed. As we have seen in the Miller trial in the case of Mrs. Baxter, even the power of the judge to have a witness treated as a court's witness rather than as a witness for one of the parties is circumscribed.

The law assumes that the best way to arrive at truth is to have the case presented to the court by the two contending factions. Whether this is really the best way to arrive at truth is a question. It is not the way we choose in other human endeavors, where we attempt to arrive at truth by a meticulous examination of the facts by an investigator who attempts to maintain an open mind during the course of his investigation. But in a criminal trial each side, broadly speaking, has the option of selecting the facts that it will present. Adverse facts tend to be presented only when side A knows that they are known to side B, and side A tries to present them first in order to diminish their import in the eyes of judge and jury. Facts known to the prosecution, which in certain aspects help the prosecution but in other aspects help the defense, may or may not be presented. Similarly equivocal facts known to the defense, may or may not be presented. Thus a whole range of facts may or may not come to the attention of the judge and jury.

The adversary system is so deeply imbedded in the judicial process and has so many virtues I do not suggest that it be abandoned. But it does suffer from this limitation as a truth determining process.

The facts, moreover, when they are presented, are presented pursuant to the "rules of evidence" designed to weed out material considered unreliable, unfair, prejudicial, or irrelevant. The rules are designed to do justice in the generality of cases. But rules designed to do justice in the generality are bound to do injustice in specific cases. Consider one of the best-known rules, the one against hearsay testimony. X is on trial for the murder of Y. There was one eyewitness to Y's death, witness W. The hearsay rule states that no one will be allowed to testify as to W's version of what took place except W himself. Thus W is present in court and subject to cross-examination. This admirable rule can work terrible injustices. If W delivers a statement to the prosecution, a positive sworn statement that he was present and saw X shoot Y, and W dies before the trial, W's statement cannot be used. If there is no other evidence, X will be acquitted and in fact may not even be brought to trial. A murderer will go free.

Suppose, on the other hand, the same set of circumstances, except that W's testimony is that it was *not* X who shot Y. Suppose further that there are various incriminating circumstances linking X to the crime and that W dies before trial. X may be convicted of murder. Thus we see that the rules of evidence can acquit the guilty or convict the innocent.

The rules of evidence are not themselves static or always clear cut. Hence the adversary system leads each side wherever possible to try to convince the court to interpret the rules to bar unfavorable evidence and accept favorable evidence.

3. *Prosecution Suppression of Evidence.*

What about prosecution suppression of evidence favorable to an accused? True, the prosecutor has a professional duty, embodied in canons of ethics and court decisions, to reveal such evidence. Unhappily, there are many instances of such supression, and when the facts come to light, the convicted man often has a long bitter battle to secure justice.

Consider the wrong done to David Almeida.[1] Armed with a .45 pistol he was one of three men who held up a Philadelphia supermarket in 1947. In the robbery Patrolman Cecil Ingling was killed. At his trial the state contended Almeida shot Ingling. The star witness against him was his fellow robber, Eddie Hough, already under sentence of death for murder.

But the prosecution had a secret which it concealed for years: Officer Ingling had been killed by a shot from a .38 pistol. Almeida therefore did not kill Officer Ingling. The State knew that he had not done so. Who did kill him? One of the several Philadelphia police officers who had responded to the robbery alarm had fired and by mistake killed his fellow officer.

True, it is a rule that if three commit a holdup during whose course one of the robbers kills someone, all are guilty of murder. It is by no means clear, however, that they are guilty of murder if a police officer accidentally kills a fellow police officer. But apart from the question of guilt, it does, or it should, make a difference in sentencing. When the facts were unearthed, the Pennsylvania State courts refused to grant Almeida a new trial. The Federal Court of Appeals, however, ultimately ordered a new trial for him.

1. U.S. ex rel. *Almeida* v. *Baldi,* 195 F. 2d 815 (C.A. 3rd, 1952)

In a Maryland case, John Brady[1] was tried for murder. The prosecution had in its possession, but suppressed, a statement from an accomplice, Donald Boblet, that Boblet had done the actual killing. When these facts came to light, the trial court refused to grant Brady a new trial. The highest court in Maryland granted him a new trial limited to the penalty. Finally the United States Supreme Court granted Brady a new trial, both on the question of the penalty and on his guilt or innocence.

In many crimes the question of whether the defendant is drunk has an important bearing on whether he has the capacity to form the requisite intent to commit the crime. Intoxication also has a bearing on the culpability and hence on punishment. In a Texas trial where there was a dispute as to whether the defendant was drunk, the prosecution permitted police officers to testify that the prisoner was not drunk when arrested. It did not, however, produce other police officers who would have testified that the defendant was drunk.[2]

In another Texas case the question of the defendant's sanity arose.[3] The defendant was examined by three sets of doctors. The prosecution produced the testimony of two sets of doctors that the defendant was sane. However, the prosecution suppressed the testimony of the third set, who had found the defendant incompetent.

The Federal Court of Appeals in New York granted a new trial to one Meers[4] after the State courts had turned him down. He was convicted of robbery on the testimony of eyewitnesses. After the trial the defendant's counsel learned that two other eyewitnesses questioned by the police had categorically denied that the defendant was the robber. These witnesses were not produced by the prosecution nor was their existence revealed to the defendant's lawyer.

In another particularly shocking case that came before the Federal Fourth Circuit Court of Appeals, a defendant was convicted of shooting a police officer.[5] The prosecution witnesses identified defendant's revolver as "similar" to the one used in the shooting. It would be hard to imagine more damning testimony. Moreover, the

1. *Brady* v. *Md.*, 373 U.S. 83 (1963)
2. *U.S.* ex rel. *Thompson* v. *Dye*, 221 F. 2d 763 (1955)
3. *Ashley* v. *Texas*, 319 F. 2d 80 C.A. 5th (1963)
4. *U.S.* ex rel. *Meers* v. *Wilkins*, 326 F. 2d 133 (C.A. 2d, 1964)
5. *Barbee* v. *Warden*, 331 F. 2d 842 (C.A. 4th, 1964)

testimony may have been true. But the prosecution did not reveal that it knew by ballistics tests that the defendant's weapon was not the weapon that fired the fatal shot. Further, there were certain crucial fingerprints which were not the defendant's prints. This fact, too, was not revealed at the trial.

In a case heard by the Philadelphia Federal Court of Appeals, a defendant was convicted of a shooting that had occurred in an automobile.[1] During the trial the prosecution refused to permit the defendant's lawyers to examine a statement obtained from the driver of the car. Later, at the penalty hearing, the prosecution finally produced the documents. In the statement the driver of the car said that a struggle had preceded the shooting. Moreover, the statement cast doubt in many respects on the driver's testimony against the defendant at the trial.

In a recent Ohio case the Supreme Court of Ohio set aside a conviction when it finally came to light that the State had suppressed the fact that it knew from ballistics tests that the defendant's gun was not the murder weapon.[2] In another New York case the prosecution suppressed the statement of a witness that the defendant was not the murderer.[3] In a Chicago case one Montgomery was convicted of rape and served a lengthy term.[4] Years later Montgomery's lawyers found out that the prosecution had in its possession a doctor's statement that when he examined the alleged victim shortly after the crime, he found no evidence of rape and that the girl was a virgin.

I could extend this list at length. No part of the country has a monopoly on such instances. How many innocent men are there in our prisons? We shall never know. By the nature of the case, the facts rarely come out. The defendants largely are poor and uneducated. The evidence that might help them lies buried in the files of the police or the prosecution. Occasionally a sensational case comes to light. There may (or there may not) be a brief flurry of interest in the press. Then again the subject of prosecution misconduct is forgotten.

1. *U.S.* ex rel. *Butler* v. *Maroney,* 319 F. 2d 622 (C.A. 3rd, 1963)
2. *McMullen* v. *Maxwell,* 3 Ohio St. 2d 160 (1965)
3. *Application of Kapatos,* 208 F. Supp. 883 (N.Y. 1962)
4. *U.S.* ex rel. *Montgomery* v. *Ragen,* 86 F. Supp. 382 (1949)

One hopeful development is the growth of pretrial discovery now penetrating the criminal law. Surprise has been largely eliminated as a factor in civil trials. Why should it not be eliminated in criminal trials?

Many prosecutors fiercely resist discovery efforts by defense attorneys. Only comparatively recently have defense attorneys made vigorous efforts for pretrial discovery, in part because overworked public defenders represent defendants in many cases and other cases may be handled by uncompensated or only nominally compensated attorneys. There may be, moreover, some defense counsel who resist vigorous discovery efforts for fear of a growing effort on the part of the prosecution to discover the defense case before trial. A genuine conflict must be resolved. The Fifth Amendment right against self-incrimination is a cherished part of our constitutional liberties. There is a need to preserve this constitutional guarantee intact. I can do little more here than touch upon the problem.

Certainly the claim of infringement of Fifth Amendment rights is strong where the State seeks to uncover evidence that will be helpful to its case and detrimental to the defendant. The claim is less persuasive when the State asks simply that it know in advance what evidence the defense intends to present so it will not be taken by surprise at the trial. But frequently the decision of what evidence the defense will present, and particularly the question whether the defendant himself will take the witness stand is not made until the trial is under way and may be governed in part by the nature of the case that the prosecution presents.

We must reconcile the Fifth Amendment with the desirability of putting all the facts before the court, whether they are in the possession of the prosecution or the defense. Scarcely less important is the requirement that each side know in advance what evidence will be presented to eliminate the element of surprise in criminal trials. If we can achieve these goals, then we will eliminate a potent source of discontent with the present system. We will minimize the unhappy spectacle of seeing convicted persons come to court year after year with requests for a new trial because this or that piece of evidence was withheld at the initial trial.

But pretrial discovery is not the whole answer to the suppression of evidence problem. Discovery will be ineffective if the prosecution

hides evidence favorable to the defense that it is supposed to produce. At least, however, discovery requirements would accomplish
this: presently, to a large extent, the prosecutor must take the ini-
tiative of offering favorable evidence to the defense, if it is to be
produced. Under a discovery system, it is produced unless the prosecution actually hides it. That is an important difference.

The foregoing assumes that the evidence has been gathered, and
in particular, that we have utilized scientific methods of crime de-
tection. Unfortunately, there are serious limitations on the use of
science in solving crimes. Moreover, science is little used even where
it can be used.

4. Science in the Courtroom.

The reader might ask, what about scientific crime detec-
tion? We live in the age of science. Our nation is pre-eminent in science and technology. Many of us have toured the crime labs of the
F.B.I. in Washington. We have heard incredible tales of criminals
trapped by a bit of dust, a speck of paint, the cast of a tire tread. We
have heard similar stories of innocent persons accused of crime who
avoided an unjust conviction through triumphs of scientific criminology.

Such events do occur, but they are rare. Only to a very limited extent, has science entered the domain of criminal jurisprudence.

The report of the President's Commission on Law Enforcement
and Administrational Justice, entitled "The Challenge of Crime
in a Free Society" (1967), stated:

> The Commission has found that the police are not making
> the most of their opportunities to obtain and analyze physi-
> cal evidence. They are handicapped by technical lacks.
> There is a very great lack in police departments of all sizes
> of skilled evidence technicians, who can be called up to
> search crime scenes not merely for fingerprints, but for po-
> tentially telltale evidence like footprints, hairs, fibers, or
> traces of blood or mud. In one 2,000-man force, for exam-
> ple, there are only 2 technicians on each shift. More often
> than not, perhaps, such evidence would not lead directly
> to the identification of a criminal about whom nothing

else is known, but it might help greatly to establish a case for or against a suspect. The two chief reasons for the lack of skilled technicians are that few persons with the requisite science education have been recruited into police operations, and that few training programs have so far been developed.

The undeveloped state of training in this field also accounts for the fact that many patrolmen and detectives have no more than a rudimentary idea of how to search the scene of a crime. (p. 118)

The foregoing indictment was amply supported in a 1967 study prepared by Dr. Alexander Joseph of the John Jay College of Criminal Justice of the City University of New York. One of the first actions of Dr. Joseph and his committee was to ascertain what crime labs existed in the United States. The list his group compiled appears to have been the first ever prepared here. Ultimately they found that there were about a hundred crime labs. Seventeen states had no crime laboratories at any level—state, county or city. The remaining thirty-three states each have a state police crime laboratory. About forty cities with populations over 100,000 had crime laboratories; but since there are about 151 such cities in the United States, about 111 such cities or three-quarters of them had no crime laboratories. Further, the committee found, "It is obvious that, with the exception of a handful of laboratories, almost all laboratories require additional facilities, equipment and personnel to enable them to meet all their responsibilities." Among existing laboratories only a small number of nonfederal, large crime laboratories can be considered fully equipped. Even the largest of the laboratories with instrumentation worth nearly a half-million dollars requires additional facilities to take advantage of new developments in science and technology. The shortages, incredibly enough, range from the lack of two instruments "to a total lack of instrumentation."

Of the 100 crime labs, fifty-three reported the size of their budgets. The total was only seven million dollars and that included those in several major cities with budgets of about one million dollars each.

Inadequately trained personnel was a serious problem. Of a total number of 459 civilian personnel, only 380 had bachelor of science degrees. There are notable exceptions in large municipal laboratories. There were only twenty Ph.D.s. All crime laboratories had at least one vacancy. Vacancies were unfilled because starting salaries were too low and the fringe benefits too few to compete with industry, universities, and other government agencies. The average starting salary was less than $8,000 a year for civilian personnel holding a B.S. degree. In some laboratories the starting salary was as low as $5,400 per year. Moreover, most laboratories indicated that they were undermanned because of budgetary restrictions. There were unresolved conflicts between civilian and police personnel because of differences in pay and working hours. In some labs civilians could not be called into a case after working hours.

One of the most serious weaknesses was that crime laboratories, with one notable exception, were run for the benefit of the prosecution. They are under the jurisdiction of the police or the prosecuting attorney. Their findings are made available to the defense only by permission of the prosecuting attorneys or by court order. The exception is the Wisconsin State Crime Laboratory, which, by statute, is an independent investigative body that serves the courts, law enforcement agencies, and defense attorneys (see Wisconsin Statutes, Sec. 165.01).

Concerning the expansion of crime laboratories, the report notes that one of the most important problems is to gain among local authorities a recognition of the need for crime labs, because "There are police departments that deny such needs." Moreover, the report stresses an important problem: to educate police officers to make them aware of the need to obtain physical evidence through use of skilled laboratory personnel. There is a shortage of such skilled personnel. Many police officers are not aware of the facilities and services available to them through a crime laboratory. Many law enforcement agencies use existing crime laboratories in only a small percentage of their cases. "This condition is not caused by the laboratory, but rather represents the failure of the majority of police and detectives to fully appreciate and understand the role of the crime laboratory in the investigative process." Some directors of large crime laboratories felt that the number of crimes that should have been serviced by the laboratory was six to twelve times greater than the number of cases actually submitted by investigating officers. Only a handful of universities prepare students for work in the field. Among the few are the University of California at Berkeley, which graduates about thirty students each year. There were even smaller programs at the Michigan State University and Florida State University. The John Jay College of Criminal Justice, which began its program in 1967, had a first-year class of thirty-six undergraduates. (A recent article indicates that conditions have changed somewhat since 1967 without improving greatly.)

The President's Commission published also in 1967, a Task Force Report, *Science and Technology*. One would suppose that the subject of "criminalistics" would receive detailed consideration in its 228 large pages of fine print. It did not. The subject warranted mention only on page 5, "The subject of criminalistics, the traditional tie between technology and criminal justice, has been treated only marginally and needs special investigation," and again on page 82, where the Task Force recommended a research institute, one of whose many functions would be to study criminalistics.

America's dismal record respecting criminalistics is reflected in another study. In 1967 a group at the Illinois Division of the American Civil Liberties Union, under my direction, undertook a study of the use of scientific evidence in capital cases. First we reviewed every capital case in Illinois between 1950 and 1965. Some form of scientific evidence was introduced by the prosecution in fifteen cases —38 percent. Such evidence consisted exclusively of the old standbys, firearm identification, blood-type evidence, and fingerprint evidence. Not a single innovative technique was advanced. We found only a single case where scientific evidence was introduced by the defense and that was the Miller case.

For the national picture we studied all available court decisions relating to individuals sentenced to death during 1963, 1964, and 1965, as reported by the Bureau of Prisons. The national pattern was much like Illinois'—scientific evidence introduced in a limited number of cases, and largely restricted to blood-typing, firearm identification, and fingerprint identification. (See "Proof of Guilt in Capital Cases—An Unscience," *The Journal of Criminal Law, Criminology and Police Science,* vol. 58, p. 310.)

In 1844, near Lawrenceville, Illinois, Elizabeth Reed was charged with the murder of her husband Leonard. The evidence against her? General storekeeper James M. Logan testified that when he saw Leonard Reed the day before his death he believed that his stomach was then in a state in "incipient mortification." He had no knowledge that Elizabeth had bought arsenic at his shop, but had reason to believe that she had done so. Eveline Deal, apparently a maid in the Reed house, testified that she saw Mrs. Reed put white powder into a cup of Mr. Reed's sassafras tea. He began to vomit immediately, dying in extreme pain. The jury found that: "Elizabeth Reed, not having the fear of God before her eyes, but being moved and seduced by the instigation of the Devil" had murdered her husband. On April 29, 1845, Betsy Reed was publicly hanged. At the gallows, a minister preached a long sermon. Then a black noose was placed over Mrs. Reed's head, the noose adjusted, and the trap sprung.[1]

Perhaps today in a poisoning case we would demand more credible proof of guilt. But in the generality of cases the sophistication of the criminal process does little credit to America. The Miller case testifies to that.

The above is a hard sell for bringing science into the criminal court. But let no one be deceived into thinking that doing so will be a ready solution for the problems of criminal justice. The crime lab can be an excellent adjunct to good police and defense work, but it can never be a substitute for them. The evidence of the crime lab must be tested and evaluated against the testimony of witnesses, the objective circumstances of a crime, and other traditional methods of determining fact. Moreover, crime labs necessarily are dependent upon the ingenuity, skill, honesty, and reliability of the police officers who make the initial examination of the scene. The crime lab can scarcely rise above the level of its on-site investigators.

Bringing science into the criminal process will be a long, slow, arduous, and costly process. For the foreseeable future it will be employed only to a limited extent for the most serious of crimes.

5. Probing the Mind of the Accused.

In this chapter I have focused on some of the limitations of the criminal process as a mechanism for seeking truth.

1. See William K. Armstrong, "The Trial and Hanging of Elizabeth Reed—The Only Woman to Die on the Gallows in Illinois," *Illinois Bar Journal,* June 1968.

We have mentioned above the extraordinary difficulty of making determinations with respect to objective "facts," questions such as whether or not the accused fired the gun that killed the deceased. But that is really only half our problem. Almost every criminal trial requires subjective determinations as well: whether a confession was "voluntary," whether a man was so drunk he could not form a specific "intent," whether he is "capable" of cooperating with counsel, whether he "understands" the charges, and on and on.

An illustration of the difficulties:

Alcorta came upon his wife one evening in a parked car kissing Castilleja. Alcorta killed his wife. The case was tried under the law of Texas, by which, if Alcorta was guilty of "murder without malice" (a murder arising from "a sudden passion from an adequate cause"), the maximum penalty was five years. The jury, however, found Alcorta guilty of murder with malice. The sentence was death. The jury sat in judgment on an essentially subjective issue: What was Alcorta's reaction to the scene in the car? Or, perhaps more precisely, what should have been the limits of his reaction had he been a reasonable man? Was the jury aware fully of the social group in which the Alcortas lived? Was Mrs. Alcorta's conduct regarded as heinous in that group? We do not know; we do not know whether the jury knew.[1]

6. *Shifting Substantive and Procedural Rules.*

To this point, I have discussed largely the problems of determining guilt. I assumed the legal rules, substantive and procedural, were largely fixed. But they are not. The rules are necessarily subtle and in constant flux. In the preceding pages we have seen numerous illustrations. I add the following because they are vivid and because in each, within a few years after a man was executed on the basis of a legal rule, the rule was changed.

Caryl Chessman[2] was executed in 1960 not for murder—he killed no one—but for "kidnapping": during an armed robbery in which

1. See *Alcorta* v. *Texas,* 355 U.S. 28 (1957). The Supreme Court reversed the conviction because Castilleja testified falsely to the knowledge of the prosecution that he had not had relations with Mrs. Alcorta.

2. See *People* v. *Chessman,* 38 Cal. 2d 166 (1951). See also *Chessman* v. *Teets,* 354 U.S. 156 (1957)

a victim was injured, another robbery victim was forced by Chessman to move about the scene of the crime. Nine years after Chessman was executed, the California Supreme Court declared that
forcing a victim to move during a robbery did not constitute "kidnapping."

For an analogous shift in the law, but procedural rather than
substantive, consider the Illinois case of Vincent Ciucci.[1] The State
alleged that Ciucci shot his wife and three children in order to marry
another woman.[2] The state elected not to try Ciucci for all four
murders simultaneously. Instead he was first tried for the murder
of his wife for which he received a sentence of twenty years. He was
then tried for the murder of one child for which he received a sentence of forty-five years. Not until he was tried for the murder of the
second child did he receive the death penalty, the goal of the state.
The Supreme Court in a five-to-four decision declared that under
Illinois law each murder was a separate crime for which Ciucci con-
stitutionally could be indicted and tried separately. Ciucci was executed in 1962.

Not long afterward the Supreme Court of Illinois disapproved
the practice of successive trials in such cases. Indeed, in 1961, even
before the execution of Ciucci, Illinois adopted a criminal code
requiring that all offenses known to the prosecuting officer be
gathered in a single prosecution.

Change and growth are essential if the law is to be a responsible,
dynamic force in society. The subtlety of life results in the subtlety
of the law. The man sentenced today is judged in the light of today's rules. Tomorrow those rules may be rejected as barbarous.

7. Conclusion.

When a crime outrages society, it pushes the authorities
to lash out, and to make a sacrifice of someone. They do so, not
usually through vindictiveness, but because of the unremitting public pressures which warp their judgment.[3]

1. *Ciucci* v. *Ill.*, 356 U.S. 571 (1958)
2. The other woman, ironically, was Carol Amora.
3. A trial is partly theatre, insofar as it is drama, and partly religion, insofar as it is
a search for justice. The Greeks saw this clearly. In Athens, the archon basileios, the
second ranking archon, who presided over the Supreme Court, was responsible for justice, religious affairs, and theatrical contests.

If the evils of the criminal law were confined to such cases, they would be unfortunate. But they are not so limited. For too many of the poor, the criminal process dispenses not justice, but harshness, cruelty, and injustice.

If the criminal law is to teach justice, it must act justly. Today, the criminal process is degraded by chicanery, deception, and deceit. These practices corrupt criminal administration and embitter the innocent. They teach the guilty that the criminal process is not more just than they are, only more powerful.

But even if we strive for reform, let us not suppose that we will achieve perfect justice. Determining "the facts" undoubtedly always will prove elusive. The adversary system, despite its strengths, will produce injustice in some cases. Rules of law designed to do justice in the general case will sometimes convict the innocent. Determining the state of mind of the accused, his "intent," his "motive," seem an inescapable part of the criminal law. We little know how to make such decisions, and we make meaningful use of only a little that we do know.

The task of perfecting our system of criminal justice is never ending. Each step should open the door to the next. Only in this way will we be a nation where "due process of law" is a reality and not merely a phrase in our Constitution.

I recall vividly one moment of the trial before Judge Perry while June Lang Gross was on the stand. Briefly, it seemed that Hayes was about to produce for the judge Superintendent Christensen's memorandum regarding her visit to him—the one in which she made wild allegations regarding many responsible residents of Canton, the one which we were reluctant to use. Perhaps that document would be the capstone of the case and would provide the final bit of proof, if any were needed, that the prosecution well knew that June's word was not to be trusted. Hayes apparently could not find the memorandum immediately, testimony turned to other things and the document was not introduced. But in that moment there flashed through my mind a single phrase from the service for the Day of Atonement: "For all things stand revealed at last."

In preparation for writing this chapter, I looked up the reference. The passage opens with a portion of the Eighth Psalm: "What is man, O God, that Thou art mindful of him, and the son of man that Thou thinkest of him." It continues with a tenth century prayer, "Over men and nations Thou stretchest the line, and who can stay Thy measurements?" A few sentences later comes the line, "For all things stand revealed at last, and all men will be called to render account for their doings. Then truth will be made manifest, and deception will be ended forever."

All things were revealed at last and in time for Lloyd Miller, not just as I envisioned it at the moment, but in time, nonetheless. Unhappily for some, truth comes too late. For some it never comes.

Nonetheless, we must recognize that a "fair trial" is a distant goal, nearly as unachievable as the Holy Grail. We have a duty to seek, knowing we will never fully achieve. In the meantime we must live in the world. Human beings must sit as judges and jurors, and human beings must function as prosecutors and defense counsel. If we truly appreciate these facts, then we can have a truer, a better, more mature, and more realistic appreciation and respect for our courts.

In the real world, the decisions of courts, right or wrong (preferably right), must be observed if society is to continue to function. But our respect for and willingness to abide by the practical consequences of a court decision does not require us to suspend judgment on the processes by which judgment is reached. To the extent that the courts conscientiously, intelligently, and truly attempt to reach results which are objectively convincing, they win our esteem and our allegiance. They also win our readiness to understand and forgive their inevitable lapses and errors, tragic as they may be in particular cases.

INDEX